Financial Fables

Financial Fables

Stories That Teach Us More Than Spreadsheets Ever Could

Adrian Vale

Mindful Pages

Published in 2025

ISBN: 9789371776363 (PB)
ISBN: 9789371771788 (eBook)

Published by

Mindful Pages
Imprint of Alpha Editions LLC
312 W. 2nd St #1834
Casper, WY 82601, USA

This book was developed using advanced writing tools to support the drafting and ideation process. All content has been thoughtfully curated, refined, and reviewed to ensure quality and relevance.

Content

Introduction
Why We Need Stories More Than Spreadsheets

Finance is often introduced to us through the cold authority of numbers. We are taught to believe that money is a matter of addition and subtraction, of compound interest tables and budget lines, of investment returns and actuarial probabilities. The textbooks speak in decimals, the news reports in percentages, and the corporate boardroom in balance sheets. Yet outside those carefully drawn columns, people make decisions about money in ways that are strikingly inconsistent with pure mathematics. A family goes into debt for a wedding celebration they can ill afford. A community rushes to buy shares in a company everyone insists will "change the world." A nation borrows endlessly because its citizens accept the promise that tomorrow's prosperity will cover today's excess. These are not acts dictated by spreadsheets. They are acts fuelled by stories.

The paradox is striking: while finance is taught as mathematics, it is lived as narrative. Every decision about earning, spending, saving, or investing takes place within a frame of meaning, a tale told about what money signifies and what it can secure. Markets move not simply because of data releases or interest-rate changes but because of the psychology and expectations those figures evoke. Entire economies rise and fall not only because of physical resources or institutional strength but because of the myths they tell about risk, reward, and resilience. Numbers inform, but stories persuade. The human imagination, more than the calculator, directs the flows of capital.

This book begins from a simple but unsettling proposition: to understand finance, we must first understand the fables by which we live. If money were purely technical, rational, and numerical, then financial crises would not repeat themselves with such grim regularity, nor would personal financial mistakes be so stubbornly predictable. But history tells us otherwise. Time and again, the same patterns appear: greed dressed up as optimism, speculation disguised as skill, promises of security masking deeper fears. The mathematics change with each era, but the underlying narratives remain astonishingly consistent.

Why, then, do stories endure while numbers fade? Statistics are precise but fragile; they lose relevance the moment circumstances change. A projection is accurate only until reality shifts. A model explains behaviour under assumed conditions but collapses in the face of uncertainty. By contrast, stories offer flexible frameworks. They are retold, reshaped, and passed down through generations, not as literal truths but as guiding myths. The tale of King Midas still colours our ambivalence about wealth. The parables of debt forgiveness in religious texts still shape modern debates about bankruptcy and relief. Even in the age of algorithmic trading, people continue to invoke metaphors of bulls and bears—creatures that never appeared on an economist's graph but linger as enduring symbols of market mood.

The purpose of *Financial Fables* is not to replace numerical reasoning with fairy tales, nor to romanticise irrationality. It is to acknowledge that human beings rarely act as the purely rational agents that economic theory imagines. We do not calculate every decision with the cold precision of a spreadsheet; we rely on shortcuts, mental models, and, above all, stories. Some of these narratives serve us well, offering perspective and restraint. Others lead us astray, seducing us into cycles of greed, fear, or denial. By bringing together parables, cultural myths, and historical episodes, this book seeks to reveal the deeper logic behind financial behaviour—a logic that is narrative as much as numeric.

To take this seriously is to confront an urgent question: if our financial lives are guided by stories, do we control those stories, or do they control us? Much of the time, the fables we live by are inherited rather than chosen. We repeat family scripts about money without even recognising them: "Always own your home," "Never talk about debt," "The stock market is a gamble," "More is always better." These sayings, passed from parents to children, form part of our cultural DNA. They determine whether we see wealth as a blessing or a curse, whether we treat debt as shameful or routine, whether we view risk as exhilarating or terrifying. Left unexamined, such stories hold extraordinary power.

The need to examine them is particularly urgent today. Modern finance presents itself as a triumph of objectivity. We are surrounded by dashboards of real-time data, forecasts generated by machine learning, investment products tailored by algorithms. Yet beneath this glittering surface, the same old narratives are at work. Technology does not eliminate our susceptibility to myths—it amplifies it. Social media spreads financial fables at unprecedented speed: the overnight millionaire, the revolutionary cryptocurrency, the looming collapse. Stories go viral, and fortunes rise or fall accordingly. We may think ourselves more sophisticated than our ancestors who read omens in the stars, but the difference is one of tools, not of psychology.

This book is an attempt to offer readers both clarity and agency. It does not present formulas to memorise or instructions to follow. Others have written excellent guides on budgeting, investing, and retirement planning. What is missing in most of them is recognition that none of those techniques will endure if they are not embedded in a narrative we can live with. People abandon perfectly sound financial strategies not because the numbers fail but because the story no longer fits. A budget feels constraining rather than empowering. An investment plan seems dull compared with the promise of quick riches. A mortgage repayment schedule feels oppressive rather than secure. Without a narrative to anchor our financial practices, we drift.

The chapters ahead take readers through some of the most powerful and persistent financial fables. We begin with the recognition that numbers, while essential, are not enough. Narratives outlast data, shaping habits and guiding cultures long after statistics are forgotten. We then confront the parable of "enough"—a concept that haunts modern societies obsessed with limitless growth. We explore greed as both temptation and cautionary tale, the gambler's fallacy as an enduring illusion, and debt as a story of morality as much as mathematics. We examine the paradoxes of gifting and generosity, the myths of scarcity and abundance, the roles of fate and fortune, and the shadows cast by inheritance. We ask why money depends so heavily on trust, why time is so often equated with wealth, and why security has always been narrated in terms of fortresses and vaults. We consider how money becomes identity, how markets are judged in moral terms, and finally, how we might choose the stories we live by rather than being captive to them.

In framing these themes, the book draws on sources that may seem unusual in a finance context: ancient myths, religious traditions, folktales, literary parables, and historical anecdotes. This is not because numbers are irrelevant, but because numbers alone cannot explain why human beings act the way they do with money. A model may predict average behaviour, but it cannot account for why individuals persist in seemingly irrational habits, or why entire societies repeat the same cycles. Stories can. They capture emotion, memory, and meaning in ways that charts cannot. They remind us that finance is a human enterprise, grounded in psychology and culture as much as in arithmetic.

The promise of *Financial Fables* is straightforward: by seeing the stories we live by, we gain the power to choose better ones. A person who recognises the myth of endless accumulation can redefine prosperity in terms of sufficiency rather than excess. A community that understands the stigma of debt as a narrative, not a law of nature, can craft healthier attitudes towards borrowing and repayment. A society that sees security not as an absolute guarantee but as a narrative of resilience can design more sustainable systems. When we understand money as story, we begin to see the possibility of rewriting those stories.

This introduction is an invitation. It invites you, the reader, to step beyond the spreadsheet and into the narratives that silently shape your financial life. You will not find promises of quick wealth here, nor prescriptions to follow blindly. What you will find is a framework for reflection: a way to understand the myths you have inherited, the parables that surround you, and the financial stories you tell yourself every day. Some of these stories may prove liberating, others may require challenge, and still others may need to be rewritten altogether.

Money is too important to be left to numbers alone. It governs our households, our markets, our politics, and our personal sense of worth. But numbers are only the visible surface. Beneath them lie stories—fables of fortune and failure, myths of scarcity and abundance, parables of trust and betrayal. To live wisely with money is not simply to calculate but to narrate. The chapters ahead are not about escaping the numbers but about placing them within their true human context. They offer no formulas, but they do offer clarity: the clarity that comes when we see that finance is not only arithmetic, but storytelling—and that the stories we choose to live by may matter more than the sums we calculate.

By the end of this book, my hope is that you will not only recognise the narratives that have shaped your financial world but also feel empowered to question them, revise them, and author new ones. For the greatest financial freedom is not measured in wealth accumulated, but in the ability to live according to a story that is both truthful and chosen. That is the work of this book, and the journey on which you are about to embark.

Chapter 1
The Stories Beneath the Numbers

Numbers have an air of authority that few other forms of communication can rival. They appear to offer certainty, precision, and objectivity. A figure, once published, seems to leave no room for debate: inflation is 3.2 per cent, the market fell by 1,000 points, unemployment stands at 6 million. Yet numbers, however sharp their edges may seem, are remarkably fragile in the face of time. They lose their power quickly, replaced by new figures, new reports, new projections. Stories, by contrast, endure. They do not expire with the next economic cycle, nor are they erased by the release of fresh data. Instead, they grow in strength as they are repeated, reshaped, and absorbed into the cultural imagination. That is why a proverb such as "money cannot buy happiness" remains widely cited centuries after its origin, while few can recall the exact GDP growth rate of their country just ten years ago. The truth is that stories persuade, while numbers merely explain.

This enduring power of narrative over numerical evidence has long been recognised by historians, psychologists, and even shrewd financiers themselves. Consider how Warren Buffett, one of the most celebrated investors of the modern age, often frames his insights not in equations but in parables. He warns against speculation by recalling the fate of tulip mania in seventeenth-century Holland, or explains patience by invoking the image of planting a tree. His point is not to dismiss numbers but to clothe them in stories that stick. The human mind remembers patterns and images far more readily than tables of data. A single story can carry across generations, passed from parent to child, mentor to student, until it becomes a silent influence shaping decisions. Statistics fade into the archives, while fables live on at the dinner table.

Finance, therefore, must be seen not only as a domain of calculation but as a cultural language. Money itself is not merely a neutral medium of exchange—it is a vessel of meaning. To pay a tithe in a religious setting is not simply to part with a percentage of one's income; it is to affirm belonging to a faith community and to acknowledge divine authority. Similarly, when a Wall Street trader rings a ceremonial bell at the close of a successful day, it is not just the arithmetic of profit being celebrated but a cultural ritual reinforcing the lore of ambition, competition, and conquest. These acts are not reducible to mathematics. They are narrative performances, reinforcing shared understandings of value, loyalty, and identity.

Indeed, the very design of financial institutions rests upon stories. A banknote is nothing more than ink on paper until a society agrees to treat it as a promise of value. Stock markets thrive not because of any intrinsic worth in their transactions but because millions of participants believe in the story of liquidity, transparency, and collective trust. Even the rise of cryptocurrencies—often presented as triumphs of pure code—has less to do with mathematics than with narrative persuasion. Bitcoin was framed not simply as a decentralised ledger but as a rebellion against established authority, a myth of liberation from corrupt institutions. Its value, volatile though it may be, is anchored more in belief than in algorithm.

If money is a language, then spreadsheets are merely one dialect within it—precise, useful, but not comprehensive. Spreadsheet thinking assumes that human beings will behave rationally if provided with sufficient data. It imagines that risk can be quantified, preferences ordered, outcomes predicted. Yet history repeatedly demonstrates the limits of such faith. Rational models cannot account for panic, nor do they capture the intoxicating pull of collective euphoria. The 2008 financial crisis is perhaps the clearest modern example. Banks and rating agencies relied on complex models that calculated the probability of mortgage defaults. Those spreadsheets suggested safety, diversification, and negligible risk. But they ignored the more powerful story that had taken hold in the culture: the belief that housing prices would always rise, that everyone deserved to own a home, that prosperity could be manufactured without end. When that narrative cracked, no equation could prevent the collapse. Numbers failed because they underestimated the stories.

The same blindness can be seen in the rise and fall of cryptocurrencies. White papers laid out elegant technical specifications, and spreadsheets projected extraordinary gains. Yet investors poured in not because they had studied cryptography or understood blockchain mathematics, but because they were captivated by a story: that ordinary individuals could escape the grip of central banks, that a new class of digital pioneers would reshape the future of money, that wealth could be minted almost magically. It was less investment than participation in a cultural myth, a twenty-first-century gold rush. When confidence wavered, prices collapsed with a speed no spreadsheet could have foreseen, because spreadsheets measure probabilities while stories move hearts.

This recurring failure of purely rational models demands a different approach. If numbers alone cannot capture the essence of financial behaviour, then we must adopt what this book calls the *fable lens*. Through this lens, we treat financial choices not as isolated calculations but as acts embedded in stories—stories about who we are, what we value, and what future we imagine. The fable lens does not deny the utility of mathematics; rather, it situates mathematics within the narratives that give it power. A compound-interest table is meaningless unless someone believes in the story of patience. An insurance policy is useless unless people share the story that protection against uncertainty is worth paying for. A national debt ceiling is arbitrary unless citizens accept the story of fiscal responsibility or, conversely, the story that endless borrowing ensures growth.

What the fable lens offers is a richer, more truthful framework for understanding why we act as we do with money. It allows us to see that financial myths are not simply childish tales to be discarded but enduring structures of thought that guide behaviour across centuries. It helps us recognise that our most sophisticated institutions are still underpinned by narratives—whether of trust, of risk, or of prosperity—that must be examined as carefully as any financial model. Most importantly, it gives us the agency to choose which stories we allow to govern our financial lives, rather than being unconsciously ruled by inherited myths.

As this chapter unfolds, we will explore how narratives outlast data, why money functions as a cultural language, how spreadsheet thinking blinds us to human behaviour, and why the fable lens provides a more reliable way of seeing finance. The aim is not to diminish the importance of numbers but to place them in their rightful context: as instruments within a larger symphony conducted by human imagination. For if we are to make wiser financial choices—whether as individuals, communities, or societies—we must begin not with numbers, but with the stories beneath them.

Why Narratives Outlast Data: Numbers explain, but stories persuade

Numbers impress us with their neatness, but they rarely survive beyond the moment that summoned them. The annual inflation rate announced by a government minister, the quarterly earnings report from a corporation, the interest rate forecast in a central banker's speech—all seem urgent and commanding when first delivered, only to fade from collective memory within days. Few people can recall the exact percentage decline of stock markets during past recessions, but many remember the story of the Great Depression: soup kitchens, dust bowls, and ruined fortunes. The human mind does not cling to statistics; it clings to meaning, and meaning is most powerfully communicated through narrative.

This tendency is not a flaw of intellect but a feature of cognition. Cognitive psychologists have long noted that memory is associative. Facts stored in isolation are difficult to retrieve, while those embedded in stories attach themselves to emotions, images, and characters, making them far more durable. Numbers, stripped of context, rarely provoke emotion. A tale, however, carries consequence. When we hear the legend of King Midas, we are not memorising a balance sheet; we are absorbing a warning about the futility of unbounded desire. When we recall Aesop's fable of the ant and the grasshopper, we are not considering percentages of savings rates, but picturing what it means to squander or prepare. These stories shape attitudes toward money far more deeply than any set of statistics ever could.

The financial world provides abundant evidence of this dynamic. Consider the 1929 Wall Street crash. Economists can furnish reams of data on price movements, margin calls, and the contraction of credit. Yet what persists in collective memory is not the data itself but the story of desperate investors leaping from skyscraper windows—a narrative exaggerated in scale, perhaps even apocryphal, but indelible nonetheless. The lasting image is not a chart line falling but a human body in freefall. That story, with all its emotional potency, has become shorthand for financial collapse itself. It continues to be invoked whenever markets wobble, reminding investors that numbers may fluctuate, but the story of panic remains constant.

This power of narrative over data is equally visible in the ways financial institutions market themselves. Banks do not attract customers by citing their capital adequacy ratios or risk-weighted assets. They tell stories about trust, stability, and reliability: a safe home for your money, a partner for your future. Investment firms do not persuade by presenting regression analyses; they narrate visions of retirement security, entrepreneurial freedom, or legacy building. Even governments, when justifying fiscal policy, speak less about bond yields than about the story of national resilience or the promise of future generations. Data may be included, but always as supporting evidence for a larger narrative frame.

Yet narratives are not merely tools of persuasion; they are also frameworks of behaviour. Behavioural economists have shown that people consistently deviate from rational-choice models in predictable ways. We overreact to stories of loss and underprepare for stories of risk. This is why a single high-profile bankruptcy can trigger fear across markets, even when underlying fundamentals remain stable. The numbers suggest one outcome; the story suggests another. And more often than not, it is the story that wins. Investors who could recite the mathematics of diversification still rushed to sell during the financial crisis of 2008, not because the numbers told them to but because the prevailing narrative of collapse overwhelmed calculation.

The endurance of stories is particularly evident across generations. Families rarely pass down spreadsheets, but they do pass down proverbs, cautionary tales, and remembered events. A grandparent who lived through the Second World War may not recall precise inflation statistics but will vividly recount the experience of rationing, the anxiety of scarcity, and the imperative to save. These stories seep into the attitudes of children and grandchildren, shaping money habits decades later. The tendency of certain households to save compulsively, to distrust banks, or to avoid debt often has less to do with objective financial analysis than with inherited narratives that have outlasted the data that first inspired them.

Religious traditions illustrate this point with clarity. The concept of tithing, for example, is underpinned not by financial calculation but by narrative obligation: the act of giving as recognition of divine providence and communal responsibility. The actual percentages may vary across denominations and epochs, but the story of duty and belonging persists. Similarly, the parables of stewardship in Christian texts or the prohibitions against usury in Islamic law endure as guiding principles long after the specific economic contexts in which they emerged have changed. Believers may not know the interest rates prevailing in medieval Europe, but they know the story of exploitation embedded in the practice of usury. Narratives, once anchored in moral frameworks, become timeless guides to financial behaviour.

There is also a pragmatic reason why stories persist. Numbers often require translation. A statistic about compound interest may be accurate, but it requires knowledge of mathematics to interpret its implications. A story, however, speaks directly. When Albert Einstein allegedly remarked that compound interest is the "eighth wonder of the world," he was not providing an actuarial calculation; he was telling a story that captured imagination. Whether or not he said it is immaterial—the attribution itself has become part of the story. As a result, people remember the principle not through formulas but through an evocative phrase.

Critics might argue that stories mislead, that reliance on narrative encourages irrationality and bias. There is truth in this concern. Narratives can distort as easily as they can guide. The story of perpetual prosperity fuelled the housing bubble before 2008; the story of a "new economy" drove the dot-com frenzy of the late 1990s; the story of technological inevitability sustains speculative bubbles in cryptocurrency. These narratives endure precisely because they are persuasive, even when they lack empirical grounding. Yet the solution is not to abandon stories but to become more discerning in how we receive them. The danger lies not in narrative itself but in unexamined narrative.

The enduring influence of stories also reminds us that financial behaviour is not simply about the present but about identity. To participate in a story is to locate oneself within a broader arc. The worker who saves diligently is not just accumulating interest; they are enacting the narrative of prudence. The entrepreneur who takes bold risks is not merely seeking profit; they are embodying the story of innovation and daring. These roles confer meaning that spreadsheets alone cannot provide. To live by numbers alone is to strip financial life of narrative resonance, leaving choices sterile and uninspiring. It is little wonder that people abandon purely numerical plans when they lack a compelling story to animate them.

The contrast between numbers and narratives is not absolute but complementary. Numbers gain their persuasive force when embedded in stories, and stories acquire credibility when supported by numbers. A health insurer's claim that preventive care saves money is far more persuasive when accompanied by both actuarial tables and stories of individuals spared from hardship. A government's argument for austerity measures is strengthened when coupled with both deficit figures and narratives of national sacrifice. The key insight is that numbers alone rarely suffice. It is the marriage of data and story that secures enduring influence, though if forced to choose, the story outlasts the statistic.

What this reveals is that financial education, policy, and practice must be attentive to the power of narrative. It is not enough to lecture on savings rates or to publish charts of historical returns. If we wish to change financial behaviour, we must also offer stories that resonate. Teaching a student that saving £100 a month at 6 per cent interest will yield a certain sum in 30 years is useful, but telling them the story of a peer who achieved security through persistence is transformative. The data may be forgotten; the story may inspire action.

Numbers explain; stories persuade. This is not a rhetorical flourish but an observable fact of human cognition and culture. Financial myths endure across centuries because they are transmitted as narratives that embody meaning, emotion, and identity. Statistics, no matter how precise, fade as circumstances change. To shape enduring money habits, we must engage with the stories that people live by. Whether those stories constrain or liberate depends on our willingness to examine them critically, to preserve the ones that serve us, and to discard those that do not. Without that recognition, we remain captive to fables we do not even realise we are following. With it, we gain the clarity to see that finance, at its core, is not only about numbers but about the narratives that give those numbers their lasting force.

Money as a Cultural Language

Money is often presented as if it were neutral, a technical medium of exchange stripped of value beyond arithmetic. Yet in practice it functions less as mathematics and more as communication. To hand over a note, to write a cheque, or to transfer funds electronically is not only to execute a transaction but to participate in a shared system of meaning. It is this cultural dimension of money—the way it signals belonging, enforces obligations, and encodes values—that gives finance its peculiar force. Numbers alone cannot explain why people tithe to their faith, why Wall Street rings a bell at the end of the trading day, or why entire societies agree to treat pieces of paper or lines of code as wealth. These are not acts of calculation alone; they are performances of shared narrative.

The anthropologist Marcel Mauss once observed that gifts are never free, and the same can be said of money. Every financial act carries a cultural signal, whether intended or not. Consider religious tithes: giving ten per cent of one's income is not a mathematically optimal decision in any conventional sense. For the faithful, however, it is a profound declaration of identity, loyalty, and gratitude. The act of parting with money in this context is not about optimising returns but about expressing a narrative of obedience and belonging. What sustains the practice over centuries is not its numerical efficiency but the cultural meaning attached to it. The same principle underpins acts of charity, philanthropy, or even conspicuous consumption. The money itself is fungible; the meaning it conveys is not.

Modern finance is no less saturated with culture, though it often cloaks itself in the language of rationality. Take the rituals of Wall Street: the opening and closing bell of the New York Stock Exchange, the shouting once heard on trading floors, the jargon of bulls and bears. These are not numerical necessities. They are cultural practices that dramatise market activity, turning abstract numbers into stories of struggle and triumph. The bell signals not just the start of trading but the continuation of a narrative about capitalism's vitality. Traders' slang, from "dead cat bounce" to "blood in the streets," transforms statistics into gripping tales. Even the architecture of financial districts, with their imposing skyscrapers and marble lobbies, speaks a language of power and permanence.

The communicative role of money becomes especially clear when we observe how different societies treat it. In some cultures, cash transactions are seen as cold and impersonal compared to barter or gift-giving, which carry narrative weight. In others, the use of credit is bound up with social status and trust. The Japanese practice of giving money in decorative envelopes at weddings, or the Chinese tradition of red envelopes during Lunar New Year, demonstrates that the *form* of money matters as much as the sum. The decoration, the ritual, the timing—all encode meanings that go far beyond the number inside. In these instances, money becomes a language of respect, blessing, and continuity.

Philosophers and historians have long noted that societies place moral weight on financial practices precisely because they recognise money as a carrier of values. Aristotle distinguished between oikonomia (the management of the household) and chrematistike (the pursuit of wealth for its own sake), suggesting that how one used money spoke volumes about character. In medieval Europe, the condemnation of usury was not based on an economic calculation of risk but on a cultural judgment about fairness, exploitation, and divine law. Similarly, in Islamic finance today, prohibitions against interest-bearing loans stem not from an inability to calculate returns but from a narrative about justice, equity, and spiritual discipline. These examples show how deeply cultural and moral codes are inscribed into the financial practices of societies, regardless of mathematical efficiency.

One might argue that modern markets, with their quantitative models and high-frequency trading, have transcended this cultural dimension. Yet the evidence suggests otherwise. The 2008 financial crisis was not triggered merely by flawed equations; it was propelled by a cultural story—that home ownership was an unquestionable good, that property prices would rise indefinitely, that the American Dream could be securitised. The mathematics of collateralised debt obligations obscured risks, but it was the narrative of ever-expanding prosperity that gave those products their cultural traction. The spreadsheet explained, but the story persuaded millions to buy into it. When that story collapsed, the numbers followed.

To see money as cultural language is also to recognise its role in shaping identity. People do not spend only to acquire goods; they spend to say something about themselves. The purchase of luxury brands, the funding of a university endowment, the display of a rare work of art—these are acts of communication. They tell a story about taste, status, allegiance, or aspiration. Sociologist Thorstein Veblen coined the term "conspicuous consumption" not to describe irrationality but to expose the narrative function of spending: wealth is performed through purchases that speak to others. The numbers on the receipt matter less than the story told by the object acquired.

There is also a darker side to money as a cultural language: it can exclude as effectively as it can include. Financial slang and rituals often act as barriers, marking insiders and outsiders. Consider the cryptic language of investment banking pitch books, or the performative aggression of trading-room banter. These are not simply efficient forms of communication but cultural codes that signal membership in a tribe. To be fluent in this language is to be accepted; to misunderstand it is to remain on the margins. Money thus becomes not just a universal medium of exchange but a marker of identity and belonging within specific cultural groups.

At the national level, the communicative function of money is even more pronounced. Currency design, for example, is rarely left to chance. Nations print symbols, leaders, and landmarks on their banknotes to tell stories of history, sovereignty, and pride. The euro, with its bridges and arches, conveys a narrative of unity across diverse states. The American dollar, with its Latin mottoes and

Masonic imagery, projects continuity and power. Even cryptocurrencies, which claim to exist beyond borders, rely on narrative design. The very name "Bitcoin" evokes both technology and coinage, straddling old and new, while the imagery of coins with a "B" symbol reinforces familiarity with a cultural object that has existed for millennia.

If money is indeed a language, then like any language it can be used to deceive. Financial frauds succeed not because the numbers add up—they rarely do—but because the narrative is compelling. Charles Ponzi promised investors easy profits by exploiting postal arbitrage, but what convinced them was not the details of his scheme but the persuasive story of opportunity. Decades later, Bernie Madoff lured billions with the story of consistent, modest returns that fit the cultural preference for steady reliability. The mathematics were secondary; the story carried the fraud.

Recognising finance as cultural language changes how we approach it. It suggests that financial literacy is not simply a matter of mastering compound interest or diversification but of understanding the stories money tells and the meanings it conveys. A technically correct financial plan will fail if it clashes with the cultural narratives a person lives by. A spreadsheet may recommend saving aggressively for retirement, but if the individual's cultural story prizes generosity in the present, they may choose to give rather than save. The numbers explain, but the story persuades. Understanding that dynamic enables us to craft financial strategies that align with human meaning rather than abstract optimisation.

To grasp finance only as mathematics is to miss its deeper significance. Money is a language in which societies narrate their values, identities, and aspirations. From the tithe that binds the faithful to the ritual of the closing bell that sustains market lore, from the symbolism on banknotes to the branding of luxury goods, finance is suffused with culture. It speaks not only in numbers but in narratives. To understand this is to gain insight not only into economics but into ourselves, for the way we use money is one of the clearest stories we tell about who we are and what we believe.

Blind Spots in Spreadsheet Thinking

One of the most striking features of modern finance is the confidence it places in models. From the algorithms used by investment banks to the risk-assessment tools employed by regulators, spreadsheets have become the apparatus through which the financial world seeks to anticipate the future. They quantify risk, forecast returns, and assign probabilities to the unpredictable. On the surface, these models represent rationality itself: a world rendered measurable, controlled, and calculable. Yet crises reveal a fundamental flaw. The spreadsheet, for all its precision, is a map that excludes the very terrain it seeks to describe. Human behaviour—the fears, hopes, narratives, and contagions of belief that move markets—is nowhere to be found in the cells and formulas.

The 2008 financial crisis stands as a cautionary monument to this blind spot. At the heart of the collapse were complex instruments—mortgage-backed securities and collateralised debt obligations—whose safety was vouched for by mathematical models. These models relied on historical data showing that mortgage defaults in different regions of the United States were uncorrelated; the failure of loans in Nevada, for example, would not coincide with defaults in Ohio. Spreadsheets, filled with elegant equations, suggested that diversification had transformed risky mortgages into stable investments. Ratings agencies blessed these products with their highest seals of approval. What the spreadsheets did not capture was the cultural story that had taken root: that home ownership was an inviolable right, that house prices could only rise, and that lending standards could be relaxed without consequence. When that narrative collapsed, correlations spiked, models failed, and the global financial system staggered. The data explained the past; the story dictated the future.

This failure is not unique to housing markets. Consider the dot-com bubble at the turn of the millennium. Spreadsheet models projected immense growth for internet companies, assigning valuations based on traffic metrics or potential market share rather than profits. Investors, entranced by the story of a "new economy," overlooked the absence of viable business models. The arithmetic of discounted cash flows was abandoned, replaced by the narrative that old valuation methods no longer applied. When reality asserted itself, trillions in market capitalisation evaporated. The blind spot was not a failure of mathematics per se, but a failure to recognise that human beings had already abandoned the logic of those models in favour of a more seductive story.

The same dynamic has played out in cryptocurrency markets. Blockchain technology, ingenious in design, lent itself to spreadsheets filled with supply limits, mining rewards, and transaction speeds. But the meteoric rise of assets such as Bitcoin and Ethereum cannot be explained by mathematics alone. What propelled their ascent was a narrative: that digital currencies represented freedom from central banks, that early adopters were pioneers in a new frontier, that the future of money itself was being rewritten. Investors bought not because they had solved cryptographic equations but because they believed in a story of transformation and rebellion. The blind spot of spreadsheet thinking lay in ignoring this cultural momentum. When scepticism spread and confidence faltered, valuations collapsed with a ferocity no spreadsheet had predicted.

Why do rational models fail so consistently in crises? The answer lies in the difference between risk and uncertainty. Risk can be quantified: the probability of rolling a six on a die, the expected return on a diversified portfolio. Uncertainty, by contrast, defies quantification. It emerges from human behaviour, from shifts in collective belief, from the sudden change in a story's plausibility. Spreadsheets excel at modelling risk but are powerless in the face of uncertainty. They offer a false sense of security, leading investors, regulators, and policymakers to believe that the future can be neatly contained within statistical distributions. Crises reveal that the real drivers of financial upheaval are not deviations from a model but the collapse of the narrative assumptions underpinning it.

The philosopher Frank Knight made this distinction almost a century ago, but modern finance has been slow to absorb it. The appeal of quantification is simply too great. Numbers appear objective, impersonal, and authoritative; they seem to remove human fallibility from decision-making. Yet this is precisely where the danger lies. By reducing behaviour to data points, spreadsheet thinking strips finance of its narrative dimension. It assumes that people will act consistently with past patterns, ignoring that human beings are storytelling creatures who respond to myths, fears, and promises. When a narrative catches fire—be it the belief in ever-rising property values, the inevitability of technological disruption, or the promise of digital utopias—no model calibrated to history can withstand the force of belief.

This is not to suggest that spreadsheets are useless. On the contrary, they are invaluable tools when used with humility. The danger arises when they are mistaken for reality itself. A spreadsheet is a model, not the world; a projection, not a prophecy. It can inform decisions but cannot replace judgment. The true challenge for finance is to integrate numerical rigour with narrative awareness. A risk model that anticipates mortgage default rates must also consider the cultural narratives of home ownership. An investment strategy that projects the growth of digital assets must also grapple with the stories of rebellion and speculation that animate the market. Without this integration, blind spots remain, and crises repeat.

The pattern of failure also underscores a broader philosophical point: markets are not machines but conversations. They are arenas in which stories compete, evolve, and sometimes collapse. Prices reflect not only discounted cash flows but the prevailing narrative of what those flows mean. To focus solely on spreadsheets is to mistake the dialogue for arithmetic. When crises strike, it is because the conversation has shifted dramatically, leaving the spreadsheets behind. Recognising this requires a different kind of literacy: the ability to read financial stories as attentively as we read financial statements.

The 2008 crisis, the dot-com collapse, and the cryptocurrency rollercoaster all teach the same lesson. Numbers explain, but stories persuade. Spreadsheet thinking blinds us to this truth, leading us to overestimate the permanence of models and underestimate the volatility of human belief. If financial wisdom is to progress, it must acknowledge that markets are shaped as much by narrative contagion as by numerical calculation. Only then can we begin to address the blind spots that have so often turned spreadsheets into instruments of delusion rather than tools of clarity.

Introducing the Fable Lens

Finance often presents itself as a science of precision, built upon models, ratios, and forecasts that appear to reduce human behaviour to neat formulae. Yet if history teaches us anything, it is that the world of money rarely obeys such tidy boundaries. Markets surge and collapse with a force that leaves analysts scrambling for explanations. Entire communities adopt financial habits that defy economic rationality but make sense when viewed through cultural or moral frameworks. What drives these patterns is not merely mathematics but narrative. People act according to the stories they believe—about prosperity, security, fairness, or ruin. To understand finance truthfully, we need a way of seeing that acknowledges these stories not as decorative embellishments but as the central drivers of behaviour. That is the work of the fable lens.

The fable lens begins with the recognition that human beings are storytelling creatures long before they are calculating ones. We can process numbers, but we make sense of the world through stories. This is as true in financial life as it is in politics, religion, or art. The stories we inherit about money—whether whispered across generations, institutionalised in law, or broadcast by the media—frame the choices we perceive as available. They influence what we consider safe, what we view as reckless, and what we believe to be "enough." In this sense, numbers are subordinate. They serve the narrative rather than dictate it. A compound-interest chart has power only when it is embedded in a story of patience and reward. A stock market graph persuades only when it confirms a broader tale of progress or resilience.

Consider the housing market. For decades, in many Western societies, the dominant narrative has been that owning a home is both a mark of adulthood and the safest form of investment. That story, deeply embedded in culture, explains why households have often taken on unsustainable debt to purchase property. The mathematics of affordability are routinely stretched, yet the narrative endures. Policymakers reinforce it with tax incentives, banks with lending practices, and advertisers with imagery of domestic stability. Numbers play their part, but the real force lies in the fable of home ownership as destiny. It is this story, not spreadsheets, that explains the extraordinary lengths to which individuals and governments go to sustain housing markets, even in the face of crises.

The fable lens also sheds light on why financial behaviour resists prediction. Classical economic theory assumes that individuals act rationally to maximise utility. Spreadsheet models embody this assumption, projecting behaviour as if it were governed by consistent equations. Yet time and again, markets defy these models because they are animated by shifting narratives. The dot-com bubble was not simply a miscalculation of earnings potential; it was the triumph of a story—that the internet had rewritten the rules of business. Investors bought into companies with no profits because the narrative of a "new economy" felt more persuasive than the arithmetic. The eventual collapse was less a failure of numbers than a collapse of belief in that story.

What distinguishes the fable lens from mere anecdote is its insistence that stories are not peripheral but structural. They are not irrational intrusions upon an otherwise rational system; they are constitutive of the system itself. Financial markets require stories to function. A currency depends on the narrative of collective trust. A bank depends on the narrative that deposits will be honoured. An insurance contract depends on the narrative that risk can be shared. Strip away these stories, and the numbers collapse into meaninglessness. The fable lens therefore positions stories not as noise but as the signal. It asks us to analyse markets as theatres of narrative exchange, where prices are shaped as much by belief and identity as by fundamentals.

This perspective also clarifies why crises are such powerful events in financial history. Crises are not merely numerical corrections; they are narrative ruptures. They occur when the dominant fable sustaining a market—such as the perpetual rise of house prices, or the inevitability of technological disruption—suddenly loses credibility. The numbers then fall into line with the new story, often with brutal speed. Understanding crises through the fable lens allows us to see them not as accidents of miscalculation but as turning points in the collective storytelling of economies. The spreadsheet tells us what has happened; the story tells us why.

The utility of the fable lens extends beyond diagnosing failure; it also illuminates resilience. Communities that weather financial storms often do so because they possess narratives that frame hardship in ways that foster endurance. Consider the idea of the "wartime spirit" in Britain during the Second World War or the "American Dream" during the Depression. These were not economic strategies in the technical sense, but cultural fables that mobilised behaviour, encouraging sacrifice, perseverance, or optimism. In modern times, societies that narrate crises as temporary and surmountable tend to recover more quickly than those that frame them as permanent decline. Again, the numbers matter, but the story matters more.

There is an important philosophical dimension to adopting the fable lens. It challenges the assumption that rationality and narrative are opposed. Too often, we imagine that numbers are objective while stories are subjective, and therefore less valuable. Yet this distinction collapses under scrutiny. Numbers themselves are meaningless without a story to interpret them. A government debt-to-GDP ratio of 90 per cent may be terrifying in one context and manageable in another, depending on the narrative that frames it. Japan has sustained debt levels that would be unsustainable elsewhere because the story of domestic trust in government bonds holds. The same number, interpreted through different fables, produces radically different outcomes. Rationality, far from being opposed to narrative, is inseparable from it.

Critics might worry that focusing on stories risks encouraging irrationality, as if narrative analysis were an excuse to indulge in superstition. Yet the fable lens does not ask us to abandon rigour. Rather, it calls for a broader conception of rigour—one that recognises stories as empirical realities in their own right. A narrative can be studied, traced, and tested. We can analyse which stories endure, which collapse, and why. We can examine how narratives interact with numbers, sometimes reinforcing them, sometimes undermining them. The fable lens thus expands the scope of financial analysis rather than diminishing it.

To illustrate this, consider the enduring appeal of gold. On paper, gold has limited practical use compared to other commodities. It yields no interest, generates no cash flow, and its industrial applications are narrow. Yet gold has held its place in human economies for millennia because of the fable that it is a store of eternal value. This story has been passed down through civilisations, from the pharaohs of Egypt to the vaults of Fort Knox. Investors still flock to gold during times of uncertainty, not because of a spreadsheet calculation of yield but because of the enduring story that gold represents safety. The fable lens makes sense of this persistence in a way that numerical models cannot.

The fable lens also equips us with practical tools. By recognising the stories at play in our own financial decisions, we gain agency. Instead of being unconsciously guided by inherited myths, we can evaluate which narratives serve us and which do not. A person raised on the story that debt is shameful may hesitate to invest in education; another raised on the story that debt is opportunity may overextend recklessly. By naming these stories, we can choose which to accept, which to revise, and which to discard. The spreadsheet can tell us the cost of a loan, but only the fable lens can tell us what that loan means to us.

Ultimately, the fable lens positions finance where it belongs: within the broader landscape of human meaning. It reminds us that money is not only an economic instrument but a narrative medium. It connects us to our past, frames our present choices, and projects visions of the future. To understand finance through the fable lens is not to romanticise it, but to see it clearly, in its full human complexity. Numbers explain, but stories persuade—and only by attending to both can we hope to understand why we behave as we do with money, and how we might behave differently.

Chapter 2
The Parable of Enough

The pursuit of wealth has always been framed as a path without end. Ancient myths and modern headlines alike attest to a cultural conviction that more is never truly enough. King Midas wished that everything he touched would turn to gold, only to discover that boundless accumulation meant starvation and despair. Centuries later, lists of the world's billionaires dominate news cycles, their net worths tracked in real time, as though each additional billion carries inherent meaning. Yet if accumulation alone guaranteed fulfilment, such figures would embody peace and satisfaction. Instead, many confess to a gnawing restlessness, perpetually comparing themselves with those even richer. The myth of limitless growth endures not because it delivers contentment but because it exploits a psychological vulnerability: the human tendency to move the goalposts of "enough" each time we approach them.

To understand why "more" rarely satisfies, we must begin with the recognition that wealth is not measured solely in material terms. It is a social construct, defined in relation to others and in relation to our own shifting desires. A farmer in antiquity who owned land sufficient to feed his family and community may have considered himself prosperous. In contrast, a modern executive with millions in assets may still feel inadequate if peers accumulate faster. The difference lies not in absolute resources but in the narrative frameworks that define sufficiency. Economic models that assume utility rises with wealth overlook this truth: that contentment depends less on the quantity of resources than on the story one tells about them.

Psychologists have documented the hedonic treadmill—the tendency for satisfaction to diminish as people adapt to improved circumstances. A pay rise, once received, quickly becomes the new baseline. A larger house, once inhabited, feels normal within months. The target shifts invisibly, keeping fulfilment just out of reach. This phenomenon is not confined to individuals; entire societies operate on similar shifting benchmarks. Economic growth is treated as an unquestionable good, regardless of whether it translates into improved well-being. Political leaders boast of GDP increases, while citizens simultaneously report stagnant happiness levels. The numbers may climb, but the story of "not yet enough" remains stubbornly intact.

History offers alternative narratives. Stoic philosophers taught that freedom lay not in accumulation but in mastering desire. Seneca observed that "he is most wealthy who is content with least," reframing prosperity as an internal disposition rather than an external possession. This philosophy, far from denying the importance of material security, sought to protect individuals from the endless dissatisfaction of moving targets. Similarly, agrarian traditions in many cultures prized sufficiency over excess. Harvest rituals often emphasised gratitude for "enough" to endure the season rather than the pursuit of limitless surplus. The rhythm of planting and reaping instilled an understanding that security derived from balance, not accumulation without end. These historical tales remind us that alternative financial logics have always existed, even if they are often overshadowed by the more glamorous narrative of expansion.

The industrial revolution and the rise of modern capitalism amplified the myth of growth. Productivity increases and technological innovations created material abundance, but they also embedded the conviction that prosperity must always mean "more than before." Economists began to treat growth as both measure and goal, and financial systems were designed to perpetuate expansion. The result is a global economy in which sufficiency is framed as stagnation, and restraint as failure. Yet cracks are visible. Climate change, resource depletion, and widening inequality expose the unsustainability of limitless accumulation. The myth of growth collides with physical and moral limits, forcing a reconsideration of what prosperity might mean.

Redefining prosperity is not an exercise in romantic austerity but a practical necessity. To view sufficiency as weakness is to misunderstand its potential. Enough can be a stabilising principle, fostering resilience rather than fragility. A household that defines prosperity as having resources to meet needs without perpetual escalation is less vulnerable to the anxiety of status competition. A society that embraces sufficiency as a measure of success can allocate resources more equitably and sustainably. The challenge lies in crafting narratives that celebrate enough, not as compromise but as wisdom. Just as myths of limitless accumulation have shaped centuries of behaviour, new stories can reframe sufficiency as strength.

Examples already exist in contemporary practice. The minimalist movement, with its emphasis on intentional living, has gained traction not because of asceticism but because it offers a compelling narrative: that freedom arises from owning less, not more. Similarly, movements advocating degrowth or steady-state economics challenge the fixation on GDP expansion, proposing instead that well-being should be measured by health, education, and environmental stability. These frameworks remain controversial, yet they represent attempts to articulate alternative fables of prosperity. Their influence demonstrates that stories can shift cultural expectations just as powerfully as statistics or models.

To approach finance through the parable of enough is to acknowledge both the danger of limitless growth and the possibility of alternative narratives. It is to see Midas not simply as a figure of myth but as an enduring warning about human psychology. It is to recognise in modern billionaires the continuation of the same restless pursuit that haunted kings and merchants before them. It is also to reclaim traditions that understood sufficiency as a foundation for freedom. Above all, it is to challenge ourselves, individually and collectively, to rewrite the story of prosperity so that "enough" becomes a mark of wisdom rather than failure.

This chapter will trace the myth of accumulation, analyse why enough is a perpetually shifting target, revisit historical models that prized balance over excess, and propose ways of reframing prosperity for contemporary life. Its aim is not to condemn wealth but to liberate us from the dissatisfaction of endless escalation. The parable of enough asks not how much more we can acquire, but whether we have the courage to recognise sufficiency when it appears—and to treat it not as a ceiling but as a source of genuine contentment.

The Myth of Limitless Growth

The belief that more is always better has proved one of the most enduring and seductive narratives in human history. It lies at the heart of ancient myths, modern economic systems, and individual ambition. Yet for all its apparent promise, the pursuit of endless growth often delivers less satisfaction than expected, leaving behind exhaustion, inequality, and a gnawing sense of incompleteness. The paradox is striking: although growth has undeniably lifted billions out of poverty and extended lifespans, the cultural obsession with accumulation reveals a deep fragility in how we measure prosperity. At the personal, corporate, and national level, "enough" remains elusive precisely because the story of "more" is never designed to end.

Classical myths capture this tension with unsettling clarity. The legend of King Midas has endured for millennia not because it describes a literal monarch cursed by golden touch, but because it expresses a timeless truth about human desire. Midas believed that endless accumulation would bring fulfilment, only to discover that abundance without limit turns nourishment into lifeless treasure and relationships into tragedy. The myth resonates because it mirrors a recurring human pattern: the hope that one more acquisition, one more deal, or one more breakthrough will finally satisfy. Yet as with Midas, the transformation of everything into gold reveals not wealth but deprivation.

In modern times, this same myth resurfaces in the way we track billionaires' fortunes as if they were athletes competing in an endless tournament. Financial news updates readers daily on shifts in net worth, celebrating individuals who climb the rankings while rarely questioning what another billion dollars represents beyond status. Interviews with ultra-wealthy individuals often reveal not serenity but anxiety: the fear of losing position, the endless comparison with peers. Sociologists studying wealth elites consistently find that the definition of "rich" shifts upwards with proximity to greater fortunes. A household with £10 million may feel comfortable until it neighbours someone with £100 million, at which point insufficiency creeps in. The cultural narrative of limitless growth fuels this cycle by framing accumulation not as a means to an end but as the end itself.

Economics as a discipline has both reflected and reinforced this obsession. Gross Domestic Product became the central metric of national success in the twentieth century, elevating growth from a means of social improvement to an unquestionable objective. Political leaders campaign on promises of ever-expanding output, and financial markets treat slowing growth as crisis regardless of underlying well-being. Yet GDP was never intended as a comprehensive measure of prosperity. Its architect, Simon Kuznets, cautioned against equating national income with welfare, warning that metrics of production could not capture distribution, quality of life, or sustainability. Despite this, the fixation on growth has hardened into orthodoxy, shaping fiscal and corporate strategies worldwide. The myth of limitless expansion has been institutionalised, transforming what should be a tool into a cultural script.

The consequences are visible both globally and individually. At the planetary level, endless growth collides with ecological limits. Rising consumption drives climate change, biodiversity loss, and resource depletion, threatening the very conditions upon which economic activity depends. Advocates of "green growth" argue that innovation can decouple prosperity from environmental harm, but critics note that efficiency gains are often offset by increased consumption elsewhere—a phenomenon known as the rebound effect. At the individual level, the relentless pursuit of more manifests as burnout, debt, and dissatisfaction. Surveys in affluent countries consistently show that once basic needs are met, additional wealth contributes little to happiness. The hedonic treadmill ensures that each increment quickly becomes normalised, fuelling the desire for the next. *More rarely satisfies because it recalibrates expectations rather than fulfilling them.*

Historical alternatives demonstrate that societies have not always equated prosperity with endless escalation. Stoic thinkers in ancient Rome urged restraint, teaching that freedom came from limiting desires rather than multiplying possessions. Agrarian communities across cultures often prized balance over expansion, embedding gratitude rituals at harvest that emphasised sufficiency. Even within religious traditions, warnings against greed are central: Christianity warns that one cannot serve both God and money; Buddhism identifies craving as a root of suffering; Islam prescribes zakat, obligating redistribution rather than hoarding. These traditions remind us that the myth of limitless growth, far from universal, is a particular cultural construction—powerful, but neither inevitable nor eternal.

Philosophical reflection adds another layer. The fixation on more presupposes that human desire can be satiated by quantity, but this misunderstands the nature of aspiration. Desire is qualitative: it seeks meaning, status, connection, identity. More money may temporarily mask these longings, but it cannot resolve them. A corporation chasing perpetual quarterly growth may satisfy investors briefly, but the narrative of "bigger" often undermines resilience, leading to reckless risk-taking or ethical compromise. Nations that prioritise expansion above all else may deliver rising GDP while neglecting education, health, and civic trust. *The myth of limitless growth mistakes scale for significance, confusing accumulation with fulfilment.*

Modern debates about sustainability reveal the need to rethink prosperity. The degrowth movement, controversial though it remains, highlights the impossibility of infinite expansion on a finite planet. Advocates propose shifting focus from quantity of output to quality of life, prioritising well-being, equity, and ecological balance over raw production. Mainstream institutions, too, are beginning to acknowledge the limits of growth as the sole metric. The United Nations' Human Development Index, Bhutan's Gross National Happiness, and various well-being budgets experiment with broader measures of success. These initiatives are not merely technocratic adjustments; they represent attempts to tell new stories about prosperity, stories in which "enough" is framed as wisdom rather than failure.

At the personal level, movements such as minimalism and financial independence echo similar themes. Individuals disillusioned by the pursuit of endless consumption increasingly embrace the idea that sufficiency, not surplus, creates freedom. The FIRE (Financial Independence, Retire Early) community, for example, redefines prosperity as having enough resources to reclaim time and autonomy rather than to perpetually chase higher income. These examples illustrate how alternative narratives can reshape behaviour as effectively as dominant myths. They reveal that growth need not be abandoned, but it must be recontextualised—treated as a means rather than an ultimate goal.

The persistence of the myth of limitless growth is a testament to its psychological and cultural power. It appeals to ambition, competition, and hope, making it deeply resistant to critique. Yet its failures—at the level of the environment, of social equity, and of individual satisfaction—are increasingly evident. If societies are to craft sustainable futures, they must confront this myth directly, questioning its assumptions and experimenting with new narratives of prosperity. Myths cannot be eradicated by data alone; they must be replaced by stories that are equally compelling. Stories that reframe sufficiency as strength, that prize balance over escalation, and that measure wealth not by accumulation but by the flourishing it enables.

To explore the myth of limitless growth is to uncover both the seduction and the danger of a narrative that has shaped civilisations. From Midas's golden touch to the net worth of modern billionaires, the story is the same: accumulation promises fulfilment but delivers dissatisfaction when treated as an end in itself. What endures are not the numbers amassed but the human need for meaning, recognition, and security—needs that no amount of "more" can fully satisfy. By recognising growth as myth rather than destiny, we open space for other stories, ones that offer a more enduring definition of what it means to prosper.

Enough as a Moving Target

Ask almost anyone how much money would make them feel secure, and the answer is usually just above what they already have. This subtle inflation of desire occurs regardless of income level. The individual earning £40,000 a year imagines stability at £60,000; the person at £200,000 longs for £300,000; and the millionaire quietly calculates that £10 million might finally be enough. This moving horizon of sufficiency is not a quirk of personality but a consistent feature of human behaviour. The definition of "enough" shifts as circumstances change, ensuring that satisfaction is always deferred.

One of the most telling pieces of research into this phenomenon was conducted by Daniel Kahneman and Angus Deaton, who found that emotional well-being rose with income up to around $75,000 in the United States (adjusted for context and living costs elsewhere), but plateaued beyond that. Life evaluation—the sense of success when reflecting abstractly—continued to rise, but the day-to-day experience of happiness stabilised. The study illuminated a paradox: even when income increases provide little added joy, people still pursue more because their perception of enough adjusts with each new benchmark. The baseline reconfigures itself, creating what psychologists call the hedonic treadmill—running harder without ever arriving.

This treadmill is not confined to personal finance; it manifests across cultures and historical periods. In Victorian Britain, middle-class families once considered a single live-in servant a sign of modest affluence. Within decades, that marker had shifted upwards, and households aspired to multiple staff, carriages, and holidays abroad. In contemporary contexts, the markers of "enough" might be private schooling, a second home, or a portfolio of investments. Each is treated as necessity rather than luxury once attained. The shifting standard demonstrates how wealth is not judged in absolute terms but relative ones—measured against peers, aspirations, and cultural expectations.

The role of comparison is particularly corrosive. Social scientists have shown that relative income predicts happiness more reliably than absolute income. A pay rise brings fleeting satisfaction until one discovers a colleague has earned more. Luxury once enjoyed privately now becomes subject to public display and comparison through social media, amplifying the sense of insufficiency. A family holiday that might once have been cherished becomes a source of dissatisfaction when measured against the curated images of acquaintances in more exotic destinations. The cultural acceleration of comparison ensures that "enough" is continually redefined by others' narratives as much as by one's own.

At the level of elites, this pattern becomes especially stark. Studies of ultra-wealthy households reveal that even those worth tens of millions often perceive themselves as only moderately well-off, citing billionaires as the true benchmark. The language used in such circles is revealing: "comfortable" replaces "rich," "secure" replaces "abundant." The bar moves so consistently upward that wealth itself ceases to provide reassurance. This perpetual deferral explains why philanthropic pledges by billionaires often coexist with continued accumulation. Their sense of enough remains unsettled, tethered to competition rather than sufficiency.

Yet dissatisfaction is not an inevitable outcome of rising wealth. Historical and philosophical traditions provide counterpoints. The Stoics urged individuals to define sufficiency internally rather than externally, emphasising mastery of desire over acquisition of goods. The Epicureans argued that pleasure derived from simple satisfactions—friendship, shelter, nourishment—was more enduring than the pursuit of endless luxuries. In agrarian societies, sufficiency was often framed through seasonal cycles: having enough grain to survive the winter or enough livestock to sustain the family was the ultimate measure. These narratives anchored "enough" to survival and gratitude rather than escalation. Their enduring relevance lies in reminding us that sufficiency is always a matter of perspective, not arithmetic.

Modern psychology reinforces these ancient insights. Research into gratitude practices demonstrates that focusing attention on what one already possesses reduces the restless search for more. Experiments in behavioural economics show that when individuals consciously cap their consumption goals, satisfaction increases and stress diminishes. Conversely, those who continually recalibrate their definition of enough report higher anxiety, regardless of their actual resources. *The moving target of sufficiency fuels dissatisfaction not because people lack resources but because they lack stability in their expectations.*

This phenomenon also has implications for policy and economics. Nations that equate prosperity with perpetual GDP growth encourage citizens to frame "enough" at a national scale as endless expansion. Alternative measures, such as Bhutan's Gross National Happiness or New Zealand's well-being budgets, attempt to re-anchor sufficiency in broader dimensions of human flourishing. These initiatives, while imperfect, recognise that the collective sense of enough can be shifted by cultural narratives as much as by material production. The challenge is to persuade societies that stability and balance can be as desirable as escalation.

It is important to note, however, that the shifting horizon of enough has adaptive functions. The desire for more has historically driven innovation, exploration, and growth. If societies had been content at subsistence levels, technological and medical advances might have stagnated. The restlessness embedded in human psychology fuels ambition. The problem arises when the horizon becomes pathological—when the pursuit of more undermines well-being, destabilises societies, or exceeds planetary boundaries. In such contexts, recognising the moving target of enough becomes a matter not only of individual wisdom but of collective survival.

Practical illustrations abound. The FIRE movement (Financial Independence, Retire Early) explicitly challenges the moving target by encouraging individuals to calculate their "enough number"—a savings threshold that allows them to exit traditional employment and reclaim autonomy. The popularity of this approach demonstrates a growing hunger for clarity about sufficiency. Similarly, minimalist lifestyles, which frame prosperity in terms of reduced clutter and intentional consumption, provide alternative narratives that resist escalation. These examples reveal that while "enough" may shift by default, it can also be anchored deliberately through conscious redefinition.

Ultimately, the moving target of enough reveals a central paradox of financial life: satisfaction is less a function of resources than of narrative stability. When enough is defined by comparison, escalation, or shifting cultural standards, it will always retreat just beyond reach. When anchored in values, sufficiency, or gratitude, it becomes attainable. The challenge, both personal and societal, lies in recognising that *enough is not a number but a story*—and in deciding which story to live by.

Historical Tales of Sufficiency

The idea that prosperity requires endless expansion is a relatively modern invention. For much of human history, sufficiency rather than excess stood as the measure of a well-lived life. Ancient philosophies, agrarian practices, and communal traditions often emphasised balance over accumulation, recognising that abundance without restraint was as likely to corrupt as it was to secure. To trace these stories is not to indulge nostalgia but to uncover alternative models of prosperity that remain profoundly relevant. They remind us that "enough" has long been understood not as limitation but as freedom.

Stoic philosophy offers one of the clearest articulations of sufficiency. Emerging in Athens in the third century BCE and flourishing under Roman thinkers such as Seneca, Epictetus, and Marcus Aurelius, Stoicism counselled that external wealth mattered little compared to internal mastery. Seneca, himself a wealthy statesman, warned that riches could enslave those who pursued them without discipline, while modest means could suffice for those who understood their own needs. *He is most wealthy who is content with least,* he wrote, not as an ascetic rejection of material life but as an invitation to recognise the futility of insatiable desire. The Stoic ideal was not poverty but self-command—the ability to remain unshaken whether fortune delivered abundance or scarcity. Their emphasis on sufficiency reframed prosperity as a state of character rather than a balance sheet.

Agrarian traditions around the world echoed this philosophy in practical form. In subsistence economies, survival hinged not on limitless expansion but on cyclical sufficiency. Harvest festivals, from the Jewish Sukkot to European harvest homes, were not celebrations of surplus alone but rituals of gratitude for "enough" to endure the coming season. Communities recognised the dangers of both scarcity and excess: too little threatened hunger, too much invited waste or envy. Agrarian wisdom therefore prized balance, reinforcing a cultural narrative that prosperity lay in moderation. These traditions also embedded reciprocity—sharing with neighbours, tithing to religious institutions, setting aside stores for times of famine. Sufficiency was never purely individual; it was collective, bound up with the survival of the community.

Eastern philosophies reinforced similar themes. In Confucian teaching, prosperity was tied to harmony and duty rather than accumulation. Wealth gained at the expense of virtue was considered hollow. Buddhist thought went further, identifying craving as the root of suffering and advocating a middle way between indulgence and deprivation. Here again, sufficiency was prized not because abundance was unavailable but because unchecked desire was seen as corrosive to well-being. These frameworks remind us that the idolisation of limitless growth is culturally specific, not universal. Many traditions independently arrived at the recognition that "enough" was the most reliable foundation for flourishing.

Even within medieval Europe, where feudal hierarchies dictated economic life, cultural narratives cautioned against excess. The Christian tradition consistently condemned avarice as one of the seven deadly sins. The concept of usury, widely prohibited for centuries, reflected suspicion of accumulation divorced from labour or need. Monastic orders, despite variations in practice, modelled lives of sufficiency, cultivating land for sustenance and teaching that spiritual wealth outweighed material stores. Jubilee laws, drawn from biblical precedent, prescribed periodic debt forgiveness, reflecting an understanding that accumulation without limit destabilised communities. These practices and stories collectively reinforced the idea that prosperity without boundaries was dangerous both morally and socially.

Contrast this with the mythologies of kings and conquerors whose legacies of expansion often ended in downfall. Alexander the Great died at thirty-two after conquering much of the known world, yet his empire disintegrated almost immediately, its scale unsustainable. Roman emperors who indulged in extravagance became cautionary figures in history, their excesses narrated as preludes to collapse. The moral embedded in these tales was not subtle: unchecked appetite leads to ruin, while sufficiency preserves order. Storytelling thus functioned as a form of cultural guardrail, reminding individuals and societies that growth for its own sake was perilous.

The relevance of these historical tales becomes clearer when set against the modern restlessness of moving targets. Where contemporary culture prizes escalation—bigger homes, higher GDP, ever-increasing consumption—ancient and agrarian traditions often told stories of contentment. The Stoic who considered a simple meal sufficient, the farmer who gave thanks for a stable harvest, the monk who renounced excess for clarity of mind—all represent alternative narratives. Their importance lies not in prescribing literal imitation but in demonstrating that prosperity has always been open to reinterpretation. The assumption that "enough" is a form of failure is a cultural choice, not an inevitability.

Practical lessons can be drawn from these traditions. Gratitude rituals, long embedded in agrarian societies, find modern expression in psychological research showing that intentional reflection on sufficiency enhances well-being. Stoic practices of negative visualisation—imagining loss to appreciate what one has—resonate with contemporary strategies for cultivating resilience. Even the communal ethos of sufficiency, emphasising shared responsibility, parallels current conversations about sustainability and inequality. Historical tales of sufficiency are not relics; they are resources for rethinking how financial life might be lived differently today.

What unites these diverse traditions is the recognition that wealth without boundaries leads to instability, while sufficiency fosters balance. The Stoics articulated it philosophically, agrarian communities practised it ritually, and religious systems codified it morally. Together they form a counter-narrative to the myth of limitless growth, reminding us that the story of "enough" has always been available, even if it is often drowned out by louder tales of conquest and accumulation. To recover these stories is not to retreat into the past but to reclaim wisdom that has guided countless generations: that true prosperity is not measured by how much more we can acquire, but by the clarity with which we can recognise when we already have enough.

Redefining Prosperity

For much of modern history, prosperity has been synonymous with expansion—more output, more consumption, more growth. Yet beneath the surface of this dominant narrative lies a tension that has become impossible to ignore. The fixation on "more" has not delivered universal satisfaction, nor has it produced stability. Instead, it has led to inequality, ecological strain, and a widespread sense that even the affluent remain restless. To move forward, we must interrogate whether our inherited definition of prosperity truly serves us, and whether sufficiency—long dismissed as compromise—can be redefined as a robust and sustainable model of flourishing.

The first step in this redefinition is to recognise the inadequacy of prevailing measures. Gross Domestic Product, the primary yardstick of national prosperity, tells us nothing about distribution, environmental impact, or quality of life. A rise in GDP may reflect increased spending on healthcare after a pollution crisis, or rebuilding efforts after a natural disaster, yet such activity is hardly a sign of genuine well-being. Equally, GDP treats unpaid care work, central to social stability, as valueless. The reliance on this single measure embodies a worldview that equates prosperity with sheer scale rather than depth. To redefine prosperity, we must be willing to question metrics that flatten human experience into narrow counts of transactions.

At the individual level, prosperity is often framed as financial abundance, but research consistently shows that beyond a certain threshold of security, additional wealth contributes little to happiness. The hedonic treadmill ensures that each increment of income quickly resets expectations, shifting the definition of "enough." By contrast, sufficiency offers stability. *When prosperity is redefined as having enough to live securely, contribute meaningfully, and sustain relationships, it becomes attainable rather than endlessly deferred.* This reframing does not negate ambition; it places ambition in service of values rather than perpetual escalation.

Contemporary movements illustrate this shift in action. The rise of the FIRE community (Financial Independence, Retire Early) reflects a growing desire to redefine prosperity as freedom of time rather than accumulation of goods. Minimalist living, often caricatured as austerity, is better understood as a deliberate reorientation: prosperity measured in clarity, autonomy, and reduced dependence on consumption. At the societal level, well-being indices, such as Bhutan's Gross National Happiness and New Zealand's Living Standards Framework, attempt to re-anchor prosperity in health, education, equity, and environmental sustainability. These examples demonstrate that redefining prosperity is not theoretical—it is already underway, challenging entrenched economic narratives.

The sustainability dimension is particularly urgent. Limitless growth collides with planetary boundaries, threatening climate stability and resource security. Redefining prosperity around sufficiency aligns economic life with ecological realities. This is not about romanticising frugality but about recognising that a definition of prosperity which undermines the conditions of its own survival is incoherent. A sustainable prosperity values resilience, stewardship, and intergenerational responsibility. It prizes efficiency not for the sake of expansion but for the sake of balance. In this light, sufficiency is not compromise but pragmatism: the art of thriving within limits.

Yet resistance to sufficiency is strong, in part because of its cultural connotations. To many, "enough" sounds like settling, as though it were the language of the resigned rather than the prosperous. The challenge is therefore as much narrative as economic. We require new stories of prosperity that celebrate balance, gratitude, and contribution. In ancient agrarian traditions, prosperity was often tied to seasonal cycles, where gratitude for "enough" grain to endure winter was central to communal rituals. Stoic philosophy, too, reframed wealth as contentment with what suffices. To recover these stories in modern contexts is to enrich the meaning of prosperity, grounding it not in relentless pursuit but in enduring satisfaction.

A critical aspect of this redefinition lies in expanding the scope of prosperity beyond individuals to communities. Prosperity cannot be reduced to private wealth when public goods—healthcare, education, safety, and trust—form the fabric of well-being. A society that tolerates vast inequality may boast high GDP figures, but it is brittle, its prosperity undermined by exclusion and resentment. A sufficiency model acknowledges that shared stability enhances individual flourishing. Prosperity is therefore best redefined not as private accumulation but as collective resilience.

Redefining prosperity also involves rethinking success in business. For decades, corporate performance has been evaluated primarily through shareholder value, encouraging strategies that maximise short-term profit at the expense of long-term stability. Alternative frameworks, such as the "triple bottom line" or "stakeholder capitalism," attempt to broaden the definition of corporate prosperity to include social and environmental outcomes. While imperfect in practice, these approaches reflect a growing recognition that financial success detached from sufficiency and sustainability is unstable. Just as individuals can be trapped in the endless pursuit of more, corporations and economies can become destabilised by the same logic.

The philosophical underpinnings of sufficiency also merit attention. To redefine prosperity is to engage with deeper questions of purpose. What does it mean to flourish? Is prosperity the ability to consume without limit, or is it the freedom to live with dignity, creativity, and security? Sufficiency, properly understood, shifts the answer towards the latter. It reframes prosperity as qualitative rather than quantitative—concerned with meaning rather than magnitude. This perspective does not dismiss material needs but contextualises them within a broader vision of the good life.

It is worth recognising that redefining prosperity is not a retreat from growth altogether. Growth remains valuable when it serves human flourishing and respects ecological balance. What sufficiency resists is growth as an unquestioned end in itself. The goal is not to eliminate ambition but to redirect it—towards innovation that sustains communities, towards efficiency that reduces waste, towards equity that broadens participation. In this way, sufficiency becomes a model not of compromise but of direction, guiding ambition towards durable outcomes rather than fleeting gains.

The task ahead is as much cultural as economic. To redefine prosperity requires changing what societies admire and reward. Today, headlines celebrate the billionaire who doubles his fortune, while barely noting the teacher who contributes to community resilience or the company that sacrifices short-term profit for long-term sustainability. If sufficiency is to be embraced as prosperity, cultural narratives must shift to honour balance as much as expansion. History offers resources here: myths that warn against greed, philosophies that prize moderation, and traditions that celebrate sufficiency as wisdom. Recasting these stories for contemporary contexts can equip societies with a richer understanding of prosperity.

Redefining prosperity as sufficiency is therefore both an intellectual and practical project. It challenges the assumption that "more" is always better, demonstrates the stability that sufficiency provides, and invites us to imagine prosperity as balance, resilience, and meaning. Far from a compromise, sufficiency offers a foundation for enduring prosperity in a world where resources, time, and attention are finite. It is not the language of resignation but of confidence: the recognition that true wealth lies not in endless accumulation but in knowing when enough is already at hand.

Chapter 3
Greed's Mirror

Few forces in human history have been as simultaneously vilified and glorified as greed. It sits at the heart of countless stories, from ancient fables to modern financial scandals, serving as both a cautionary tale and a seductive promise. Greed is rarely acknowledged in neutral terms; it is portrayed as a corrupting impulse, a shadow of ambition that crosses an invisible threshold. From Aesop's tale of the dog who loses his bone by snapping at its reflection to Charles Dickens's portraits of avarice in figures such as Scrooge, greed has been cast as a mirror in which societies examine their own appetites and anxieties. What these stories reveal is that greed is not simply an individual failing but a cultural barometer. It helps define the line between acceptable aspiration and destructive excess.

The persistence of these tales suggests that greed cannot be eradicated, only contained. Its presence across cultures and epochs points to a universal human struggle: desire that grows faster than reason. The recurring pattern is clear and recognisable: opportunity presents itself, ambition rises to meet it, overreach follows, and collapse ensues. The cycle repeats not because people fail to learn the lessons of the past but because the allure of excess has always been more persuasive than the caution of moderation. The stories endure precisely because each generation must grapple anew with the temptation. By narrating the fall of the greedy, cultures encode boundaries of acceptable behaviour, using vivid narrative rather than abstract principles.

Modern finance provides abundant evidence of this cycle in action. The collapse of Enron at the beginning of the 2000s epitomised corporate greed disguised as innovation. Executives constructed elaborate schemes to inflate profits, creating the illusion of limitless success until the edifice crumbled, leaving employees without pensions and investors with catastrophic losses. Two decades later, the implosion of the cryptocurrency exchange FTX revealed strikingly similar dynamics: charismatic leadership, promises of boundless returns, reckless risk-taking, and eventual ruin. These scandals are not aberrations but modern iterations of an old story. They illustrate that greed is not confined to individuals but can infect institutions, markets, and entire sectors, creating collective delusions sustained until reality intrudes.

The resonance of such stories lies in their memorability. Charts and data sets documenting financial mismanagement may be accurate, but they rarely linger in public consciousness. The narrative of downfall, however, sticks. People remember the hubris of Icarus, not the structural analysis of aerodynamics; they recall the image of a CEO led away in handcuffs more readily than the fine print of regulatory reports. Stories of greed and collapse function as cultural touchstones, embedding moral lessons that statistics cannot. They remind us not merely of technical missteps but of the psychological and ethical dimensions of financial behaviour. *It is not the balance sheet that captivates but the arc of ambition and fall.*

Why societies demonise greed is therefore not simply moral posturing but a form of self-preservation. By casting greed as vice, communities attempt to contain its destabilising potential. Yet the relationship is ambivalent, for the same societies that condemn greed also celebrate ambition, competition, and achievement. The line between virtue and vice is intentionally blurred. Greed is thus the mirror: when we condemn it, we also confront our own aspirations and the discomfort of seeing how easily they could tip into excess. This duality explains why stories of greed resonate so deeply—they are not about others alone but about ourselves, our neighbours, our institutions.

This chapter examines greed not as an abstract sin but as a recurring human pattern, a force that shapes financial systems as powerfully as spreadsheets or models. It will trace how cultures have used stories to delineate the boundaries of ambition, why the cycle of temptation and collapse repeats, and how modern financial scandals echo ancient fables. By the end, the reader will see why moral lessons conveyed through narrative endure longer than warnings delivered through numbers, and why understanding greed's mirror is essential for navigating both personal choices and collective financial life.

Why We Demonize Greed

Greed has always been more than a personal flaw; it is a story that societies tell themselves to mark the limits of acceptable ambition. Cultures across time have relied on cautionary tales of avarice to regulate behaviour, translating the abstract dangers of unchecked desire into vivid images that could be remembered, repeated, and internalised. We demonise greed not because wealth or aspiration is inherently suspect, but because greed represents the moment ambition turns corrosive—when individual desire threatens communal stability. To understand why this narrative recurs so insistently, one must see greed not as an occasional lapse but as a cultural mirror that reflects anxieties about power, inequality, and excess.

The earliest fables establish this function clearly. Aesop's tales, circulating orally long before they were written down in the sixth century BCE, captured human tendencies in concise, memorable form. In the story of the dog with a bone who, greedy for the reflection in the water, loses what he already holds, the moral is simple but profound: in grasping for more, one risks losing enough. Such fables endure because they distil complex truths into images a child can grasp but an adult can still find unsettling. They warn that greed destabilises by turning sufficiency into insufficiency, contentment into hunger. The demonisation here is pedagogical: society codifies greed as a vice in order to preserve moderation as a virtue.

The moral weight of greed becomes even more pronounced in religious traditions. Christianity identifies avarice as one of the seven deadly sins, pairing it with images of spiritual decay and eternal peril. Medieval sermons often depicted misers as damned figures, their hoarded gold transformed into chains that dragged them to perdition. Islam emphasises zakat, the obligation to redistribute wealth, explicitly as an antidote to greed, while Buddhism frames craving as the root of suffering. Across traditions, greed is not condemned merely for its effect on individuals but for its threat to community cohesion. By demonising it, religions reinforced norms of generosity, stewardship, and shared responsibility.

Literature amplified these themes by embodying greed in characters whose fates served as stark warnings. Shakespeare's Shylock, Dickens's Scrooge, and Balzac's Père Grandet represent greed not simply as a personal defect but as a distortion of humanity. Dickens in particular wielded avarice as a moral foil to expose Victorian anxieties about industrial capitalism and widening inequality. Scrooge is memorable not because of his ledger but because of his transformation, dramatising the possibility of redemption when greed is renounced. Stories such as these did not merely entertain; they instructed, reminding readers where society believed the boundaries of ambition lay. *Greed became legible through narrative in ways that economic theory could never achieve.*

The demonisation of greed also performs a political function. By casting excess accumulation as immoral, societies draw attention to the destabilising effects of inequality. Ancient Rome witnessed periodic attempts to curb land accumulation by elites, often justified by appeals to fairness and the dangers of avarice. In more recent history, public outrage at financial scandals often takes narrative form. The South Sea Bubble of 1720, which ruined investors across Britain, gave rise to pamphlets and plays portraying speculators as dupes of their own greed. The 2008 financial crisis produced similar stories, with bankers cast as reckless villains whose insatiable pursuit of profit collapsed global systems. Data on derivatives or mortgage-backed securities may have explained the mechanics, but it was the narrative of greed that mobilised public anger and reform.

Yet the demonisation of greed is never straightforward, for societies also celebrate ambition, innovation, and competition. The boundary between aspiration and avarice is porous, and cultures rely on narrative to manage the ambiguity. Entrepreneurs are lauded for vision, until their success appears excessive; investors are admired for boldness, until their risk-taking topples institutions. Demonising greed thus functions as a flexible tool: it allows societies to draw lines retrospectively, condemning excess after collapse while tolerating or even encouraging aggressive pursuit beforehand. This is why scandals like Enron or FTX so readily become parables. Their stories confirm long-standing archetypes of greed's overreach, reminding communities of the risks of celebrating ambition without limits.

The persistence of these narratives suggests that greed is best understood as a cultural category, not a fixed behaviour. What is labelled greedy in one era may be praised as ambition in another. Charging interest was once condemned as usury; today it is a pillar of global finance. Lavish displays of wealth might once have been derided as wasteful; today they are often packaged as lifestyle aspiration. By demonising greed, societies negotiate these shifting boundaries, deciding which behaviours protect communal stability and which threaten it. The tales endure not because they deliver immutable truths but because they adapt, providing moral orientation in changing contexts.

Philosophically, the demonisation of greed speaks to a deeper discomfort with insatiability. Unlike hunger or thirst, which can be satisfied, greed has no natural endpoint. It promises fulfilment but produces restlessness. By telling stories of downfall—Aesop's dog, Dickens's miser, the ruined speculator—cultures externalise this anxiety, giving form to the fear that unchecked desire may unravel both individual lives and social orders. Demonising greed becomes a way of containing the uncontainable, offering reassurance that communities can name and punish the vice even if they cannot eradicate it.

Ultimately, we demonise greed because stories of its dangers do the cultural work that data, law, and policy cannot. They shape moral imagination, teaching through narrative where ambition ends and vice begins. In condemning greed, societies are not simply attacking individuals who want too much; they are defining, for themselves, what counts as enough. These stories endure not because they resolve the tension but because they illuminate it, reminding us that the struggle between desire and restraint is one of the most enduring features of financial life.

The Temptation Cycle

Financial history is littered with patterns that seem unique in their details but strikingly familiar in their structure. A new opportunity emerges, promising wealth to those bold enough to seize it. Enthusiasm swells into overconfidence, and restraint is cast aside. Then, inevitably, comes the collapse—shattering fortunes, reputations, and sometimes entire economies. This recurring cycle of opportunity, overreach, and downfall is not simply an economic rhythm but a human one. It reflects our deepest psychological impulses: hope, fear, desire, and denial. What makes the cycle so persistent is not the novelty of the instruments involved—whether tulips, railroads, dot-com stocks, or digital tokens—but the enduring vulnerability of human beings to temptation.

One of the earliest and most famous examples of this cycle can be traced to the Dutch tulip mania of the seventeenth century. What began as fascination with exotic flowers quickly transformed into speculative frenzy. Tulips were no longer admired for their beauty but traded as financial instruments, their prices spiralling far beyond intrinsic worth. The opportunity was alluring: to turn a bulb into a fortune. As overreach set in, stories spread of single bulbs commanding the price of a townhouse. When the collapse inevitably arrived, it exposed not only the fragility of speculative markets but also the psychology of a society enthralled by the promise of effortless gain. Tulip mania has since become shorthand for irrational exuberance, yet its significance lies less in the flowers themselves than in the cycle of temptation they embodied.

The South Sea Bubble of 1720 illustrates a similar trajectory on a grander scale. Investors in Britain poured money into the South Sea Company, enticed by visions of immense profits from trade in South America. Shares skyrocketed as enthusiasm snowballed, driven not by rational assessments of opportunity but by the contagious excitement of others' apparent success. The overreach was spectacular, with fortunes staked on promises that could not possibly be delivered. When the collapse came, it devastated households and tarnished the reputations of prominent politicians and financiers. Once again, the narrative of temptation unfolded predictably: opportunity misread, ambition unchecked, reality reasserted. The cycle was not about maritime trade; it was about human susceptibility to the allure of quick gain.

Modern finance has offered countless iterations of this pattern. The dot-com boom of the late 1990s mirrored tulip mania in digital form. The internet promised revolutionary opportunities, and in many respects delivered them, but investors conflated genuine innovation with speculative excess. Start-ups with no profits—or even products—attracted valuations in the billions. The mantra was that the old rules no longer applied, a familiar justification in moments of overreach. When the bubble burst, trillions were wiped from markets, yet the underlying cycle had played out as it always had. Likewise, the housing market collapse of 2008 followed the same arc. The opportunity of accessible home ownership, combined with financial engineering that disguised risk, morphed into reckless lending and frenzied speculation. When collapse came, it triggered the worst global financial crisis since the Great Depression.

The cryptocurrency boom and subsequent bust of the past decade provides a contemporary case study. Bitcoin and other digital assets began as opportunities to reimagine finance outside traditional systems. For some, they represented legitimate innovation in decentralised technology. But as enthusiasm surged, speculation overtook utility. Stories of overnight millionaires spread like wildfire, fuelling a culture of risk-taking in which restraint seemed obsolete. Exchanges like FTX rode the wave of overreach, their founders celebrated as visionaries. Yet when reality punctured the bubble, what remained was ruin: investors lost savings, firms collapsed, and trust evaporated. The cycle had played out once again, this time amplified by global media and real-time trading platforms.

What is striking in each of these cases is how predictable the structure becomes when viewed in hindsight. Opportunity ignites imagination, overreach clouds judgement, collapse delivers a brutal reckoning. Yet in the moment, participants believe they are living through something new, unprecedented, exempt from history's lessons. *The temptation cycle persists because it exploits fundamental human biases: overconfidence, herd behaviour, and the belief that this time will be different.*

Psychologists have studied these dynamics extensively. Prospect theory, developed by Daniel Kahneman and Amos Tversky, demonstrates that people are more sensitive to losses than to gains, leading them to take disproportionate risks in the hope of avoiding loss. Behavioural finance highlights how herding behaviour amplifies bubbles, as individuals take cues from others rather than independent analysis. Neuroscientific studies reveal that the anticipation of reward activates the brain's dopamine system, fostering a sense of euphoria that overwhelms caution. These findings confirm what historical narratives already show: temptation is not merely a cultural phenomenon but a cognitive and emotional one.

The temptation cycle also reveals an uncomfortable truth about collective memory. Each collapse prompts vows of reform and resolutions to learn from mistakes. Yet within a generation, new opportunities emerge, and the lessons fade. This amnesia is not accidental; it is part of the cycle itself. The pain of collapse recedes, while the allure of opportunity shines brightly once more. The very stories told to warn against greed often end up fuelling curiosity about how fortunes were made before they were lost. History, instead of inoculating societies against repetition, sometimes inspires them to try again with different instruments.

Understanding the temptation cycle requires grappling with its dual nature. On one hand, it exposes the dangers of unchecked desire, reminding us of the fragility of financial systems built on exuberance. On the other, it highlights the very impulses that drive innovation and progress. Opportunity is not in itself destructive; it is the fuel of enterprise. Overreach is not inevitable; it is the consequence of forgetting restraint. Collapse, though devastating, often clears the ground for new systems to emerge stronger. The cycle is destructive, but it is also generative, shaping the evolution of economies and cultures.

The enduring challenge is whether societies can retain the dynamism of opportunity without succumbing to the inevitability of collapse. Regulations, safeguards, and cultural narratives all attempt to temper overreach, but none can fully eliminate the pull of temptation. Stories of past bubbles and scandals therefore remain essential, not as historical curiosities but as active tools of memory. They remind us that the cycle is less about markets than about human nature. *To understand finance is to understand the psychology of temptation, the way opportunity transforms into overreach, and why collapse is so often required to reset the balance.*

The temptation cycle will recur as long as human beings are drawn to the promise of more. Recognising its structure does not guarantee escape, but it equips us with perspective. By studying the patterns—ancient and modern—we learn not to believe in immunity from history. Opportunity will always tempt, overreach will always threaten, and collapse will always teach. The question is not whether the cycle can be eradicated but whether individuals and societies can learn to navigate it with greater clarity, resisting the illusion that the next opportunity is exempt from the laws of human behaviour.

Greed in Modern Finance

Few words capture the public imagination in times of financial crisis as sharply as "greed". It is invoked in headlines, parliamentary debates, and protest chants because it provides a human face for systemic collapse. Numbers and models may explain the mechanics, but greed tells the story. Modern financial scandals such as Enron's collapse at the dawn of the twenty-first century and the implosion of FTX in the digital age reveal greed not as a relic of ancient parables but as a recurring, dynamic force embedded in global markets. These episodes remind us that when ambition mutates into avarice, the consequences spread far beyond boardrooms, reshaping economies and eroding trust.

The Enron scandal stands as one of the most emblematic cases of greed's destructive potential in modern corporate history. Founded in 1985, Enron rose rapidly from a regional energy supplier to a global powerhouse, hailed as a pioneer of financial innovation. Its executives projected an image of brilliance, embodying the narrative of visionary capitalism. Yet beneath the rhetoric of innovation lay a labyrinth of deceit. Complex accounting manoeuvres—special purpose entities designed to keep debt off the balance sheet—were used to mask losses and inflate earnings. Investors, dazzled by soaring stock prices, ignored warning signs. Employees poured retirement savings into the company, convinced that they were part of an unstoppable success story. The opportunity seemed boundless. But when the truth emerged in late 2001, Enron's share price collapsed from ninety dollars to under one in weeks, wiping out tens of billions in shareholder value. Thousands lost jobs and pensions, while executives such as Jeffrey Skilling and Kenneth Lay became symbols of corporate greed unbound. The scandal was not merely a financial collapse but a cultural one, shattering faith in corporate governance and leading to sweeping reforms like the Sarbanes-Oxley Act. *Greed, not energy, had powered the company's meteoric rise and catastrophic fall.*

The lessons of Enron were widely proclaimed, yet two decades later, remarkably similar dynamics played out in the world of cryptocurrency. FTX, once valued at thirty-two billion dollars and hailed as the future of digital finance, imploded in 2022 with equal speed and devastation. Its founder, Sam Bankman-Fried, cultivated an image of scruffy genius and altruistic philosopher-king, promising not only to revolutionise finance but also to deploy profits for the greater good. Investors, politicians, and celebrities alike were drawn into the orbit of his charisma. Yet behind the façade, client funds were misused, risks concealed, and corporate controls virtually absent. When liquidity dried up, the edifice collapsed almost overnight, leaving millions of customers stranded and billions in value destroyed. The parallels to Enron are striking: complexity used as cover, charisma masking irresponsibility, and an ecosystem too willing to suspend disbelief in the face of extraordinary promises. Here again, greed functioned as the hidden engine—driving executives to expand recklessly, investors to ignore due diligence, and regulators to hesitate until collapse was unavoidable.

What these scandals demonstrate is that greed in modern finance is rarely a solitary vice. It is collective, thriving in environments where opportunity outpaces oversight and where cultural narratives celebrate boldness more than caution. In both Enron and FTX, greed was institutionalised, woven into the very culture of the firms. Employees were encouraged to take ever greater risks, often rewarded handsomely for short-term gains while the long-term stability of the enterprise was neglected. Shareholders clamoured for growth without asking how it was achieved. Auditors and regulators, either compromised or complacent, failed to act. Greed, in these cases, is not reducible to the moral failings of a few individuals but reveals how entire systems can be corrupted when restraint is abandoned.

The cultural resonance of such stories lies in their ability to translate complex technical failures into memorable narratives. Few members of the public could explain Enron's accounting fraud in detail or the mechanics of FTX's trading algorithms, but they remember the images: executives cashing out millions while employees lost pensions; a billionaire wunderkind arrested in the Bahamas. These are modern morality tales, functioning much like the fables of old. They crystallise abstract lessons into vivid examples, reminding us of the consequences of unbridled desire. The fact that they remain reference points years after their collapse testifies to the enduring power of narrative in shaping collective memory of financial crises.

Yet greed is not demonised in isolation; it exists in tension with cultural admiration for ambition. Both Enron and FTX were celebrated as disruptors before they were condemned as frauds. Investors were complicit, not merely victims, because they willingly embraced the prospect of extraordinary returns. Greed, in this sense, is a mirror, reflecting back not only the excesses of executives but also the credulity and appetite of broader society. The cautionary tale is therefore double-edged: it condemns the avarice of leaders while also warning against the temptation of those who enable them.

The challenge for modern finance lies in distinguishing ambition that drives genuine progress from greed that undermines stability. Innovation is indispensable to economic growth, yet when narratives of disruption become shields for opacity, the temptation cycle accelerates towards collapse. Scandals such as Enron and FTX are not aberrations but reminders of the fragility of systems that fail to check the human impulse for more. Regulation and oversight matter, but so too does cultural memory—the stories we tell about greed and its consequences. Without them, each generation risks repeating the same pattern, convinced that this time the opportunity is different.

Greed in modern finance is therefore best understood as both a vice and a signal. It signals when ambition has crossed the line into excess, when opportunity is being distorted into illusion, and when the costs of desire will inevitably exceed the gains. By studying these stories—Enron's collapse, FTX's implosion, and others like them—we gain more than technical lessons. We acquire cultural tools to recognise patterns of behaviour before they metastasise into crises. *The moral clarity of narrative endures long after the numbers have faded, reminding us that unchecked greed remains one of the most potent risks in financial life.*

Moral Lessons That Stick

Numbers may clarify, but they seldom linger. Charts can warn, yet their authority often fades once the immediate crisis has passed. What endures, generation after generation, are the stories of financial downfall—the cautionary tales of individuals and institutions undone by their own excesses. Human beings are narrative creatures; our memory is tuned less to data points than to parables, and our moral imagination more easily grasped by vivid downfall than by abstract statistical warnings. It is this asymmetry that explains why the stories of collapses like Enron, Lehman Brothers, or the implosion of FTX become embedded in collective consciousness, while the technical details of price-to-earnings ratios, capital buffers, or liquidity spreads slip into obscurity. *Moral lessons endure because they are lived as drama, not read as figures.*

The fall of Icarus in Greek mythology is one of the oldest templates of this narrative power. Few remember the exact details of wax and feathers, yet the enduring image of a young man soaring too close to the sun continues to define our cultural understanding of overreach. The moral survives not because it is the only story of hubris but because it is one of the most striking. In the same way, financial scandals provide modern myths: we remember Bernie Madoff's clients queuing outside offices in disbelief, the shredded documents of Arthur Andersen, or Sam Bankman-Fried's tousled hair and defiant interviews, long after the precise mechanics of Ponzi schemes or fraudulent accounting have been forgotten. The lesson—beware of promises too good to be true—retains force precisely because it is told through narrative images that engage emotion and imagination.

This dynamic is not accidental. Cognitive psychology demonstrates that people retain information more readily when it is embedded in narrative form. Experiments show that statistics alone rarely shift behaviour, while stories can dramatically increase recall and persuasion. When health campaigns, for example, pair data with personal stories of suffering or recovery, they consistently achieve stronger behavioural change. Finance operates no differently. A chart warning that housing prices are unsustainable may be ignored, but the story of a neighbour losing their home can reshape perception of risk immediately. *It is not rational indifference to numbers but the primacy of narrative in human cognition that makes moral stories stick.*

The financial crisis of 2008 offers striking evidence of this principle. While regulators issued technical reports for years about systemic risk, it was not until the collapse of Lehman Brothers that the public grasped the severity of the crisis. The image of employees leaving headquarters with boxes in hand became the symbol of a wider catastrophe. Few recall the specific levels of collateralised debt obligations or the Basel capital requirements that were breached. What endures is the story: hubris in the housing market, bankers enriching themselves, and ordinary families paying the cost. The enduring moral lesson—unchecked greed brings ruin—was captured more effectively through the story of collapse than through any spreadsheet of failing balance sheets.

Enron provides another illustration. The intricate accounting fraud involved special purpose vehicles and mark-to-market accounting so complex that even analysts struggled to grasp them. Yet what the public remembers are the executives cashing out shares while employees lost pensions, or the hubris of Jeffrey Skilling proclaiming brilliance until the edifice collapsed. The story communicates the moral lesson more forcefully than any technical breakdown could: brilliance without integrity collapses into farce. Similarly, with FTX, the esoteric world of cryptocurrency derivatives and exchange structures was incomprehensible to most. Yet the vivid image of a once-celebrated "genius" arrested in the Bahamas made the moral unambiguous: charisma and apparent innovation are no substitutes for honesty.

Part of why stories of downfall endure is their dramatic arc. They follow a structure that human beings instinctively understand: rise, hubris, and fall. It is the same shape found in literature, theatre, and religion, from Shakespeare's tragedies to biblical accounts of kings undone by pride. Financial collapses map neatly onto this archetype.

Investors are enthralled by meteoric rises, unsettled by overreach, and fascinated by the spectacle of collapse. The arc satisfies both curiosity and caution, leaving a moral imprint more durable than technical lessons. The story of Long-Term Capital Management in the 1990s illustrates this perfectly: two Nobel laureates applied sophisticated models to markets, achieved astronomical returns, then collapsed when assumptions failed. The detail of volatility spreads is forgotten; what remains is the moral: no model is immune to reality.

Critics sometimes argue that such stories oversimplify, turning systemic crises into morality plays centred on villains. There is truth in this observation. Enron was not the fault of a single executive, nor was the 2008 crisis caused by one reckless bank. Yet simplification is precisely what makes stories memorable. They do not serve as forensic reports; they operate as cultural tools to transmit lessons across time. The risk is that nuance is lost, but the benefit is that lessons remain accessible. *If we remembered only the technical causes of collapse, history's warnings would be locked away from most of the public, unavailable to shape behaviour.*

The enduring moral resonance of downfall also reflects the deep human preference for negative lessons. Research in behavioural psychology demonstrates that negative experiences carry greater weight than positive ones, a principle known as negativity bias. People remember losses more vividly than gains, and cautionary tales more powerfully than success stories. This is why investors who lived through the Great Depression remained risk-averse for decades, shaping entire eras of financial behaviour. Success stories may inspire, but downfall stories protect, anchoring communities against repeating costly mistakes.

Yet the persistence of these stories also raises an uncomfortable paradox. While they endure in cultural memory, they do not always prevent recurrence. Despite centuries of cautionary tales—from tulip mania to the South Sea Bubble to dot-com euphoria—new generations continue to repeat the same patterns. This reveals that while moral lessons stick, their deterrent power is limited. Memory may not be enough to counter temptation when opportunity arises anew. Still, their value lies in providing frameworks for interpretation. When the next bubble inflates, society instinctively searches for narrative analogues, invoking past scandals as warnings. Even if behaviour does not change, understanding is enriched, and scrutiny sharpened.

The most powerful function of downfall stories may be their capacity to connect individual morality with systemic critique. When we hear of Madoff's deceit or FTX's implosion, we are reminded not only of personal dishonesty but also of regulatory failure and collective gullibility. The story personalises the lesson without erasing structural critique. It tells us that greed and corruption matter at the individual level, but also that systems designed without transparency or accountability are prone to collapse. This dual resonance is what makes such stories particularly effective in shaping public discourse: they allow us to blame individuals while questioning institutions.

In the end, the endurance of moral lessons from financial downfall reflects the way human societies learn. We do not internalise technical manuals; we internalise drama. Charts and warnings can be dismissed as predictions, subject to dispute. But stories of failure, once told and retold, acquire the weight of inevitability. They survive because they resonate with our cognitive and emotional wiring, and because they distil complex systems into simple, memorable truths. *It is through stories of downfall, not data alone, that finance becomes legible to the wider public and that moral boundaries are preserved across generations.*

Chapter 4

The Gambler's Folly

Few domains reveal the tension between human rationality and human desire as starkly as gambling. It is here, in the roll of dice, the turn of a card, or the flicker of numbers on a lottery machine, that centuries of cultural attitudes towards chance, fate, and calculation converge. Some societies elevate the gambler as a daring risk-taker, flirting with destiny and trusting to fortune. Others scorn the act as reckless folly, a moral failing that undermines the virtues of work, prudence, and skill. Yet even in cultures that preach restraint, gambling in its various guises continues to exert a magnetic pull. This chapter examines why, despite its predictable odds and the near certainty of loss, the allure of gambling has never faded—and why understanding its narratives is essential for making sense of financial behaviour more broadly.

At its heart lies the enduring contrast between luck and skill. In many societies, chance has been treated as a divine or mystical force, a reminder of humanity's dependence on powers beyond control. Ancient dice carved from animal bone were not merely tools of entertainment; they were instruments through which individuals sought signs of favour or punishment from the gods. To cast dice was to ask a question of destiny. In China, fortune sticks and the I Ching provided frameworks through which randomness was imbued with meaning, transforming arbitrary outcomes into signals for life choices. Such practices framed luck not as frivolity but as a language through which the universe communicated. In contrast, mercantile societies that depended on trade, calculation, and contract developed cultures that privileged skill. Success was to be earned, not gambled for. Investments, however speculative, were justified as exercises of knowledge and foresight. This divide continues to echo in modern attitudes: lotteries attract the desperate and the hopeful, while trading floors celebrate calculation, though both rely on elements of chance far greater than participants admit.

The ancient allure of chance has proven remarkably persistent. Roman soldiers, between campaigns, wagered on dice not simply for amusement but for the thrill of yielding control to fate. Religious prohibitions against gambling across different faith traditions reveal how seriously its appeal was regarded: prohibitions are rarely placed on trivialities. The persistence of state lotteries across centuries testifies to the same truth—that societies, even while condemning gambling as wasteful, often harness it as a source of revenue and social control. To buy a ticket is to purchase a dream, however improbable, and in that sense lotteries are less about mathematics than about hope. The stories of miraculous wins—paupers turned into millionaires overnight—fuel participation far more effectively than statistical tables showing the infinitesimal odds of success.

Modern behavioural finance has provided language for what gamblers across millennia have intuited: the illusion of control. People routinely overestimate their influence in environments governed by randomness. A gambler who throws dice harder when seeking a high number demonstrates the same fallacy as an investor who believes that timing the market consistently is within grasp. This illusion is not limited to casinos or trading floors; it pervades everyday financial decisions. Home buyers believe they can forecast housing markets; entrepreneurs assume skill where survival often reflects timing. Psychological research on the gambler's fallacy—the belief that past random outcomes influence future ones—shows how deeply flawed intuitions about chance are. If a coin lands heads five times in a row, many assume tails is "due," despite the independence of each flip. Casinos exploit these biases, but so too do financial markets, where investors often double down after losses, convinced a reversal is imminent.

The folly lies not in risk itself but in the stories we attach to it. Risk-taking is essential to progress; no great venture, artistic, scientific, or commercial, has ever succeeded without it. Yet when risk is framed through narratives of destiny or inevitability, it becomes destructive. The gambler's myth is not that risk is avoidable, but that luck alone can substitute for skill and preparation. Conversely, the myth of pure calculation—that with sufficient information, chance can be eliminated—is equally deceptive. The financial crises of recent decades have shown that models laden with complex mathematics are no less vulnerable to the unpredictability of human behaviour. Both extremes—blind faith in luck and blind faith in numbers—represent distorted lenses through which risk is misunderstood.

A healthier relationship with risk requires reframing. Instead of treating risk as a gamble against fate or as an equation to be solved, it is better understood as a spectrum of possibility where preparation, resilience, and humility matter more than certainty. In investment, as in life, acknowledging uncertainty is a safeguard against overreach. The successful entrepreneur does not eliminate chance but manages exposure, ensuring that a single failure cannot wipe out all. The prudent investor accepts that no model guarantees success but spreads bets in recognition of unpredictability. The healthiest risk-takers are those who recognise that fortune is fickle and that skill, while essential, is bounded by forces beyond control.

The gambler's folly, then, is not simply that people lose money on games of chance. It is that the stories of luck and inevitability seep into wider financial decision-making, shaping markets and economies as much as individual lives. Whether in Roman dice games, Chinese fortune rituals, or contemporary cryptocurrency manias, the same narrative pattern recurs: opportunity, illusion of control, overcommitment, and collapse. By examining these stories with clarity, we can learn to distinguish between destructive myths and productive narratives. Risk is unavoidable; folly is not. Recognising the difference may be one of the most valuable financial lessons history has to offer.

Luck vs. Skill

Across human history, wealth has been pursued through two broad narratives: one grounded in fortune, the other in foresight. Some cultures prize the hand of fate, casting dice or buying tickets in the belief that destiny can intervene to transform lives. Others elevate the virtues of calculation, discipline, and measured risk, framing prosperity as the product of skill rather than chance. The tension between these two logics—luck and skill—has shaped not only individual choices but entire economies, determining which societies cultivate gamblers and which cultivate merchants, which venerate fortune and which reward foresight. To understand money as more than numbers, one must examine how cultures embed their financial systems in stories of randomness and mastery.

The persistence of luck as an organising principle is striking. Archaeological evidence shows dice made from bones as far back as 3000 BCE in Mesopotamia, suggesting that the casting of lots was not merely amusement but a practice bound up with religion and fate. For ancient Greeks, Tyche—the goddess of fortune—was worshipped as one who could elevate or ruin with a whim, her capriciousness both feared and courted. Romans rolled dice not only in taverns but as acts of divination, reading the fall as an omen. In China, fortune sticks and the I Ching framed randomness as a coded message, a way of interpreting the will of heaven. To embrace luck was to accept that human agency is limited, and that wealth flows from forces beyond comprehension. The persistence of state lotteries and gambling traditions into modernity reflects this deep-rooted belief. People may acknowledge the odds, but *they still invest in the story that luck can rewrite destiny in an instant.*

By contrast, other cultures sought to diminish the role of chance by elevating skill as the true driver of prosperity. Merchant republics like Venice or the Dutch Republic built institutions that rewarded calculation—contracts, credit markets, and the careful weighing of risk. Here, wealth was not to be prayed for but managed. In Confucian traditions, discipline and foresight were emphasised in household management, positioning skill as both moral and practical. Early Islamic finance prohibited games of chance, while structuring trade to align with fairness and predictability. To prize skill was to assert that humans could tame uncertainty through intellect and order. This ethos underpins modern investment: financial analysts, fund managers, and entrepreneurs construct entire identities around the premise that foresight, not fortune, determines outcomes.

Yet the divide between luck and skill is far less absolute than it appears. Consider the casino and the trading floor. At first glance, they seem opposites: one a temple of chance, the other of calculation. Yet behavioural finance has shown that the same cognitive biases drive both. The roulette player doubling bets on red mirrors the investor who "chases" a rising stock, assuming momentum guarantees future gain. The lottery ticket, bought for the dream it represents, finds its counterpart in the speculative cryptocurrency investment, justified as skill but often little more than gambling with digital tokens. In both domains, narratives of control clash with the reality of uncertainty. The gambler exaggerates their ability to influence dice with the flick of a wrist; the trader overestimates their capacity to outguess the market. Both underestimate the brute force of chance.

Modern societies wrestle with this ambiguity. The United States, for example, is culturally ambivalent: it champions the "self-made" entrepreneur, suggesting prosperity stems from skill, while simultaneously running one of the world's largest lottery systems, feeding on the belief that luck can bypass systemic barriers. In parts of Europe, gambling is often framed as vice while financial speculation is framed as rational, though both involve betting on uncertain futures. Emerging markets frequently embody both tendencies at once: lotteries flourish among populations excluded from credit markets, while elites turn to investment vehicles that purport to reward skill. The coexistence of these approaches reveals a deeper truth: *cultures rarely choose between luck and skill; they weave them together in varying proportions, depending on historical experience and social needs.*

This interplay raises philosophical questions about agency and justice. If wealth depends on luck, then outcomes appear arbitrary, raising questions of fairness and the role of redistribution. If wealth depends on skill, then disparities can be justified as meritocratic, even when chance played a hidden role. Narratives of luck often provide comfort to the disadvantaged—after all, anyone might win tomorrow—while narratives of skill flatter the successful, allowing them to attribute outcomes to effort rather than fortune. Neither narrative is purely descriptive; both function as cultural tools for legitimising inequality and structuring aspiration.

The consequences for financial behaviour are profound. When people believe luck governs outcomes, they may engage in riskier behaviours, investing in lotteries, betting, or speculative bubbles. The appeal lies not in probability but in possibility—the story that life can change instantly. When people believe skill governs outcomes, they may devote themselves to disciplined saving, investment, or entrepreneurship, yet risk overconfidence, mistaking chance successes for personal genius. Markets oscillate between these poles. The dot-com boom of the late 1990s and the cryptocurrency surge of the 2010s both blended narratives of skill—technological insight, early adoption—with narratives of luck—being in the right place at the right time. In hindsight, the boundary between gambler and investor blurred almost entirely.

Anthropologists and historians remind us that both narratives serve collective purposes. Cultures that emphasise luck often do so to explain volatility and preserve hope in the face of limited control. Societies that emphasise skill cultivate habits of prudence and accountability. But both leave blind spots. Overreliance on luck breeds fatalism, while overreliance on skill fosters hubris. Sustainable financial cultures emerge not from choosing one narrative but from recognising their interaction: skill increases probabilities, luck determines outcomes. To tell the story otherwise is to indulge in myth, whether the myth of destiny or the myth of mastery.

What unites these perspectives is the recognition that neither luck nor skill alone can explain wealth. Even the most disciplined investor cannot eliminate chance; even the luckiest lottery winner requires some measure of management to retain their windfall. The stories we tell about luck and skill matter because they shape not only how individuals act but how institutions are built. Laws regulating gambling, education systems teaching financial literacy, and media celebrating entrepreneurs all reflect implicit decisions about where societies place the boundary between fate and foresight. These boundaries are not fixed; they evolve as crises, technologies, and cultural shifts rewrite the balance.

The enduring tension between luck and skill is therefore not a problem to be solved but a lens through which to interpret financial life. It explains why lotteries remain popular despite impossible odds, why traders insist on their edge despite markets that humiliate predictions, and why cultures oscillate between praising fortune and praising calculation. To navigate finance wisely requires recognising that both narratives carry truth, but also distortion. The art lies not in denying one in favour of the other but in discerning when chance dominates and when skill can genuinely tip the balance. Only then can individuals and societies craft financial practices that are both realistic and resilient.

The Ancient Allure of Chance

To modern eyes, the throwing of dice or the drawing of sticks may appear as quaint diversions, relics of simpler times when probability was poorly understood. Yet to ancient societies, these practices carried weight far beyond entertainment. They were instruments for discerning fate, distributing resources, and testing the limits of human control in a world governed by uncertainty. What we today might dismiss as games of chance were in fact cultural laboratories for negotiating risk, shaping beliefs about fortune, and embedding financial behaviour in ritual and story. The endurance of these traditions across millennia is testimony to the deep psychological and social allure of chance, an allure that continues to structure markets and money-making even in supposedly rational financial systems.

Consider the Romans, whose obsession with dice reflected more than a taste for gaming. Archaeological excavations have unearthed thousands of dice across the empire, carved from bone, ivory, and even precious metals. These cubes were not confined to taverns or military barracks; they appear in elite households and temples, suggesting their role extended beyond leisure. Roman writers noted the symbolic power of dice throws, with outcomes sometimes interpreted as omens or messages from the gods. Soldiers, uncertain of whether they would survive battle, cast dice in rituals that mingled play with fatalism. Merchants, too, were known to settle disputes or make decisions by lot, implicitly acknowledging that fortune, not calculation, often determined outcomes. It is telling that Julius Caesar's decisive move to cross the Rubicon was memorialised with the phrase *alea iacta est*—the die is cast—a metaphor that embedded political risk in the imagery of chance.

In China, the tradition of fortune sticks reveals a parallel narrative of chance fused with destiny. Known as *kau cim* or lottery divination, the practice involved shaking a bamboo container filled with numbered sticks until one fell out. The stick was then interpreted using verses and oracles, offering guidance on matters ranging from marriage to trade. Unlike Roman dice, which celebrated randomness as spectacle, fortune sticks framed chance as encoded wisdom. The randomness of the stick's fall was not meaningless but rather a mechanism through which the universe revealed hidden truths. Merchants travelling along trade routes consulted such divinations before major ventures, treating chance not as chaos but as signal. In both Rome and China, randomness was not trivial—it was embedded in systems of meaning that informed practical, often financial, decisions.

This framing of chance as socially useful extended across cultures. In India, the Mahabharata recounts a pivotal dice game in which the Pandava brothers lose their kingdom, their wealth, and even their freedom, underscoring both the thrill and devastation bound up in games of chance. In Norse tradition, tales describe gods playing dice to determine the distribution of power, entwining divine order with randomness. Among indigenous communities in North America, dice games using peach stones or carved bones served not only as entertainment but as ritualised ways of redistributing goods. What links these diverse practices is the recognition that *chance was not idle; it was a tool for rebalancing, revealing, or reconfiguring the distribution of fortune within society.*

The economic dimensions of these practices are crucial. To stake money, land, or goods on a throw of dice was not merely to gamble; it was to engage in a microcosm of risk-taking that echoed larger patterns of trade, war, and investment. Games of chance were laboratories of loss and gain, training individuals to cope with uncertainty long before the rise of formal markets. They also provided mechanisms for redistributing wealth in societies where direct transfer might have been socially fraught. A noble losing to a commoner at dice allowed wealth to change hands under the cover of fate, preserving dignity while altering material outcomes. In this way, chance created a socially acceptable channel for economic mobility, however limited.

The persistence of these traditions reflects a deeper psychological pull: the human desire to make meaning out of randomness. To cast dice or draw sticks is to confront the limits of control, but in a manner framed by ritual, story, and expectation. Unlike pure chaos, these games impose boundaries: a set of rules, a clear outcome, and the possibility of extraordinary reversal. The tension between predictability and unpredictability is precisely what captivates. The thrill lies not in ignorance of the odds but in the recognition that, despite knowledge, anything might happen. This emotional experience of chance has profound implications for financial behaviour, explaining why speculative markets often mimic gambling despite claims to rationality.

Modern behavioural finance echoes these insights. The gambler's fallacy—the belief that past outcomes influence future ones in independent events—is not a quirk of contemporary casino-goers but a bias rooted in millennia of cultural practice. Ancient players of dice and sticks were likely subject to the same cognitive distortions, convinced that a streak signalled divine favour or impending reversal. The persistence of such beliefs shows that narratives of chance are not easily displaced by statistics. Even when probability is understood, *the story of fortune exerts stronger influence than the calculation of odds*. This helps explain why lotteries flourish today despite their negative expected value, and why speculative bubbles emerge even in sophisticated financial systems.

The Roman gambler, the Chinese diviner, and the modern cryptocurrency trader are not as far apart as they might seem. Each participates in a culture that uses chance to negotiate uncertainty, to create hope, and to legitimise outcomes. What has shifted is not the allure of chance but the scale and complexity of its application. Where dice once decided a feast's redistribution, derivatives now shift billions in capital. Yet the same psychological and cultural forces are at work: the search for meaning in randomness, the thrill of risk, and the enduring belief that chance can deliver extraordinary transformation.

To revisit these ancient practices is not to dismiss them as superstition but to recognise their enduring relevance. They remind us that financial life is not only about calculation and control but also about the narratives we construct to manage uncertainty. Chance is not an aberration from rationality but a constant companion to it, shaping behaviour in ways that no spreadsheet can fully capture. By understanding the ancient allure of chance, we gain insight into why markets still lurch into bubbles, why people still queue for lottery tickets, and why risk remains as much a cultural story as a mathematical one. The dice may have changed, the sticks replaced by algorithms, but the fascination with fortune endures, as deeply human as the desire for wealth itself.

The Illusion of Control

Few forces are more seductive in financial decision-making than the belief that outcomes rest securely within our grasp. Behavioural finance has repeatedly demonstrated that investors, gamblers, and even policymakers frequently overestimate their ability to predict or influence events governed largely by chance. This misplaced confidence—what psychologists term the *illusion of control*—remains one of the most persistent cognitive biases shaping markets and personal finance alike. It is a subtle distortion: rarely do individuals consciously assert mastery over randomness, but rather they behave as if patterns exist where none can be discerned, or as if their choices can tilt probability in their favour.

The illusion is most famously observed in the gambler's fallacy, the conviction that a random event is somehow "due" after a series of contrary outcomes. If a coin has landed on heads five times in a row, many believe tails becomes increasingly likely, when in fact the probability remains unchanged at fifty per cent. Casino studies have shown gamblers raising their stakes after losing streaks, convinced that their fortunes are about to reverse, or celebrating wins as if skill had intervened in games where chance rules absolutely. Financial markets echo this dynamic. Investors buy into slumping stocks because they "must" rebound, or cling to speculative assets because a run of losses makes recovery seem imminent. Such patterns are not random mistakes but rather expressions of a deeply ingrained human discomfort with unpredictability.

What is striking is how even well-informed individuals succumb. Daniel Kahneman and Amos Tversky, whose work underpins much of behavioural finance, revealed through experiments that trained statisticians could still fall prey to the gambler's fallacy. Knowledge of probability does not inoculate against the bias; the brain seems wired to seek equilibrium where randomness reigns. Studies of traders have shown that after a string of losses, they take larger risks, subconsciously expecting a correction in their favour. Others, after a series of wins, reduce caution, believing they have developed a "hot hand". In both cases, narrative replaces arithmetic: outcomes are woven into a story of streaks and reversals, rather than understood as independent probabilities.

The illusion of control extends beyond gaming tables or stock tickers. Consider the investor who studies patterns in price charts, convinced that a particular configuration—a "head and shoulders" or a "double bottom"—signals future movement. While technical analysis may sometimes capture momentum effects, much of its appeal lies in its promise of deciphering randomness. The human mind is exquisitely attuned to patterns, a trait that once ensured survival in nature but now lures people into over-interpreting noise as signal. Research on financial forecasting has shown that expert predictions fare little better than chance in complex markets, yet the experts themselves often remain confident in their models. The same misplaced confidence that leads a gambler to believe they can influence dice throws leads a fund manager to insist they can outguess market volatility.

The psychology of lottery players illustrates the bias in everyday life. Surveys reveal that many believe choosing their own numbers improves their chances, despite identical odds to quick-pick selections. Others hold onto tickets because they feel a stronger likelihood of winning with numbers they "own". Here the illusion is not about improving the odds but about claiming a semblance of agency in an uncontrollable process. This perceived control, however false, provides psychological comfort, transforming passive waiting into active participation. In finance, the illusion serves a similar function: investors prefer strategies that let them feel in control, even if the results differ little from random allocation. Active fund management, with its high fees and often poor performance compared to passive indexing, persists in part because it feeds this appetite for agency.

Crucially, the illusion of control is not merely an error but a double-edged bias. On one side, it drives reckless behaviour: gamblers chasing losses, investors holding onto doomed positions, policymakers overestimating their ability to stabilise crises. On the other, it can provide the confidence necessary to act in environments of uncertainty. Economies depend on people taking risks—starting businesses, investing in ventures, committing resources with no guarantee of return. If individuals fully recognised the degree of randomness shaping outcomes, many might retreat into paralysis. *A measure of illusory control may therefore be adaptive, encouraging risk-taking and persistence in the face of long odds.* The challenge is to balance this motivating illusion against its destructive extremes.

Behavioural experiments shed light on where that balance fails. Ellen Langer's studies in the 1970s found that people believed they had greater control when they threw dice themselves rather than when another person did, or when they chose their own lottery ticket rather than receiving one randomly. Such illusions are benign at small stakes but catastrophic when transposed into financial systems where billions ride on similar psychological distortions. The global financial crisis of 2008 illustrates the point. Banks constructed elaborate models of mortgage-backed securities, convinced their calculations controlled for risk. When defaults cascaded, the illusion collapsed, revealing how confidence in models had disguised the fundamental unpredictability of human behaviour and housing markets. The gambler's fallacy and its cousins had been institutionalised at systemic scale.

Contemporary financial technology introduces new layers to the illusion. Algorithmic trading platforms claim to harness vast datasets to control outcomes, yet their predictions often falter in periods of genuine uncertainty. Retail investors on platforms such as Robinhood or Binance engage in rapid trades, buoyed by a sense that technology gives them mastery over markets. Cryptocurrency, with its wild swings and opaque valuation, provides fertile ground for illusions of control. Traders believe they can spot patterns or time entry points, even though the underlying drivers are often sentiment-driven rather than calculable. When prices crash, the belief persists that recovery is just around the corner, echoing the casino gambler waiting for the dice to fall differently next time.

The persistence of these illusions raises a philosophical question: why does the human mind resist acknowledging randomness? One answer lies in narrative. Randomness is unsatisfying; it denies causality and undermines meaning. By imposing control—illusory though it may be—people can transform uncertainty into a coherent story. This makes losses tolerable, sustains hope, and maintains a sense of fairness in systems otherwise indifferent to human striving. Financial narratives, whether about "corrections," "recoveries," or "cycles," reflect this impulse. They frame randomness as part of a larger order, persuading participants to stay engaged. In this sense, the illusion of control is not a flaw to be eradicated but a cultural force to be managed.

What behavioural finance contributes is not the elimination of illusion but the awareness of its contours. Recognising the gambler's fallacy does not prevent it, but it allows individuals and institutions to build safeguards. Casinos impose betting limits; regulators mandate disclosure of risks; investors diversify portfolios. These structures acknowledge human vulnerability to illusion while channelling it into more sustainable practices. The most effective strategies do not attempt to eradicate bias but to design around it, accepting that people will always seek patterns in noise and control in chaos.

The financial world will never be free of illusions of control, nor should it be. They animate the risks on which economies are built, sustaining participation in uncertain ventures. But unchecked, they also fuel bubbles, crises, and personal ruin. The task is to cultivate humility alongside confidence: to act boldly in the face of uncertainty without mistaking boldness for mastery over chance. The gambler's fallacy remains a cautionary tale not only for those at gaming tables but for all who navigate markets and money. Its lesson is deceptively simple yet endlessly difficult to internalise—that randomness is indifferent, that probability does not bend to desire, and that recognising the limits of control is itself a form of wisdom.

Healthy Risk-Taking

Risk is often spoken of as a danger to be minimised, a hazard standing between us and security. Yet the reality is more nuanced: to live without risk is to forego opportunity, growth, and innovation. The issue is not whether we take risks, but whether we take them wisely. History and behavioural science both show that humans are prone to framing risk through the lens of myth—luck, fate, or misplaced confidence—rather than through clear-eyed assessment. The challenge, then, is to reimagine risk not as reckless speculation or paralysing fear but as a disciplined engagement with uncertainty, one that sustains ambition while reducing self-destruction.

One way to begin reframing risk is to distinguish between risk and uncertainty, a distinction made famous by the economist Frank Knight in the 1920s. Risk refers to scenarios where probabilities can be estimated—the odds of a coin toss or the actuarial tables of an insurance company. Uncertainty, by contrast, covers the vast domain where probabilities are unknowable: geopolitical shifts, technological revolutions, or cultural transformations. Most destructive financial misjudgements arise when uncertainty is mistaken for risk, when investors assume they can calculate odds in situations that are fundamentally unpredictable. *Healthy risk-taking starts by recognising the limits of calculation, accepting that some of life's most consequential decisions cannot be reduced to spreadsheet models.*

Examples abound of where this misrecognition leads to folly. Before the 2008 financial crisis, bankers believed they had mastered risk through complex derivatives that supposedly diversified and hedged exposure. In truth, they had treated deep uncertainty about human behaviour—whether millions of homeowners would default at once—as if it were a calculable probability. When the models collapsed, the illusion of control was laid bare. Contrast this with the entrepreneurs of Silicon Valley who invest in ten start-ups knowing that most will fail, but that one or two may transform industries. They acknowledge uncertainty, spread exposure, and frame risk not as the avoidance of loss but as the pursuit of asymmetric outcomes.

The concept of *optionality*, popularised by Nassim Nicholas Taleb, provides a useful framework for healthy risk-taking. Optionality emphasises small, affordable bets that preserve the ability to benefit disproportionately from favourable surprises while limiting downside exposure. Venture capital portfolios embody this principle, but it is equally applicable to individual finance. Rather than betting one's savings on a single "sure thing", a healthier approach is to hold a diversified portfolio, invest in continuous learning, and retain flexibility in career and life choices. *The essence of healthy risk is not fearlessness but resilience: ensuring that no single failure is fatal while leaving space for upside possibilities.*

Cultural attitudes towards risk further shape behaviour. In East Asian traditions influenced by Confucian thought, financial conservatism and collective responsibility often temper individual risk-taking, creating more gradual but sustainable growth patterns. By contrast, American culture has long celebrated the entrepreneur as a risk-taker, with failure often reframed as valuable experience. These differences highlight that risk is not simply an objective calculation but a cultural narrative. Healthy risk-taking requires recognising when cultural myths encourage either excessive caution or reckless daring. The lottery player who spends more on tickets than they can afford participates in a destructive myth of sudden fortune; the corporate executive who never invests in innovation succumbs to a paralysing myth of stability. Both mistake unhealthy extremes for prudence or opportunity.

Behavioural finance offers additional insight into how framing influences risk decisions. Kahneman and Tversky's prospect theory shows that people are more sensitive to losses than gains, leading them to avoid risks even when potential rewards outweigh potential harms. This aversion can prevent individuals from investing in markets that, over the long run, deliver growth despite volatility. At the same time, the same individuals may engage in reckless short-term gambles, such as day trading or speculative bubbles, because those risks are framed as chances for extraordinary gain. *Healthy risk-taking depends on reframing: to see long-term investments as disciplined exposure to productive risk, and short-term speculation as unnecessary volatility dressed up as opportunity.*

Historical examples illustrate the difference between destructive and constructive risk. The Dutch tulip mania of the seventeenth century exemplifies the danger of myth-driven speculation, where prices became detached from any reasonable assessment of value. Yet just decades later, the Dutch pioneered joint-stock companies and global trade ventures that transformed capitalism. The former was destructive risk driven by frenzy, the latter calculated risk that spread exposure across many investors and voyages. Similarly, the difference between gambling at a roulette wheel and investing in an index fund is not the absence of risk in the latter but the way it is structured, managed, and connected to real productive activity.

Healthy risk-taking also involves an honest appraisal of time. Many destructive risks arise from impatience: the desire for rapid returns, immediate gratification, or the avoidance of short-term discomfort. Long-term perspectives, by contrast, allow for volatility without panic. Pension funds, for example, can tolerate market swings that would devastate a day trader, because they are structured around decades-long horizons. For individuals, cultivating patience transforms risk from a threat into a companion of growth. *The disciplined acceptance of volatility over time is one of the most effective forms of healthy risk management.*

There is also a moral dimension. Risks that jeopardise others while protecting personal gain are often destructive, not only financially but socially. The managers of Enron and the architects of FTX pursued risks that shifted losses onto employees, customers, and the wider economy while enriching themselves temporarily. By contrast, risks that distribute both rewards and losses fairly—such as co-operatives, mutual funds, or community investment schemes—can build trust and resilience. Healthy risk-taking is not merely a technical calculation but an ethical practice, aligning one's appetite for uncertainty with responsibility to others.

Modern applications of these principles are increasingly urgent in a world facing systemic risks: climate change, pandemics, technological disruption. Here, healthy risk-taking involves collective as well as individual choices. Societies must invest in renewable energy, public health infrastructure, and adaptive technologies, even when payoffs are uncertain. To delay because outcomes cannot be precisely calculated is itself an unhealthy gamble. Just as the entrepreneur embraces uncertainty for potential growth, societies must embrace uncertainty for survival. The destructive myth in such cases is that inaction is safer than engagement, when in reality the greater danger lies in paralysis.

Reframing risk, then, is less about suppressing our appetite for uncertainty and more about cultivating the wisdom to engage it constructively. Risk is not the enemy but the raw material of progress. The difference lies in whether we allow myths—of luck, of control, of stability—to dictate behaviour, or whether we adopt frameworks that balance boldness with resilience, opportunity with responsibility, and ambition with patience. Healthy risk-taking is a discipline, a cultural practice, and a moral stance. It recognises uncertainty not as a flaw to be eradicated but as a condition to be navigated. The more we internalise this reframing, the more we can harness risk not as a destructive force but as the quiet architecture behind sustainable prosperity.

Chapter 5
The Debt Trap

Debt has always been more than an entry in a ledger. Across centuries and cultures, it has carried moral weight, social meaning, and emotional burden, shaping not only economies but also human identities. To owe is rarely a neutral state. It conjures stories of guilt and duty, of chains and redemption, of shame hidden behind closed doors and the occasional hope of forgiveness granted from above or decreed by law. Unlike other financial instruments—savings, investment, or trade—debt is infused with narrative, its mathematics overlaid with myths that dictate how societies treat debtors, how individuals experience their obligations, and how entire nations interpret their responsibilities to one another.

The moral undertones of debt reach back to some of humanity's oldest stories. In religious texts, debt is often equated with sin: both are obligations one must atone for, both invite judgment, and both promise redemption through forgiveness. Medieval Europe institutionalised this association, treating debt as a form of moral failure, punishable not merely by confiscation of property but by imprisonment or exile. These practices reflect a cultural insistence that debt was not simply a transaction but a breach of trust, a disruption of order requiring correction. *To borrow without repaying was to trespass not only against another person but against society itself.* Even today, the vocabulary of debt retains this moral residue: we "pay our debts" to friends and institutions alike, and we speak of being "indebted" in gratitude or obligation, as if every favour or kindness places us on a moral balance sheet.

Yet if debt has long carried the stigma of sin, it has also been regarded as a necessary evil, a tool of survival, expansion, and ambition. Farmers borrowed against future harvests, merchants against future profits, nations against future tax revenues. Without debt, few could have built empires, financed voyages, or industrialised. The paradox lies in the fact that debt fuels progress while simultaneously burdening its carriers with suspicion. It empowers while it enslaves, enabling vast undertakings even as it leaves borrowers vulnerable to collapse should their calculations fail.

Stories of debt, then, oscillate between condemnation and necessity, each culture navigating this ambivalence by weaving cautionary tales and rituals of forgiveness.

The stigma that clings to debt is striking when compared to other financial topics. Few speak openly of their credit card balances, their mortgage arrears, or their student loan struggles. Unlike the pride that accompanies discussions of investments or income, debt stories are often told in whispers, if at all. This secrecy reinforces cycles of shame, discouraging individuals from seeking help or confronting realities until it is too late. Contrast this with cultures or historical moments where debt relief was public and communal: the biblical tradition of Jubilee, where debts were cancelled every fifty years, was a collective acknowledgment that perpetual bondage corrodes both individuals and society. In such settings, forgiveness was not seen as indulgence but as necessary recalibration, ensuring that financial obligations did not harden into lifelong chains.

The persistence of debt myths also reveals how societies define power and hierarchy. Ancient debt slavery, in which unpaid obligations transformed free citizens into bondsmen, underscored the link between economic failure and social subordination. Centuries later, debtor's prisons in Europe embodied the same logic, punishing those who failed to meet obligations by stripping them of liberty altogether. Both practices highlight a common theme: debt is a mechanism not only of finance but of control. The stories that surround it justify the social order, reinforcing who may command credit and who must submit to obligation. Even today, credit scores and lending practices embed narratives about who is trustworthy, who is "risky," and who deserves another chance. These are not merely numerical calculations but cultural judgments clothed in statistical garb.

Modern societies often present debt in technical terms—interest rates, repayment schedules, credit ratings—but beneath the arithmetic lie personal narratives that shape behaviour. A debtor who frames their situation as a temporary setback, part of a broader life story of resilience, is more likely to take proactive steps toward repayment. Another, who internalises debt as evidence of failure or moral deficiency, may spiral into avoidance and deeper entrapment.

Debt becomes self-fulfilling not because of the numbers alone but because of the stories people attach to those numbers. Financial counsellors increasingly recognise this dynamic, framing repayment not merely as a technical process but as an exercise in rewriting personal narrative—from one of shame to one of agency.

The cultural myths of debt also shape national politics and global economics. Nations too are judged by their obligations, praised when they repay and condemned when they default. The Eurozone crisis a decade ago revealed how debt discourse could fracture alliances, with creditor nations casting themselves as prudent and debtor nations as reckless. Here again, debt was not treated as a neutral economic condition but as a moral drama of discipline and indulgence, virtue and vice. These narratives often obscure structural realities—imbalances in trade, inequalities in productivity, or the impact of external shocks—but they endure because they resonate with the deeper human tendency to moralise obligation.

What makes debt so enduringly potent as a narrative device is its universality. Few escape it entirely. Whether through mortgages, student loans, or national deficits, debt touches individuals and collectives alike. This universality gives the stories we tell about debt extraordinary influence: they shape laws and policies, influence personal decisions, and colour cultural identities. The myth of debt as servitude warns us of dependency; the myth of debt as investment entices us with visions of growth; the myth of debt forgiveness reminds us that no society can thrive if obligations are allowed to harden into permanent shackles.

This chapter seeks to illuminate these narratives—not to resolve the ambivalence of debt but to reveal how it is framed, interpreted, and lived. By examining tales of sin and servitude, shame and secrecy, historical forgiveness and modern entrapment, we come to see that debt is not merely about balances owed and repaid. It is a cultural script, one that dictates how we treat each other, how we judge ourselves, and how we imagine the possibilities of the future. To understand the debt trap, then, is not only to calculate interest and principal but to read the stories behind them, stories that can either reinforce cycles of despair or open pathways toward liberation.

The Weight of Obligation

Debt is one of the few financial concepts that transcends arithmetic to become a matter of morality. To owe is rarely described in neutral terms. Instead, debt has been portrayed for millennia as a burden, a form of servitude, or even a stain upon one's character. Unlike wealth, which is celebrated, or trade, which is seen as a skill, debt carries with it the language of guilt and obligation. Its metaphors are heavy: we "shoulder" debt, we "labour under" it, and we "repay" not only money but an implied moral failing. The sheer persistence of these narratives suggests that debt has always been more than a contractual arrangement—it has functioned as a cultural device for defining trust, discipline, and justice.

Ancient societies often interpreted debt as a violation of order. In Mesopotamia, clay tablets record not only loans but also periodic proclamations of debt forgiveness, known as "clean slates." These were not acts of generosity but pragmatic responses to the corrosive effects of perpetual bondage. Left unchecked, debt created cycles where farmers lost land, families lost liberty, and societies lost stability. The act of wiping obligations clean was a way of restoring harmony, underscoring the sense that debt was an abnormal condition—tolerated for survival, but morally dangerous if allowed to fester. *Debt was thus never a neutral exchange but a force requiring constant narrative management.*

Religious traditions amplified these moral framings. In Judaic thought, debt was intertwined with sin, both requiring forgiveness and atonement. The Christian Lord's Prayer famously uses the word "debts" in place of sins in some translations, a linguistic fusion that has shaped Western consciousness for centuries. To be indebted was not merely to fall short financially; it was to stand in deficit before God or community. Islam, too, treats debt as a serious moral obligation, warning against dying in debt as a state of spiritual imbalance. These traditions linked financial obligation to cosmic order, framing repayment not as a business transaction but as an ethical duty with eternal consequences.

Such narratives were not confined to scripture. Classical literature often cast debt as the first step toward ruin. Roman playwrights used indebted characters to symbolise weakness, corruption, or impending downfall. Debt was dramatised not as liquidity management but as a moral compromise leading to servitude. Roman law itself institutionalised this view: debtors unable to repay could become bonded labourers, their freedom surrendered as collateral. In this sense, debt was not simply about money but about hierarchy—it marked the boundary between autonomy and dependence, virtue and vice.

Medieval Europe carried these associations forward with striking severity. The rise of debtor's prisons transformed private obligations into public punishments. To fail financially was to fail morally, deserving confinement until restitution was made. The practice reinforced the narrative that debt was not a temporary misfortune but a shameful breach of responsibility. The imprisoned debtor was a cautionary tale made flesh, warning others against imprudence or dishonesty. At the same time, usury laws sought to curb the exploitative side of lending, casting excessive interest as sinful greed. The result was a dual moral code: borrowing too much was a vice, but lending exploitatively was also condemned. Debt, in this frame, was tolerated only within strict ethical boundaries.

The Enlightenment and the rise of modern capitalism did little to dissolve these moral overlays. While credit became the engine of commerce and industrial expansion, debt retained its aura of suspicion. Literature from this period reflects this tension vividly. Charles Dickens' depictions of debtors and their prisons, particularly in *Little Dorrit*, painted indebtedness as both systemic injustice and personal failing. For Dickens' readers, debt was not an abstract economic mechanism but a deeply human drama—of desperation, humiliation, and entrapment. Such cultural portrayals hardened the stigma, embedding the sense that debt is an obligation weighted with shame, even as it became indispensable to economic progress.

In modern times, debt has been rationalised through spreadsheets and credit scores, yet its moral undertones endure. Credit ratings purport to measure risk, but they also function as judgments of character, categorising people as "responsible" or "reckless." Bankruptcy law is presented as an administrative process, yet those who file often experience it as a confession of failure. Even the language of national debt is infused with morality: nations are praised for "fiscal discipline" and condemned for "profligacy." Markets punish countries perceived as irresponsible, echoing the ancient conflation of debt with sin. *The numbers may be modern, but the narratives remain ancient.*

The framing of debt as sin or servitude persists because it serves a social function. It disciplines behaviour by embedding financial obligations within moral expectations. To pay debts is to demonstrate integrity; to fail is to risk exclusion from trust networks. These cultural expectations can encourage prudence but also foster shame that inhibits transparency. For individuals, this often means concealing debt until it spirals out of control; for nations, it can mean austerity policies that inflict social harm in the name of fiscal virtue. The weight of obligation, when moralised, can create perverse outcomes—solvency maintained at the expense of wellbeing.

Yet the persistence of these narratives also reveals their adaptability. Debt is not always demonised; in certain contexts it is reframed as a necessary tool or even a badge of ambition. Entrepreneurs often leverage debt to build businesses, their risk valorised as vision rather than condemned as recklessness. Governments justify borrowing for infrastructure or wartime expenditure as investment in collective futures. These examples show how the same act—incurring debt—can be cast either as moral failure or as prudent courage, depending on the story told. The boundary between sin, servitude, and necessity is porous, negotiated continually through cultural narrative.

Understanding debt through this lens helps explain its enduring emotional charge. Unlike other financial commitments, debt implicates identity. It speaks to how one is perceived—trustworthy or dishonest, prudent or reckless, free or bound. The moral stories we inherit about debt are not just historical curiosities; they shape everyday experience. A student hesitating to admit loan struggles, a family hiding credit card arrears, a nation imposing austerity—all are guided less by numbers than by inherited scripts about what debt means. To grasp the weight of obligation, therefore, is to see beyond the balance sheet and recognise the centuries-old narratives that continue to govern financial life.

Debt endures because it is both indispensable and uncomfortable. It enables growth, opportunity, and survival, but it carries with it the shadows of sin and servitude. Societies have sought to tame its dangers with laws, forgiveness rituals, and financial innovation, yet the moral residue remains. To explore the weight of obligation is to uncover how cultures have disciplined debt through story, turning arithmetic into morality, and obligation into identity. It is only by recognising this narrative inheritance that we can begin to engage with debt more honestly—not as a simple economic fact but as one of humanity's most enduring moral dramas.

Shame and Secrecy

Debt occupies a peculiar place in the landscape of finance: omnipresent yet rarely discussed in candid terms. People will boast of income, investments, or property, but few admit to the size of their credit card balances or the months they have fallen behind on mortgage payments. This asymmetry of disclosure suggests that debt, unlike other financial realities, is shrouded in stigma. It is not simply a matter of numbers owed; it is a matter of identity and moral standing. To speak of debt openly is to risk social judgement, to reveal vulnerability in a society that prizes autonomy and control. *Shame, not arithmetic, explains why debt is a uniquely silenced financial condition.*

The roots of this silence are historical and cultural. In many societies, debt was tied to personal honour. To owe meant to be beholden, stripped of independence and reliant on the grace of another. This dynamic was intensified in communities where reputations determined access to trade, land, or marriage prospects. One public revelation of indebtedness could stain an individual's family for generations. In rural villages or tightly knit urban quarters, gossip about unpaid debts was not trivial—it was a form of social policing. To avoid disgrace, debtors learned to conceal their obligations, creating a culture of secrecy that persists even in today's anonymous economies.

Religious traditions deepened this association by equating debt with sin. In the Christian Lord's Prayer, "forgive us our debts" intertwines financial and moral obligations. To fall into debt was to fall short, not only before one's creditors but before God. This conflation encouraged a sense that debt was not a neutral transaction but evidence of flawed character. Islam similarly emphasises the moral seriousness of debt, warning that a soul may remain unsettled until debts are repaid. These teachings instilled a powerful legacy: borrowing was not merely financial—it was moral exposure. The shame of debt, then, is not incidental but the outcome of centuries of cultural narratives equating it with spiritual deficiency.

Modern capitalism has complicated this picture without erasing it. Credit is marketed as empowerment—mortgages to build homes, loans to fund education, credit cards to smooth consumption. Yet beneath this language of opportunity, debt remains coded as weakness when mismanaged. The paradox is stark: societies encourage borrowing while condemning indebtedness. Governments promote student loans as pathways to mobility, yet young graduates speak of their balances in hushed tones, fearing judgement for financial choices they were effectively pushed into making. The stigma has not disappeared but shifted, now reserved for those who fail to manage debt with apparent ease. *Secrecy flourishes in this contradiction, as people attempt to reconcile the normalisation of borrowing with the shame of indebtedness.*

Psychology provides further insight into why debt is uniquely stigmatised. Shame differs from guilt: guilt arises from recognising a bad act, while shame attaches to the self. To be in debt is often felt not as "I borrowed unwisely" but as "I am irresponsible." Debt thus becomes a proxy for personal inadequacy. Studies in behavioural finance show that individuals are more likely to lie about their debts than their savings, even to close friends or partners. This concealment can perpetuate isolation, as the fear of disclosure delays problem-solving. By contrast, other financial topics, even losses in investments, are often shared as stories of misfortune or learning. Debt rarely receives that framing; it is seen not as bad luck but as personal failure.

The consequences of secrecy are tangible. On an individual level, hiding debt can lead to spirals of avoidance—bills unopened, collectors ignored, opportunities for negotiation missed. At a societal level, the shame of debt discourages open dialogue about systemic issues. The stigma attached to personal borrowing obscures the structural forces that drive indebtedness, such as wage stagnation, predatory lending, or inflated education costs. Silence ensures that debt remains framed as an individual failing rather than a collective challenge. When families hide their struggles, policymakers feel less pressure to address the underlying conditions, reinforcing cycles of secrecy and blame.

The contrast with other financial narratives is telling. Risk-taking in investments is often glamorised: entrepreneurs who gamble with capital and fail are admired for their daring. Even bankruptcy can be reframed as a rite of passage in certain entrepreneurial cultures, a sign of resilience. Debt, however, resists such rebranding. Rarely does society celebrate the courage of those who borrow to survive illness, keep a family business afloat, or pursue education. Instead, the narrative defaults to imprudence. *The shame of debt lies in its invisibility: it is endured silently, stripped of the legitimacy granted to other financial risks.*

Yet secrecy is not immutable. Historical examples show how collective acknowledgment can soften stigma. In ancient Mesopotamia, rulers periodically declared debt amnesties to reset the social order, recognising that widespread indebtedness threatened stability. These "clean slates" reframed debt from individual failure to societal imbalance, lifting shame through communal recognition. Similarly, in modern contexts, movements advocating student debt forgiveness have sparked more open conversations. When millions acknowledge shared burdens, secrecy loses some of its hold. The challenge lies in extending this collective reframing beyond moments of crisis or protest, embedding it into everyday financial discourse.

Technology, paradoxically, both worsens and relieves secrecy. Digital credit scoring systems quantify indebtedness with clinical precision, reducing a complex human experience to a number. This systematised judgement reinforces shame: a low score becomes a scarlet letter in a data-driven society. Yet digital platforms also create spaces for anonymous disclosure. Online forums where people confess their debts attract massive participation, suggesting a deep hunger to break silence without risking social stigma. These communities demonstrate that while debt stories remain hard to tell in public, the impulse to share persists. *Secrecy is thus less about disinterest than about fear of judgement; where judgement is suspended, disclosure follows.*

The persistence of shame and secrecy around debt reminds us that financial life is always cultural life. Debt does not merely measure economic transactions; it shapes and is shaped by stories of character, morality, and belonging. Unlike other financial metrics, which can be recounted with pride or detachment, debt is narrated through whispers and omissions. This silence is not accidental but a survival strategy in societies that equate owing with failing. To analyse debt properly, then, is to move beyond numbers and confront the cultural scripts that keep people quiet. Only by understanding the roots of secrecy can we begin to dismantle the stigma and imagine a financial culture where obligation is acknowledged without shame, and transparency replaces silence as the foundation of trust.

Historical Debt Myths

Few financial institutions have carried as much symbolic weight as debt, and few have been as deeply entwined with questions of morality, justice, and mercy. From ancient codes to modern legislation, debt has been narrated not merely as an economic arrangement but as a moral drama in which forgiveness and punishment define the limits of social order. To study historical debt myths is to uncover how cultures grappled with the tension between obligation and release, responsibility and reprieve. These stories reveal that societies have long recognised the destructive potential of unpayable debt and, at different moments, sought to contain its corrosive effects through ritual, law, and narrative. *Debt is never just about money; it is about how communities imagine fairness and continuity in the face of imbalance.*

The Jubilee tradition of the Hebrew Bible remains one of the most striking attempts to narrate forgiveness into the very structure of society. Every fiftieth year, according to Leviticus, slaves were freed, land returned to original families, and debts cancelled. This was not an act of sentiment but a radical recognition that perpetual debt corrodes communal life. Without periodic reset, inequality hardens into permanence, the poor become trapped, and social bonds fracture. The Jubilee embedded mercy into law, not as charity but as justice, reframing debt cancellation as a collective obligation to preserve stability. In doing so, it challenges the modern instinct to treat repayment as inviolable. The myth endures because it forces us to ask: should all debts be enforceable forever, or does there come a point where forgiveness serves the greater good?

In the Greco-Roman world, by contrast, debt myths often revolved around harsh consequences rather than merciful release. Roman law permitted creditors to enslave or even kill debtors under certain conditions in the early Republic. The legend of the plebeian debtors—peasants and soldiers who fell into bondage after borrowing—was central to political struggles between patricians and plebeians. Narratives of indebted citizens chained or sold into servitude fuelled calls for reform and helped shape the institutions of the Republic itself. Debt here was not only an economic fact but a rallying point for class struggle, dramatizing the balance between creditor power and debtor survival. *The myth of debtor bondage persisted because it crystallised the fear that financial obligation could reduce free citizens to slaves.*

Medieval Europe added another layer of moral interpretation. Christian teaching, rooted in biblical injunctions, condemned usury—the charging of excessive or any interest—as a sin, reflecting suspicion toward the very act of profiting from another's need. Debt forgiveness was woven into the sacramental system: to forgive debts was to embody divine mercy, while to enforce them ruthlessly was to risk damnation. Yet alongside these teachings emerged the institution of debtor's prisons, where those who failed to repay were confined indefinitely. This paradox—preaching forgiveness while practicing punishment—illustrates the ambivalence of cultural debt narratives. On one hand, societies acknowledged that mercy was necessary; on the other, they relied on shame and coercion to uphold the sanctity of obligation. The tension between these poles created enduring myths of the debtor as both pitiable victim and moral failure.

The image of the debtor's prison haunts European history, immortalised in literature as much as in law. Charles Dickens, whose own father was imprisoned for debt, depicted the Marshalsea prison as a site where families disintegrated and dignity was destroyed. Such portrayals were not exaggerations but reflections of lived reality, where imprisonment rarely led to repayment and often entrenched poverty further. These narratives helped galvanise public opinion against the practice, leading to reforms in the nineteenth century. The myth of the prison served as a moral reckoning: by locking up debtors, societies symbolised the triumph of creditors' rights over human dignity. The eventual abolition of debtor's prisons was not only a legal reform but a cultural shift, an acknowledgment that excessive punishment of debt undermines rather than secures social trust.

Beyond Europe, traditions of debt forgiveness took other shapes. In Mesopotamia, rulers proclaimed periodic amnesties, wiping clean the debts of peasants to prevent social collapse. These "clean slate" decrees were politically motivated—designed to maintain loyalty and prevent rebellion—but they also reflected an understanding that debt could destabilise the very foundations of power. Ancient China too wrestled with cycles of peasant indebtedness, with dynasties rising and falling in part because rulers failed to relieve burdens that drove populations to revolt. In these contexts, myths of debt were bound up with the legitimacy of rulers: a wise king relieved his subjects; a tyrant who clung to strict enforcement invited ruin. *Forgiveness was framed not as weakness but as the wisdom of rulers who recognised that the health of the whole outweighed the claims of the few.*

What unites these diverse traditions is the recognition that debt, if left unchecked, generates unsustainable inequalities and threatens social cohesion. Myths of forgiveness—from Jubilee proclamations to debt amnesties—served as reminders that economies are built on trust and interdependence, not merely on contracts and calculations. By embedding these resets into law or narrative, cultures sought to prevent obligation from ossifying into servitude. At the same time, the punitive myths—from Roman bondage to European debtor's prisons—served as cautionary tales, warning that forgiveness could be exploited and that obligation was not to be taken lightly. The oscillation between these poles reflects the enduring tension in human societies: how to balance justice for creditors with mercy for debtors.

The endurance of these myths has implications for modern debates. Calls for student debt forgiveness in the United States, for instance, echo Jubilee logic, framed as necessary to restore opportunity and prevent generational inequality. Critics respond with Roman sternness, insisting that forgiveness undermines responsibility and rewards imprudence. The fact that both sides draw, knowingly or not, on ancient narratives reveals how debt myths still shape moral imagination. *Contemporary debates are not novel but modern enactments of age-old stories about the meaning of obligation and the possibility of release.*

Historical debt myths remind us that repayment is never a purely economic matter. It is a stage on which societies negotiate power, morality, and belonging. Forgiveness has always carried political weight, while punishment has always raised ethical questions. The stories we inherit about debt—whether of mercy, shame, or servitude—continue to structure how we think about credit, default, and reform. To understand debt today requires listening to these older voices, for they show that behind every spreadsheet lies a narrative about what it means to owe, to pay, and, sometimes, to be forgiven.

Debt as Story, Not Just Numbers

Debt is often presented as an equation—a ledger of liabilities and repayments, a schedule of interest, a matter of arithmetic precision. Yet beneath the numbers, what truly determines how individuals experience, manage, and escape debt is the narrative they attach to it. For some, debt is framed as a temporary bridge, a rational tool for building a future; for others, it becomes a mark of shame, an inherited curse, or a lifelong trap. The arithmetic may be identical, but the story makes all the difference. *It is not the balance sheet alone that dictates outcomes, but the meaning people assign to their debts.*

Consider two university graduates with identical student loans. One views the debt as an investment in their human capital, a loan taken not out of desperation but ambition. They narrate repayment as part of a broader trajectory of growth: an obligation that, though burdensome, validates their journey toward a professional life. The other graduate interprets the same debt as evidence of systemic injustice, a punishment for pursuing education, or a personal failing.

In the first case, repayment becomes part of a story of resilience; in the second, it risks spiralling into resentment and avoidance. The figures on the statement are the same, but the narratives surrounding them diverge profoundly, shaping not only financial behaviour but mental health and identity.

This is not a modern phenomenon. Throughout history, debt has carried moral and emotional weight precisely because it has been cast in stories. Ancient myths of divine forgiveness, mediaeval condemnations of usury, and nineteenth-century tales of debtor's prisons all embedded debt within moral dramas. These stories were not neutral—they influenced how individuals internalised their obligations. A farmer in ancient Mesopotamia might have perceived his debt not simply as a private matter but as a weight that, if unrelieved by royal amnesty, threatened the very stability of the community. In Victorian England, a debtor might interpret their confinement as proof of personal dishonour. Across time, the same economic mechanism has been lived as either temporary duty, irredeemable shame, or potential redemption, depending on the story told.

Modern psychology reinforces this view. Behavioural finance research shows that individuals do not respond to debt in purely rational terms. People are prone to "mental accounting"—segregating debts into categories of meaning. A mortgage is often narrated as "good debt," tied to stability and asset-building, while credit card debt is cast as reckless or shameful. These categories are not dictated by mathematics but by cultural narratives about legitimacy and responsibility. *The classification of debt reflects values, not calculations, and those values in turn influence repayment behaviour.* Someone may prioritise mortgage payments at all costs, even when carrying higher-interest credit card balances, because one form of debt is integrated into a socially acceptable narrative while the other is perceived as moral failure.

Personal narratives also influence how individuals approach repayment strategies. Research into debt repayment psychology reveals that many people prioritise clearing small balances first—even when it is mathematically optimal to tackle high-interest debts—because the act of "closing a chapter" in their debt story provides a motivational boost. This is sometimes called the "debt snowball" effect, and while it defies spreadsheet logic, it makes sense when understood as narrative closure. To pay off a small debt is to rewrite part of one's financial story: a burden lifted, a shame resolved, a victory achieved. The emotional impact of progress, however incremental, reinforces momentum. Here again, story shapes financial outcomes as much as numbers do.

The destructive power of negative debt narratives can be seen most starkly in cycles of poverty. When debt is internalised as inescapable—an inherited destiny passed from parent to child—it can perpetuate fatalism and disengagement from financial systems. Families that view debt as proof of moral weakness or systemic exploitation may avoid formal credit altogether, relying instead on high-cost informal lending. The narrative of debt as trap becomes self-fulfilling, reducing access to the very tools that might enable upward mobility. Yet the inverse is also true: debt framed as a stepping stone can encourage risk-taking, entrepreneurship, and investment in education or housing. The same financial instruments produce wildly different life trajectories depending on the stories that surround them.

Cultural contexts intensify these dynamics. In the United States, debt has often been narrated as both a personal failing and a tool of aspiration. Homeownership, historically tied to the "American Dream," has legitimised mortgages as virtuous commitments, while bankruptcy law has offered a narrative of second chances. By contrast, in parts of Southern Europe, where family honour and reputation weigh heavily, debt carries deeper stigma, and individuals may go to great lengths to conceal financial struggles. In Japan, indebtedness has historically been associated with dishonour to such an extent that some have resorted to extreme measures, including suicide, rather than face public shame. These cultural stories shape not only personal choices but also policy approaches to credit, default, and forgiveness.

Financial institutions themselves exploit the narrative dimension of debt. Credit card companies advertise not only access to funds but lifestyles—travel, freedom, prestige—embedding debt in aspirational stories rather than cautionary ones. Student loan systems frame borrowing as an "investment in the future," casting repayment as a natural consequence of opportunity. Meanwhile, payday lenders cloak predatory terms in narratives of immediate relief or empowerment. In each case, the underlying numbers are secondary to the story being sold. *The creditor who controls the narrative often controls the behaviour of the debtor.*

Yet stories of debt are not solely imposed from outside; they are also crafted by individuals to cope, resist, or reframe their situation. Narratives of debt survival and eventual triumph—memoirs of overcoming bankruptcy, for example—circulate widely because they offer counterweights to shame, suggesting that indebtedness need not define identity permanently. Grassroots debt forgiveness campaigns, such as those targeting medical debt in the United States, work not only by clearing balances but by rewriting the cultural script: they frame debt forgiveness as an act of justice rather than indulgence. Such reframing has powerful consequences, challenging the inevitability of financial suffering and reshaping what communities deem acceptable.

The practical lesson is clear. For individuals and policymakers alike, addressing debt requires more than designing repayment schedules or interest caps. It requires attending to the stories people tell about debt—stories that influence repayment, avoidance, and reform. *Debt literacy must include narrative literacy.* To teach financial resilience is not only to provide technical knowledge but also to help people craft healthier narratives: debt as manageable obligation rather than moral stain, as opportunity rather than fate, as temporary stage rather than permanent identity.

The significance of debt as story lies in its ability to determine whether individuals spiral into cycles of despair or chart paths of recovery. A ledger records obligations; a story gives them meaning. Numbers may calculate what is owed, but narratives decide how it feels, how it is managed, and whether it becomes a weight that crushes or a challenge that galvanises. To see debt only as numbers is to miss its human core. To recognise it as story is to understand why it endures as one of the most powerful forces shaping lives, not merely in the economy, but in the imagination.

Chapter 6
The Gift and the Ledger

Modern life is often narrated through the lens of exchange: salaries earned, bills paid, receipts issued, and balances settled. Yet money, for all its reputation as the most transactional of inventions, has always carried with it another dimension—one that defies the arithmetic of markets and veers into the territory of obligation, generosity, and meaning. To see finance solely as the settlement of accounts is to ignore the subtler ledger that runs parallel to every transaction: the social and psychological record of what is given, received, owed, and remembered. *A gift, though seemingly free, is never without consequence.*

Anthropologists have long recognised that exchange does not begin with coins or contracts but with gifts. Long before formal markets, societies created complex systems of reciprocity where value circulated in ways that reinforced bonds and established hierarchies. In the potlatch ceremonies of the Indigenous peoples of the Pacific Northwest, lavish feasts and the distribution of goods were not acts of reckless generosity but carefully staged performances of prestige, cementing the giver's status through obligation placed upon the receiver. In parts of Polynesia, the act of giving a prized item—whether shell, feather, or food—was imbued with the notion that the object carried a spirit of its giver, binding the recipient into an ongoing relationship. To give was not to lose, but to entangle. What looked like a dispersal of wealth was in fact a redistribution of power, meaning, and future expectation.

These traditions reveal a truth that extends into our supposedly rational financial systems: *"free" is rarely free.* When a parent gives money to a child, it is not merely an economic transfer; it embeds lessons of dependence, gratitude, or sometimes guilt. When a company sponsors a public festival, it is not charity in its purest form but a bid for reputational capital. Even in the world of digital crowdfunding, where strangers contribute to a stranger's cause, the act of giving is never neutral. It signals solidarity, buys symbolic association with a narrative, and—at times—creates pressure for recipients to perform worthiness in return. In each case, the ledger is not confined to the bank statement; it is etched in memory, reputation, and expectation.

Understanding this duality—gift and ledger—is essential to making sense of how people experience money beyond arithmetic. One might pay off a mortgage with regular instalments that close neatly on a spreadsheet, but a gift lingers. A birthday present, a philanthropic donation, a bailout by a friend: these remain unfinished, their meaning replayed and reinterpreted over time. The giver may recall the moment with pride or resentment; the receiver may feel gratitude, indebtedness, or quiet unease. Unlike a purchase, where the exchange is neatly sealed, gifts reopen themselves again and again in the mind. This is why anthropologist Marcel Mauss argued that the gift is never truly free: it carries the "spirit of the gift" that insists on return, whether immediate, delayed, or symbolic.

Modern finance appears to distance itself from this messiness by priding itself on precision and neutrality. Yet beneath its surface, the language of gift and obligation still shapes practice. Corporate philanthropy is justified not by return on investment but by narratives of responsibility and reputation. Government relief payments, while accounted for in budgets, also signal values about who deserves support and under what conditions. The popularity of crowdfunding platforms such as GoFundMe illustrates this tension vividly. A contribution is framed as generosity, yet it also writes a story of belonging: the donor becomes part of the recipient's struggle or triumph. The campaign itself performs worthiness, and the gift legitimises the narrative. Each pledge, therefore, is less a financial donation than a social alignment, recorded as much in memory as in money.

This has profound implications for how we think about generosity in the modern world. Economists may measure charitable giving in terms of GDP percentages or tax deductions, but individuals rarely experience giving in such sterile terms. To give is to express values, to define identity, to forge ties. In business, a discounted service offered to a loyal client may be entered into accounts as a loss, yet it operates as a gift that deepens relational capital and increases the likelihood of reciprocity later. In personal life, a neighbour offering childcare, a friend covering a meal, or a community pooling resources for someone in need all embody the same principle: the act carries meaning far beyond the immediate utility.

At the same time, gifts can entangle in ways that are troubling. To receive without the ability to reciprocate can feel humiliating. Cultures that emphasise equality often mask generosity with ritual or formality to reduce this imbalance: consider the reciprocal gift-giving of Christmas, where the act of giving is staged as mutual rather than hierarchical. Conversely, in contexts where hierarchy is accepted, gifts reinforce power. Patronage systems, both historical and modern, thrive on this asymmetry: a benefactor provides, and the beneficiary remains tied in loyalty, gratitude, and sometimes silence. *The gift, then, is both a bridge and a shackle.*

As finance becomes more digital and global, it is tempting to assume that gifts will fade into irrelevance, replaced by the anonymity of transactions. Yet the opposite seems true. The rise of online tipping, Patreon subscriptions, and micro-donations reveals how individuals crave the symbolic weight of giving. They are not simply paying for content or service; they are inscribing themselves into a relationship, signalling recognition and allegiance. Even blockchain experiments with "social tokens" and decentralised funding communities show how deeply humans continue to conflate money with meaning. Numbers alone do not satisfy; stories of generosity, obligation, and reciprocity remain indispensable.

The challenge, then, is to reframe generosity not as a distraction from financial rationality but as integral to it. To give wisely is not merely to budget for donations but to recognise the symbolic and relational economies one participates in. A gift to a colleague may smooth collaboration more effectively than a contractual incentive. A gesture of generosity in business negotiations may build goodwill that no clause can guarantee. And on a societal level, recognising the role of generosity can help explain why welfare policies succeed or fail, not by economic efficiency alone but by whether they resonate with citizens' narratives of fairness and solidarity.

The gift and the ledger are not opposing worlds. They are intertwined, each shaping how the other is perceived. The ledger records the measurable; the gift records the meaningful. When we pretend money is purely about numbers, we obscure the obligations, expectations, and opportunities that truly define its role in our lives. To understand finance today requires more than charts and contracts—it requires recognising that every balance sheet has a shadow ledger of relationships, memories, and meanings that can amplify, distort, or redeem the arithmetic. To ignore this is to miss the most enduring truth: money, whether given or exchanged, is never just about value—it is always about connection.

Money Beyond Transaction

To see money purely as a mechanism of exchange is to misunderstand its place in human life. Markets, prices, and contracts dominate modern thinking about finance, but long before coinage or credit ledgers, communities organised their economies around giving, receiving, and reciprocating. Anthropologists have shown that in many societies, *value was not measured by efficiency of trade but by depth of relationship*. The act of giving bound people together in webs of obligation and meaning that outlasted any single transfer of goods. Money in its transactional sense, stripped of this richness, is a relatively recent innovation, and even today it cannot fully displace the older logic of reciprocity.

One of the most influential works in this field, Marcel Mauss's *The Gift* (1925), revealed that gifts in traditional societies were never "free" in the modern sense. They created a binding cycle: to give, to receive, and to return. This cycle was not reducible to barter, because the return was often delayed, symbolic, or transformed. The Maori concept of *hau* suggested that the gift retained the spirit of the giver, demanding its circulation rather than its retention. Among the Kwakiutl and Tlingit peoples of the Pacific Northwest, potlatch ceremonies transformed giving into an assertion of prestige: chiefs staged elaborate feasts, distributing wealth in order to secure honour and obligation. Far from being wasteful extravagance, these events reinforced hierarchies, alliances, and collective memory. To withhold gifts in such systems was not prudence—it was social death.

Reciprocity, then, functions less like a contract and more like a narrative. Each gift tells a story of who belongs, who owes, and who stands apart. In many agrarian communities, harvest festivals and collective feasts redistributed food not only to prevent hunger but to reaffirm community bonds. The person who shared was not simply generous; they were publicly weaving themselves into the fabric of the group. Likewise, in pastoral societies where cattle functioned as wealth, gifting an animal was a profound gesture of alliance, a statement of trust, and a claim upon future solidarity. *The economic dimension was inseparable from the symbolic.*

Even when money entered circulation, its use was often framed by these older logics. Ancient Rome operated both a market economy and a gift economy. Senators might transact in coin, but their reputations were secured through largesse: sponsoring games, building aqueducts, or extending loans to allies. The financial loss was offset by the accrual of honour and influence. In medieval Europe, gift-giving among the nobility—whether jewels, land, or favours—functioned as political currency. In this sense, money and gifts were never separate domains but overlapping instruments in the pursuit of social and cultural capital.

The persistence of gifting logics into the modern era suggests that reciprocity is not an archaic stage superseded by rational markets but a permanent feature of human exchange. Charitable donations, for instance, are rarely motivated by abstract altruism alone. They often carry implicit expectations: recognition, social belonging, or even the subtle return of self-respect. Philanthropy at scale magnifies this dynamic. When a billionaire donates to a university, the institution may rename a building in their honour, enshrining the gift in collective memory. The ledger records expenditure, but the cultural record immortalises prestige. The donor gives, but also receives—status, influence, and sometimes moral redemption.

On a more intimate level, family finances illustrate how gifting logic remains central. Parents who fund a child's education do not regard the expense as a market transaction; it is a gift laden with expectation. The child may feel gratitude, pressure to succeed, or even guilt. The story of that gift shapes identity, influencing career choices or the willingness to care for parents in old age. These dynamics reveal why money is never neutral within families: it always carries the weight of narrative.

Digital culture has only amplified this interplay between transaction and gift. Online crowdfunding platforms blur the line between donation and investment. A contributor may give to a stranger's medical fund not for financial return but for the story: the satisfaction of alignment with a cause, the symbolic participation in another's struggle. Yet the giver also expects something intangible in return—updates, acknowledgement, or the affirmation of being part of a community. Streaming platforms where fans "tip" creators display similar dynamics. The payment is voluntary, not compulsory, but its meaning lies less in the amount than in the recognition it communicates. What looks like commerce is often theatre of reciprocity.

The significance of these insights extends far beyond anthropology. They suggest that economic models which treat humans as rational actors maximising self-interest capture only half the picture. In reality, much of economic behaviour is structured by *the need to be seen, remembered, and connected.* This explains why people often make decisions that appear inefficient in transactional terms. They may over-give, undercharge, or persist in unprofitable generosity because the value lies not in material gain but in social return. From a purely financial perspective, this may look irrational. From a human perspective, it is entirely logical.

At the same time, gifting economies raise tensions. Reciprocity can liberate but also entangle. To receive a gift without the means to reciprocate may feel humiliating, creating a burden rather than a blessing. In some cultures, elaborate etiquette evolved precisely to mitigate this imbalance: the ritual exchange of equivalent gifts at holidays or ceremonies, ensuring that generosity remained balanced. In others, asymmetry was accepted, even valorised, reinforcing status differences between patron and client. The history of philanthropy often illustrates this ambivalence: admired as generosity by some, condemned as self-serving dominance by others.

To reframe money beyond transaction, therefore, is not to romanticise gifts but to acknowledge their complexity. *Every act of giving carries power, symbolism, and expectation.* Economists who ignore this dimension risk misunderstanding why people act as they do. A development programme that delivers aid as a purely transactional transfer may falter if it ignores the narratives of reciprocity within local communities. Conversely, initiatives that frame aid as partnership or shared responsibility often secure deeper trust. The anthropology of the gift is not antiquarian curiosity; it is a toolkit for interpreting the lived experience of finance today.

The enduring lesson is that humans rarely see money as numbers alone. Whether in the feasts of the potlatch, the patronage of Renaissance elites, or the micro-donations of digital culture, money functions simultaneously as currency and as story. It carries the weight of relationship, obligation, and memory. To reduce it to transaction is to flatten a multidimensional reality into arithmetic. To understand it as gift as well as payment is to restore the richness of human exchange—and to recognise that our economic lives are always moral lives too.

The Hidden Obligations of Gifts

Nothing in human exchange is ever truly free. A gift may appear spontaneous or altruistic, but across cultures and history, receiving it invariably creates a bond that carries expectations—whether of gratitude, reciprocity, loyalty, or acknowledgement. Anthropologists have long noted that gifts are never simply objects or resources transferred from one person to another. They are charged acts that bind giver and recipient in webs of obligation. *The cultural and psychological weight of a gift lies precisely in its inability to be neutral.*

The anthropological classic here is Marcel Mauss's *The Gift*, which demonstrated that in many traditional societies, gifts are part of a tripartite obligation: to give, to receive, and to reciprocate. Failure in any stage is not merely a social faux pas but a breach of moral order. The gift is not just a transfer of goods; it is the medium through which trust, honour, and community cohesion are maintained. In Polynesian societies, for example, the concept of *hau* expressed the idea that a gift carries the spirit of its giver, pressing upon the recipient a duty to return it in some form. What appears to the outsider as generosity is in fact a system that keeps communities bound together through cycles of mutual indebtedness.

This logic did not vanish with the rise of money economies; rather, it persists in subtler ways. Consider the modern workplace, where an unsolicited gift from a manager to an employee—a bottle of wine, an expensive meal, or even extra time off—carries an implicit demand. The employee may feel obliged to show heightened loyalty, gratitude, or performance in return. The object itself is secondary; what matters is the psychological ledger it opens. The same is true in politics: lobbyists rarely hand over cash, but gifts in the form of dinners, travel, or campaign contributions create soft obligations that shape decision-making. The transaction is technically "free," yet its weight can be decisive.

Psychology provides further evidence of this dynamic. The principle of reciprocity, well-documented in behavioural research, shows that humans feel an almost automatic compulsion to give back when something is received. In experiments, participants who were given small, unexpected gifts—even a simple soft drink—were more likely to return favours or comply with requests. This mechanism explains why marketing strategies rely so heavily on samples, free trials, or promotional giveaways. The company is not simply losing money by offering something gratis; it is triggering a deep-seated psychological rule that predisposes customers to repay the kindness, often far in excess of the original cost.

The obligation of gifts also carries a moral weight. In many cultures, to refuse a gift is tantamount to rejecting the relationship itself. Among certain Indigenous groups of North America, declining to participate in a potlatch ceremony—where goods were lavishly distributed—signalled an unwillingness to belong. Similarly, in Mediterranean cultures, refusing hospitality can be interpreted as a grave insult, because the gift of food and shelter is understood not as a convenience but as a profound assertion of connection. *The gift is never only about the object—it is about the bond it creates, and the moral duty to honour that bond.*

Yet gifts also generate tension, because they place the recipient in a position of indebtedness. Debt here is not measured in currency but in social weight. A lavish wedding present, for instance, may delight the recipient but also pressure them to respond with a gift of equivalent value in the future. The act of generosity, therefore, is never free of calculation. This tension can even become oppressive. In contexts where power differentials are stark—patron-client relationships, colonial encounters, or philanthropy from the ultra-wealthy—the gift can be a veiled instrument of domination. The recipient may be placed in a permanent state of obligation, unable to "repay" the gift in any meaningful way, effectively bound in asymmetrical dependency.

Philanthropy provides a striking modern example. When a billionaire donates vast sums to a university or hospital, the gesture is publicly framed as altruism. Yet institutions often respond by naming buildings after the donor, awarding honorary degrees, or providing privileged access. The gift transforms into a platform for prestige, and the institution becomes an unspoken debtor. Critics argue that such philanthropy allows the wealthy to launder reputations or entrench influence while still being praised for their benevolence. The "free" gift here is not free at all—it reconfigures relationships of power.

On a smaller scale, consider the way digital culture has reintroduced gifting dynamics into daily life. Crowdfunding platforms thrive on contributions framed as donations. While contributors may not expect financial return, they do anticipate updates, gratitude, or social acknowledgement. Streamers and online creators receive "tips" or donations not purely as income but as visible symbols of belonging: the act of giving establishes a tie between giver and recipient. Here, too, the psychology of obligation plays out. A creator who receives support may feel compelled to produce more, respond directly to supporters, or otherwise "repay" the generosity. These exchanges demonstrate that gifting has not been erased by market logic—it has simply adapted.

The paradox of gifts lies in their dual character. They are both voluntary and obligatory, both freeing and constraining. A parent who pays for a child's university tuition does not frame it as a debt, yet the child may carry a lifelong sense of owing. A friend who insists on covering dinner may be resented rather than appreciated if the gesture feels like a way of asserting superiority. What is intended as generosity can be received as control, depending on the balance of power and the subtle expectations attached. *The gift binds because it changes the story of the relationship, whether or not either party acknowledges it outright.*

Understanding the hidden obligations of gifts also clarifies why societies develop rituals to regulate them. Gift-giving at Christmas or weddings is often standardised precisely to reduce the tension of imbalance: everyone gives, everyone receives, and equivalence is loosely maintained. Likewise, formal philanthropy is accompanied by transparency reports, tax structures, and governance to mitigate the distortions of power. These rituals and regulations are cultural technologies designed to manage the obligations that gifts inevitably generate.

To grasp the true significance of gifts, then, is to move beyond the illusion of "free." Gifts create circuits of value that operate outside market pricing yet remain deeply binding. They can build trust, solidarity, and belonging, but they can also entangle, manipulate, and dominate. Their hidden obligations remind us that money is not the only ledger we live by; we also carry moral, emotional, and symbolic accounts that are every bit as consequential. Recognising this does not diminish the beauty of generosity, but it sharpens our awareness of its power. To give or to receive is never trivial. It is to enter a story that demands a response, shaping the bonds we live within and the balance of our shared lives.

Case Studies of Gift Economies

Across history, societies have developed systems of exchange that operate not on strict calculation but on generosity, obligation, and symbolism. These gift economies reveal that the circulation of wealth cannot be understood purely through market terms. They show that value often lies as much in relationships as in material goods, and that generosity can be both a social performance and a practical means of survival. Examining case studies from traditional cultures to modern digital platforms underscores that while the forms evolve, the underlying dynamics remain strikingly consistent: gifts shape communities by binding people into networks of mutual recognition and responsibility.

Perhaps the most famous example is the *potlatch* ceremonies of Indigenous peoples along the Pacific Northwest coast of North America. These elaborate feasts, held to mark events such as marriages, funerals, or status transitions, involved the public distribution—and sometimes the deliberate destruction—of wealth. Families would give away blankets, canoes, food, or even copper shields, often to the point of personal impoverishment. To outsiders, such practices appeared wasteful or irrational. Yet within their cultural context, the potlatch was a highly sophisticated economic and social system. Status was not derived from hoarding resources but from the ability to give them away. Generosity was both competitive and communal: a chief who could distribute the most displayed not only personal wealth but also the strength of the networks that supported him. *The act of giving, far more than the material itself, was the true currency of prestige.*

Anthropological studies reveal that the potlatch was also a mechanism of redistribution. Resources that were abundant in one area—such as fish or furs—could circulate across communities through the medium of these feasts. In effect, the ceremonies ensured that no single group monopolised wealth, even as they reinforced hierarchies of honour. The state attempted to ban the potlatch in the late 19th century, viewing it as a barrier to assimilation into capitalist norms. Yet the practice persisted underground, testifying to its resilience as a social glue. It is a reminder that economies centred on gifting are not primitive precursors to "real" markets but alternative systems that organise power and meaning in ways capitalism struggles to comprehend.

Comparable practices existed elsewhere. In the Trobriand Islands, the *kula ring* exchange system bound chiefs in an endless circuit of ceremonial trading. Shell necklaces and armbands circulated clockwise and counter-clockwise between islands, carrying not only material but also symbolic value. The objects could not be retained permanently; their worth derived from their movement and the prestige attached to their temporary custodianship. Like the potlatch, the kula ring exemplified how gifts are not simply about goods but about the maintenance of social ties and hierarchies. The refusal to participate, or the failure to reciprocate, would signal exclusion from the network of alliances.

Fast forward to the modern world, and the same principles of symbolic generosity underpin phenomena as diverse as philanthropy, crowdfunding, and open-source collaboration. Consider platforms such as Kickstarter or GoFundMe. At first glance, these are mechanisms for raising money; yet closer inspection reveals that they operate more like digital potlatches than conventional markets. Supporters often contribute not because they expect a tangible financial return but because they seek belonging, recognition, or the satisfaction of enabling a project to exist. A musician's album funded through fans' contributions or a neighbour's medical expenses covered through online donations exemplifies the modern gift economy: the act of giving affirms identity, solidarity, and trust.

Importantly, these systems also retain the same tensions as traditional gift economies. Backers on crowdfunding platforms often expect symbolic reciprocity—updates, acknowledgements, or tokens of appreciation. Failing to deliver on these can fracture trust, just as failing to reciprocate in the kula ring or potlatch could lead to loss of status. The so-called "free" generosity of digital communities is thus never entirely without expectation. It is framed in terms of belonging, recognition, and relational debt rather than strict accounts. *Modern crowdfunding reminds us that money is never purely transactional—it is also expressive of values, stories, and communal ties.*

Corporate practices can also be analysed through the lens of gift economies. Open-source software, for instance, thrives not because contributors are paid but because of reputational capital and the reciprocal expectation of future contributions. A programmer who contributes code "gifts" their labour to the community, but in return gains visibility, influence, and often access to others' work. This mirrors the anthropological insight that gifts are both altruistic and strategic. Even acts of apparent generosity carry embedded calculations, whether of honour, reciprocity, or symbolic capital.

What unites these case studies is the recognition that gift economies are not marginal curiosities but enduring systems that coexist with markets. They persist because they address human needs that markets alone cannot satisfy: the need for recognition, for belonging, for symbolic affirmation. Whether in the dramatic potlatch feasts of the Pacific Northwest, the ritualised kula exchanges of the Trobriand Islands, or the digital pledges of crowdfunding platforms, generosity is never a neutral act. It is an investment in relationships, a performance of identity, and a recalibration of power.

The endurance of gift economies also raises important questions about modern finance. If the most successful crowdfunding campaigns are those that build strong narratives of trust and belonging, what does that reveal about the limits of purely transactional models of investment? If philanthropists earn prestige and influence through their donations, how different is this from the chiefs who distributed wealth at potlatch ceremonies? And if open-source communities thrive on reciprocity rather than price, what lessons might that hold for rethinking collaboration and innovation?

The anthropology of gift economies insists that money is never just about numbers; it is always about meaning. These case studies demonstrate that generosity is both symbolic and financial, a medium through which societies express their deepest values. To study gift economies is to confront the fact that we are never free from the invisible ledgers of obligation and recognition. Whether in feasts, shells, or crowdfunding pledges, the logic is the same: giving is not the opposite of economy, but its most revealing expression.

Reframing Generosity in Modern Finance

The language of finance is usually dominated by precision, measurement, and efficiency. We speak of optimising portfolios, balancing budgets, or maximising returns. Within this vocabulary, generosity is often treated as an indulgence, a pleasant but secondary feature of human life that sits outside the central logic of markets. Yet history, anthropology, and modern behavioural science all suggest that this is a profound misunderstanding. *Giving is not peripheral to finance but constitutive of it; generosity is not a side activity but one of the most enduring forces shaping relationships, trust, and meaning in human economies.* Reframing generosity as a core principle rather than a charitable afterthought offers not only a deeper understanding of money's role in society but also a more sustainable framework for modern economic life.

One striking way to see this is to look at the companies and communities that thrive not because they extract the maximum from every interaction but because they embed giving within their operating model. Consider the success of microfinance initiatives such as Grameen Bank. At its heart, microcredit is not simply about lending small sums of money but about creating networks of trust and mutual accountability. Borrowers often form solidarity groups where repayment is not enforced by collateral but by shared responsibility. What sustains these systems is less the technical architecture of the loans than the cultural expectation of reciprocity and the symbolic value of being entrusted. Here, generosity takes the form of institutional trust: the lender chooses to extend credit without traditional guarantees, and in turn, borrowers feel compelled to honour that trust. The result is an economy of meaning rather than a mechanical transfer of funds.

This dynamic plays out in philanthropy at scale. When wealthy individuals or corporations donate substantial sums, the act is rarely reducible to a simple calculation of tax benefits. It is an exercise in reputation, legacy, and social influence. Andrew Carnegie's libraries were as much about shaping civic identity as they were about literacy. More recently, the Giving Pledge, through which billionaires commit to giving away the majority of their wealth, demonstrates how generosity is used to craft narratives of responsibility and stewardship. Critics point out that such initiatives allow the wealthy to retain disproportionate control over public goods, bypassing democratic processes. Yet whether praised or questioned, the phenomenon underscores the same lesson: giving reshapes power dynamics and redefines relationships between individuals, institutions, and society. *Generosity, in finance, is never neutral—it always signals meaning and creates obligations.*

The digital era has amplified these dynamics in unexpected ways. Crowdfunding platforms not only enable individuals to fundraise for causes ranging from creative projects to medical expenses, they also transform giving into a visible, relational act. Backers often give not because they expect material return but because the act of contribution is bound up with identity and belonging. A fan supporting an independent artist, or a community rallying to support someone's healthcare costs, demonstrates that the financial transfer is inseparable from symbolic affirmation. In this sense, platforms like Kickstarter or GoFundMe function as theatres of generosity, where giving is performed publicly, and meaning is co-created between giver and recipient. Traditional finance, with its emphasis on anonymity and numerical efficiency, fails to account for this dimension of money as a medium of identity.

Behavioural economics adds further nuance by showing that people do not always act in narrowly self-interested ways. Experiments in "dictator games," where participants are free to divide money between themselves and strangers, consistently show a willingness to give even when there is no expectation of reciprocity. Economists once treated such behaviour as anomalies, deviations from rationality. Today, these acts are recognised as evidence that generosity is a built-in part of human decision-making, an expression of fairness norms and moral intuitions that guide economic life as much as rational calculation does. *Far from being irrational, generosity can be seen as an adaptive mechanism for building trust and cooperation, assets that are every bit as valuable as cash flows or balance sheets.*

The corporate world has also begun to recognise generosity as more than branding. Companies that invest in employee wellbeing, community engagement, or open innovation often find that the returns—though not immediate—are profound. For example, firms that adopt profit-sharing schemes or employee ownership models frequently benefit from greater loyalty and productivity. Similarly, businesses that engage authentically in corporate social responsibility programmes often secure more resilient customer bases. These cases demonstrate that giving, whether in the form of shared profits, environmental stewardship, or community investment, functions as a strategic lever, not merely a moral flourish. To view generosity as a cost centre is to misunderstand its role as an engine of long-term value creation.

Yet the reframing of generosity requires careful attention to its risks. Not all forms of giving are emancipatory. History is littered with examples where generosity was wielded as a tool of domination. Colonial authorities often framed their extraction of resources as benevolent "gifts of civilisation," while contemporary geopolitics still sees foreign aid used as a vehicle of influence. Even on an individual level, acts of generosity can create uncomfortable obligations or perpetuate inequalities. The psychological weight of debt, explored in earlier chapters, mirrors the weight of the "gift that cannot be repaid." Thus, reframing generosity in modern finance cannot simply mean celebrating giving uncritically; it must also involve acknowledging how generosity shapes hierarchies and responsibilities. *The gift binds as well as liberates, and true wisdom lies in recognising both dimensions.*

What emerges from these perspectives is that generosity in finance is not about subtracting from one's resources but about adding layers of meaning to transactions. A budget may track income and expenses, but it cannot capture the symbolic value of a donation that cements a relationship, or the reputational capital of a company that gives back to its community. By reframing generosity as a central economic practice, we begin to see that financial health is not measured only by solvency ratios or stock prices but also by the strength of networks and the trust embedded in them. This has profound implications for how individuals, institutions, and policymakers think about prosperity.

For individuals, reframing generosity means recognising that acts of giving—whether small contributions to a friend's project or larger commitments to community organisations—are not simply drains on personal wealth but investments in social capital. For institutions, it means designing financial systems that acknowledge and encourage reciprocity rather than treating giving as irrational. And for societies, it means questioning the tendency to reduce all forms of value to monetary terms, acknowledging instead that finance is inseparable from culture, meaning, and identity.

Generosity is not the opposite of finance. It is finance at its most human. To give is to acknowledge interdependence, to shape the stories that connect us, and to leave a trace that endures beyond the numbers on a ledger. In recognising this, we move from seeing giving as a discretionary line item in the budget to understanding it as a vital architecture of modern economic life. The challenge is not whether generosity has a place in finance—it always has—but whether we are prepared to treat it not as an afterthought but as a guiding principle that shapes relationships, sustains communities, and creates meaning in a world too often reduced to spreadsheets.

Chapter 7
Scarcity and Abundance Myths

Scarcity and abundance are not simply economic conditions; they are stories that societies tell themselves, myths that shape behaviour as much as material reality. The mere whisper of shortage can send rational individuals into irrational spirals of panic, while promises of limitless plenty can seduce entire cultures into overconsumption and complacency. Both narratives have proven extraordinarily resilient across history, surviving changes in technology, political systems, and global trade. What matters is not merely whether resources are objectively scarce or plentiful but how people *believe* them to be, and how those beliefs structure financial systems, cultural norms, and individual decisions. To understand modern financial anxieties—whether the rush to empty supermarket shelves at the hint of disruption or the relentless optimism of speculative bubbles—one must look not only to balance sheets but also to the stories of scarcity and abundance that underpin them.

The fear of running out has deep roots in human memory. Pre-industrial societies often lived at the edge of subsistence, where poor harvests could mean famine, and the instinct to store, hoard, and prepare was not irrational but essential for survival. These experiences left cultural imprints that outlasted the conditions themselves. Folktales of famine, from European cautionary stories of empty granaries to African parables of hunger spirits, carry the same core lesson: resources are fragile, and prudence requires vigilance. Modern economies, for all their technological sophistication, are not immune to these echoes. The psychology of the bank run, for example, mirrors the ancient fear of famine: the very act of fearing shortage creates the shortage itself. When depositors queue to withdraw their savings, the institution collapses not because its assets have vanished overnight but because collective belief makes collapse inevitable. *Scarcity, in this sense, is as much a narrative contagion as an objective state of affairs.*

Yet alongside these warnings of insufficiency are equally enduring myths of abundance. Agrarian societies often celebrated the promise of unearned plenty, from the biblical land of milk and honey to the medieval legend of the Land of Cockaigne, where roasted geese flew directly into one's mouth and rivers ran with wine. Such stories reassured communities that life was not only hardship but also held the possibility of magical bounty. In the modern era, abundance myths re-emerge in different guises: advertising slogans promising a life of effortless consumption, investment pitches touting endless growth, or technological utopianism suggesting that human ingenuity can overcome any limitation. *The danger of abundance myths lies not in hope itself but in the illusion that prosperity requires no discipline, no trade-offs, no stewardship.*

What complicates matters is that many cultures tell both stories at once. Scarcity for others, abundance for insiders. Colonial empires justified extraction by portraying conquered lands as inexhaustibly rich, ripe for exploitation, while simultaneously cultivating fear among their own populations about the dangers of shortage. Contemporary consumer economies often sustain themselves by selling scarcity to some (limited editions, exclusive access) while projecting abundance to others (cheap mass production, perpetual credit). Even in personal finance, individuals may oscillate between the two narratives: fearing financial ruin if they do not save aggressively, while simultaneously believing in the possibility of sudden windfalls through lotteries, speculative investments, or entrepreneurial success. These contradictions are not anomalies but structural features of how societies organise economic meaning.

Modern finance continues to reflect these mythologies in subtle but powerful ways. The panic buying of toilet paper during the COVID-19 pandemic was not triggered by any objective shortage but by the fear of shortage, amplified by images of empty shelves. Conversely, the rise of cryptocurrency markets demonstrated how abundance myths operate: investors were drawn by the promise of exponential, almost magical returns, often disregarding the fundamental volatility of the assets. Both phenomena demonstrate that financial behaviour cannot be understood through rational models alone. *People do not simply manage resources—they interpret them through the lens of cultural stories that frame what is possible, desirable, and threatening.*

The relevance of these myths is not confined to crises or speculative bubbles; they permeate everyday choices. A family may overstock their pantry, not because it is efficient, but because stories of past hardship haunt them. A start-up founder may chase unsustainable growth because the abundance narrative suggests that scaling endlessly is both possible and necessary. Governments, too, invoke these stories when framing policy: austerity measures are often justified by scarcity narratives—"there is no money left"—while expansionary projects rely on abundance narratives that promise boundless prosperity. Recognising these underlying myths reveals how financial policy debates are rarely just technical arguments but moral dramas about whether society faces a desert of deprivation or a cornucopia of wealth.

What makes these narratives so powerful is that they are not mutually exclusive but mutually reinforcing. The fear of scarcity can drive individuals to seek refuge in fantasies of abundance, while the disappointment of abundance myths collapsing—such as during financial crises—can intensify scarcity fears. Together, they form a cycle that perpetuates instability, oscillating between hoarding and excess, caution and recklessness. The task for modern readers is not to banish these myths—they are too deeply woven into human imagination—but to interrogate which narrative is at play when making decisions, and whether that narrative serves clarity or distortion.

This chapter invites readers to pause before reacting instinctively to the stories of shortage and plenty that permeate financial life. By tracing their origins, recognising their cultural contradictions, and examining their contemporary manifestations, we can begin to see how much of economic behaviour is governed not by numbers but by inherited myths. The practical question is both personal and collective: when we act out of fear of running out, or seduction by endless bounty, what choices do we make, and whose interests do they serve? *Scarcity and abundance myths are not relics of folklore—they are living scripts guiding our financial systems, our policies, and our private anxieties. To master them is to reclaim agency over money's most powerful illusions.*

The Fear of Running Out: Shows how scarcity narratives fuel hoarding and panic, from famine tales to bank runs

Few forces shape human behaviour more predictably than the anticipation of shortage. Long before modern finance, the spectre of running out drove families to fill cellars with grain, shepherds to guard pastures, and rulers to hoard treasures. What distinguishes scarcity narratives from simple prudence is their capacity to multiply beyond proportion: the moment a community *believes* supplies are dwindling, behaviour changes dramatically, and scarcity can be created where none previously existed. The fear of running out is not merely a reaction to material reality; it is a cultural script, a psychological reflex, and often a self-fulfilling prophecy.

Historical memory preserves this reflex in vivid stories of famine. In medieval Europe, hunger loomed over every harvest. When rains failed or blight struck, villages faced starvation, and the tales that survived reflect not only hardship but also the moral codes forged in desperation. Chronicles describe villagers accused of hiding stores, of profiting unfairly, or of failing to share. Religious sermons framed famine as divine punishment for collective sin, and scarcity became a moral lesson as much as a physical crisis. In China, dynastic histories are punctuated by accounts of floods or droughts that wiped out crops, with the legitimacy of emperors often judged by their ability to secure grain reserves. These examples underscore how *fear of running out is woven into narratives of morality, governance, and survival.* It is rarely just about the food; it is about trust, responsibility, and power.

This cultural inheritance explains why scarcity stories exert such force even in conditions of plenty. Take the case of modern supermarket panics. During the early months of the COVID-19 pandemic, households across the globe stockpiled flour, rice, and toilet paper. In most places, supply chains were robust enough to handle demand, but the *image* of empty shelves transmitted the message of shortage faster than any official reassurance. The result was circular: people bought more because they saw others buying more, and scarcity was produced not by collapse of supply but by collapse of confidence. Economists describe such phenomena as coordination failures, but from a cultural perspective, they are simply the old famine story re-enacted in fluorescent aisles.

Finance provides parallel examples, the most iconic being the bank run. In 1907, before the creation of the US Federal Reserve, a cascade of withdrawals nearly destroyed the American banking system. In 2008, the collapse of Lehman Brothers triggered panic across global markets. In both cases, the actual problem was compounded by perception: if depositors or investors fear they will not be able to access funds, their rush to withdraw ensures that prediction becomes true. A bank run is less a rational audit of balance sheets than a collective rush of scarcity psychology. The difference between solvency and collapse is not always the asset column but the stories people believe about whether money is available. *Fear manufactures the very shortage it dreads.*

Anthropology helps to explain why scarcity narratives strike so deeply. In many traditional societies, survival was linked to seasonal cycles, with lean months expected and abundance fleeting. Hoarding was not stigmatised but seen as prudence. Yet cultural frameworks added a moral overlay. Among the Igbo of Nigeria, yam barns were both a sign of wealth and a test of generosity, as a man who hoarded too much without redistribution invited social censure. In biblical texts, the story of Joseph advising Pharaoh to store grain during years of plenty is framed as wisdom, while the subsequent famine becomes a narrative of divine providence and human foresight. Scarcity, in these stories, is not only about material insufficiency but about whether one has behaved rightly in preparing for it.

Modern behavioural finance adds another dimension: cognitive biases intensify scarcity fears. Psychologists note that people overweight losses compared to equivalent gains, a principle known as loss aversion. Scarcity amplifies this effect, narrowing attention to immediate resources and heightening risk-averse behaviour. Studies show that individuals under conditions of perceived scarcity make more short-term decisions, even if these undermine long-term welfare. This is why the poor, faced with credit shortages, may accept predatory loans despite exorbitant interest rates: the fear of running out overrides rational calculation. *Scarcity does not just deplete resources; it depletes cognitive bandwidth.*

The persistence of scarcity myths in consumer culture reveals their adaptability. Luxury industries trade on the allure of limited editions, persuading buyers that exclusivity itself is a form of value. Sales promotions emphasise "while supplies last" or "only three left in stock," harnessing the same instincts that once drove peasants to horde grain against winter. Scarcity has become not only a fear but a marketing strategy, commodified to generate urgency. What was once the terror of famine is now the psychology behind flash sales.

Scarcity narratives also influence public policy and political rhetoric. Calls for austerity often invoke the metaphor of the household budget, suggesting that governments, like families, must tighten belts when resources appear thin. Yet states with sovereign currencies can create liquidity in ways households cannot, and framing the problem as scarcity may be more ideological than economic. Similarly, debates about immigration frequently mobilise scarcity fears—jobs, housing, and welfare benefits are said to be finite, and newcomers portrayed as threats to existing shares. Whether or not resources are objectively constrained, the language of scarcity provides a potent justification for exclusion. *Fear of running out, in this sense, becomes a political technology as well as an economic reflex.*

There are, however, counter-narratives worth noting. Some cultures have sought to ritualise release from scarcity fears. The biblical Jubilee commanded the periodic forgiveness of debts and return of lands, breaking cycles of perpetual shortage for the disadvantaged. In contemporary economics, universal basic income proposals appeal to the idea that guaranteeing a floor of security can reduce the destructive psychology of scarcity. Experiments show that when individuals receive unconditional cash transfers, they often make longer-term, more rational decisions—evidence that easing the fear of running out can liberate better judgement.

Yet scarcity stories endure precisely because they are anchored in real vulnerability. Resources are not infinite, and the instinct to prepare for shortage has genuine evolutionary value. The challenge is not to dismiss scarcity narratives but to interrogate when they serve adaptive functions and when they distort perception. Hoarding grain in a premodern village might be wise; hoarding toilet paper during a pandemic, less so. Withdrawing funds from a failing bank might protect an individual, but if everyone follows suit, the collective collapses. The paradox is that *scarcity stories that once helped us survive can, in new contexts, undermine collective resilience.*

Ultimately, the fear of running out is not just a relic of the past but a living force shaping financial behaviour today. It governs how households budget, how markets respond to shocks, and how societies define fairness in the distribution of resources. The lesson is not to dismiss scarcity fears as irrational but to recognise them as cultural scripts that require conscious interrogation. Are we reacting to actual constraints, or to inherited stories of famine and collapse? Are we amplifying shortages by anticipating them? The difference between prudence and panic, between resilience and fragility, lies in how we answer these questions. Scarcity may begin as a fact, but its true power comes from the story it tells—and from how completely we believe it.

The Myth of Unlimited Plenty: Contrasts with abundance myths promising bounty without work

Every civilisation has told stories of inexhaustible abundance. They range from the Greek tale of the cornucopia, a magical horn spilling out endless fruit and grain, to the medieval European dream of Cockaigne, a land where roasted geese flew into people's mouths and rivers flowed with wine. What unites these myths is their promise of bounty divorced from toil. They reflect a deep human longing to escape the grind of labour and the anxiety of scarcity, yet they also expose cultural anxieties: if wealth can be had without work, what happens to the values built on restraint, effort, and discipline? The myth of unlimited plenty has always been more than idle fantasy—it has been a contested narrative about morality, fairness, and the very meaning of wealth.

Anthropologists note that abundance myths often flourish in societies where scarcity is an ever-present threat. For medieval peasants, Cockaigne was not merely comic invention; it was an inversion of their lived reality of hunger and hard field work. The very absurdity of roasted animals serving themselves underscored the harshness of ordinary life. Similarly, in agrarian China, legends of magical fields that replenished themselves overnight surfaced in times of famine, functioning as psychological release valves. *Imagining abundance without labour was a way to endure scarcity by temporarily suspending its logic.* Yet such fantasies also served as veiled critiques of elite privilege. In Cockaigne, monasteries collapse into fountains of ale, mocking the Church's wealth and leisure; in other cultures, stories of inexhaustible food highlight resentment towards rulers whose granaries were full while peasants starved.

In modern contexts, the myth has migrated into the language of economics and finance. The promise of perpetual growth—measured in rising GDP, expanding markets, and technological productivity—echoes the old dream of unlimited plenty. When governments speak as though economies can grow indefinitely without environmental or social cost, they are telling a secular version of the same story. The logic of compound interest itself appears to suggest an endless bounty, with wealth multiplying if left untouched. Yet the 2008 financial crisis exposed the fragility behind such promises: mortgage-backed securities and derivatives were sold as instruments of inexhaustible profit until the underlying reality—overextended borrowers—brought the system crashing down. The dream of plenty, unmoored from labour or limits, became a nightmare of collapse.

The rise of consumer culture has deepened the allure of this myth. Advertising routinely conjures visions of effortless abundance: credit cards that "open up worlds without limits," shopping platforms promising next-day delivery of anything imaginable, diets where one can "eat all you like and still lose weight." These promises are less about material sufficiency than about freedom from constraint. What they sell is not the object itself but the fantasy that desire can be endlessly gratified without cost. *The danger of such narratives is that they displace responsibility: if the world is one great cornucopia, then limits—whether financial, ecological, or moral—can be ignored until they violently assert themselves.*

Historical contrasts sharpen this point. The Protestant ethic, famously analysed by Max Weber, prized thrift, discipline, and deferred gratification. Wealth was framed not as a magical gift but as the fruit of labour and evidence of moral character. Yet this ethic coexisted uneasily with abundance myths that persisted in folklore and popular culture. The tension reveals a cultural double-bind: societies depend on discipline to generate productivity, but they also dream of escaping discipline's burdens. This duality persists today. On the one hand, financial advice columns urge budgeting, saving, and compound interest. On the other, lottery jackpots and speculative bubbles dangle the possibility of sudden, unearned wealth. Both discourses coexist because humans desire both order and release, both prudence and miracle.

Psychology explains why abundance myths remain compelling. Scarcity narrows focus, but the promise of limitless supply frees imagination. Experiments show that when people are primed to think in terms of abundance, they take more risks, trust more readily, and even report higher levels of happiness. The myth works because it taps into a genuine cognitive and emotional need: to believe that struggle can end, that effort will not always be required. At its healthiest, this narrative inspires generosity, as people who feel secure in abundance are more likely to share. At its most dangerous, it lulls individuals and societies into complacency, ignoring constraints until crisis forces recognition.

Modern financial products often straddle this line. Consider multi-level marketing schemes that promise effortless riches for those who recruit friends, or cryptocurrency projects that advertise limitless upside without real productivity behind them. These phenomena are not simply financial frauds; they are cultural expressions of the myth of plenty. They flourish because they repackage an ancient fantasy in contemporary form, offering liberation from the grind of work while cloaked in the language of innovation. The collapse of FTX in 2022 illustrates how abundance myths persist even among sophisticated investors: the belief that digital assets could deliver endless returns without the grounding of labour or real value was a modern retelling of Cockaigne.

Environmental debates sharpen the critique. The idea that growth can continue indefinitely on a finite planet is, in essence, the myth of unlimited plenty in political form. Economists such as Kenneth Boulding warned decades ago that "anyone who believes exponential growth can go on forever in a finite world is either a madman or an economist." Yet public discourse often sidesteps this reality. Renewable energy and technological innovation are sometimes framed not as difficult transitions requiring discipline but as silver bullets that will allow business-as-usual to continue. Here again, the old fantasy of bounty without effort re-emerges: salvation without sacrifice, plenty without price.

Still, the myth is not wholly destructive. It carries aspirational energy, fuelling art, invention, and generosity. Belief in abundance underpins philanthropy, open-source collaboration, and community projects where participants give without expecting direct reciprocation. When the internet was first described as an "information superhighway" where knowledge could be shared freely, it evoked a utopian abundance that motivated extraordinary creativity. *The key is distinguishing between myths that liberate potential and those that deny reality.* Unlimited generosity may expand human possibilities; unlimited extraction depletes them.

Abundance myths, then, must be understood as cultural tools. They are not innocent fantasies, nor are they mere errors to be corrected. They shape how societies frame labour, fairness, and obligation. When balanced against scarcity narratives, they reveal the dialectic at the heart of economic life: the tension between recognising limits and longing to transcend them. To ignore scarcity entirely is dangerous; to imagine nothing but scarcity is equally paralysing. The myth of unlimited plenty reminds us of the seductive appeal of freedom from work, but it also challenges us to ask whether that freedom is illusory or whether it can be channelled into new forms of productivity and generosity.

In the end, what makes these myths enduring is not their literal truth but their emotional resonance. They speak to the universal human wish that effort might one day cease and sufficiency remain. The lesson for modern finance and culture is not to eradicate such dreams but to scrutinise their consequences. Do they encourage innovation and generosity, or do they disguise unsustainable exploitation? Do they release us from fear, or do they cultivate denial? By answering these questions, we can separate the empowering elements of abundance myths from their most destructive illusions, and in doing so, navigate between fantasy and responsibility.

Cultural Contradictions: Examines societies that tell both stories simultaneously—scarcity for others, abundance for insiders

One of the most revealing truths about human societies is that they rarely speak with one voice when it comes to wealth. Cultures construct parallel narratives: for some, scarcity is emphasised as natural, inevitable, or even morally correct, while for others, abundance is celebrated as destiny or entitlement. These contradictions are not accidents of rhetoric. They serve as instruments of power, shaping who is permitted to live in plenty and who must accept deprivation. *The coexistence of scarcity and abundance myths is not simply hypocrisy; it is a deliberate cultural logic, one that structures economies, hierarchies, and worldviews.*

Colonial histories provide some of the clearest examples. European empires justified conquest with claims of scarcity at home: land was insufficient, resources were dwindling, and citizens required new territories for survival. At the same time, they presented abundance to their own populations through tales of vast overseas riches—gold, spices, and fertile lands—waiting to be claimed. Scarcity explained the necessity of expansion, while abundance legitimised it as providence. For colonised peoples, however, the rhetoric was reversed: their resources were depicted as underutilised, their labour insufficient, their cultures stagnant. They were cast as unworthy stewards of abundance, needing European extraction to "unlock" value. *The same fields that were said to feed empires were told, to their original custodians, to be barren unless cultivated under foreign control.*

Modern consumer economies sustain similar contradictions. Advertisements bombard affluent consumers with messages of endless plenty—new products, limitless credit, a global marketplace designed for convenience. Yet when governments or institutions address poorer populations, the language shifts towards scarcity and austerity. Welfare recipients are told that resources are finite, budgets must be cut, belts tightened. The contradiction is striking: *for insiders, markets promise infinite choice; for outsiders, policies insist on perpetual shortage.* This duality conditions not just access to material goods but also cultural dignity. To be positioned within abundance is to be invited to dream and desire; to be positioned within scarcity is to be reminded constantly of limits and discipline.

Religious traditions also exhibit this dual logic. In Christian theology, heavenly abundance is promised to the faithful, while earthly scarcity is framed as a test of virtue. Prosperity gospel movements invert this by claiming material abundance here and now, but only for believers, often implying that non-believers or the insufficiently faithful must endure want. In Hindu traditions, karma shapes who enjoys wealth and who suffers deprivation, suggesting that abundance for some is cosmically justified, while scarcity for others reflects moral debts. Across cultures, the same stories that comfort insiders with visions of plenty are wielded to explain away or justify the suffering of outsiders.

The language of national economies reveals the persistence of this pattern. In times of financial crisis, governments routinely call for austerity, arguing that resources must be conserved. Citizens are urged to accept cuts, rationing, or increased taxes. Yet within the same societies, elites often insulate themselves with narratives of abundance: tax loopholes, corporate bailouts, and luxury consumption are framed not as waste but as engines of growth. Scarcity becomes a story told downward, abundance a story told upward. *The contradiction is not hidden—it is normalised, internalised, and made part of the cultural grammar of economics.*

Banking and finance provide sharp illustrations. The rhetoric of "tightening belts" and "living within means" is frequently aimed at households, urging them to avoid excess debt. Yet at the level of governments and corporations, the language flips: deficit spending is framed as investment, and massive borrowing is justified as a path to prosperity. Individuals are warned against greed and imprudence; institutions are excused for the same behaviours, as long as they are described as "growth strategies." The insider/outsider divide functions not by accident but by systemic design, delineating who must carry the burdens of scarcity and who is entitled to the fruits of abundance.

Anthropology shows how deeply this pattern is embedded. Gift economies, such as those of the Pacific Northwest potlatch, embodied both generosity and exclusion. Chiefs distributed lavish gifts to insiders as a demonstration of wealth and power, but the system simultaneously reinforced social stratification, marking outsiders as permanently marginal. The spectacle of abundance relied on carefully maintained scarcity elsewhere. In many societies, elite feasting traditions achieved the same effect: nobles or rulers staged abundance to display status, but the ability to do so was premised on withholding surplus from commoners. *Abundance for the few was made possible by scarcity for the many, and stories told around these practices reinforced that balance as natural or divinely ordained.*

Contemporary globalisation continues this paradox. Affluent societies often frame themselves as living in abundance, with access to technology, healthcare, and consumer goods that signal prosperity. Yet this abundance is built upon global supply chains that depend on scarcity narratives elsewhere: labour in developing nations is treated as cheap and expendable, environmental damage as an acceptable cost, local shortages as unfortunate but peripheral. The rhetoric of "cheap goods" presumes scarcity for those who produce them while guaranteeing abundance for those who consume them. When shortages do arise in wealthy societies, as during the COVID-19 pandemic, panic sets in because the myth of uninterrupted abundance collides with the sudden reality of scarcity. Toilet paper hoarding became a symbol of this cultural dissonance, revealing how fragile abundance narratives can be when tested.

The contradictions are not only economic but psychological. People are often taught to think of themselves as both constrained and free, limited and unlimited, depending on context. A middle-class professional may experience scarcity in terms of time—endless deadlines, insufficient hours—while simultaneously living in abundance materially, surrounded by goods, services, and opportunities. Scarcity and abundance are not objective realities but frames that govern perception. *To be told one lives in scarcity or abundance is to be positioned within a story about what is possible, permissible, and deserved.*

Perhaps the sharpest tension lies in how these narratives shape moral judgement. Those who are insiders to abundance are often praised for their wealth, framed as innovators, job creators, or visionaries. Those who are outsiders are blamed for their scarcity, labelled as irresponsible, lazy, or undeserving. The same condition—access to or lack of resources—is narrated differently depending on who experiences it. This moral asymmetry ensures that cultural contradictions are sustained not just by policy or economics but by deeply ingrained stories of virtue and vice.

Recognising these contradictions allows us to see that scarcity and abundance are rarely objective descriptors of resources. They are stories that divide insiders from outsiders, privilege from poverty, legitimacy from marginality. The enduring lesson is not that one story is true and the other false, but that societies choose which story to tell to whom, and when. *The real power lies in controlling the narrative: deciding who must live with scarcity and who may live as though abundance were their birthright.* By examining these contradictions, we come closer to understanding how cultures manage inequality—not only through laws or markets, but through the stories they tell about what is limited, what is limitless, and who belongs on either side of that divide.

Shaping Mindsets Today: Invites readers to recognise which narrative governs their choices

The most enduring power of economic myths is not in markets or policy, but in the minds of individuals who absorb them without noticing. The stories we tell about scarcity and abundance are not abstract cultural relics—they shape the logic of everyday decision-making, from the way a household manages its pantry to the way a government allocates its budget. *Recognising which narrative governs one's choices is not merely an intellectual exercise but a practical tool for understanding why certain actions feel necessary, inevitable, or beyond question.*

Consider the ordinary experience of shopping during a crisis. When shelves begin to look empty, many feel compelled to buy more than they need, fearing future shortage. The behaviour is not driven solely by the actual availability of goods but by the narrative of scarcity: the belief that if one does not act quickly, one will be left without. The panic buying of essentials during the COVID-19 pandemic illustrates how swiftly scarcity stories override reason. Rationally, there was enough supply to meet demand in most wealthy nations, but the fear of running out spread faster than the virus itself. *What people hoarded was not just toilet paper or pasta—it was a sense of control over an uncertain world.*

On the other end of the spectrum are abundance narratives, which encourage confidence, sometimes to the point of recklessness. Credit-fuelled consumer cultures rely heavily on the myth that more is always possible, that one can borrow against tomorrow without consequence. Individuals persuaded by this story often conflate availability of credit with availability of wealth, forgetting that abundance provided by lenders carries obligations that can transform into scarcity later. The housing bubble of the early 2000s exemplifies this mindset: homeowners believed rising property prices would continue indefinitely, treating abundance as permanent, only to face scarcity when debt obligations caught up and values collapsed. *Believing in unlimited plenty can be as destabilising as fearing unrelenting shortage.*

These narratives operate not only at the level of material goods but also in professional and personal lives. Employees conditioned to see time as scarce may hoard hours, declining opportunities to rest or explore new ventures, fearing that they will fall behind. By contrast, those steeped in abundance narratives about time may overcommit, convinced that they can always do more, absorb more projects, and stretch themselves endlessly. Both mindsets distort reality. Time is finite but renewable; hours cannot be stored like commodities, yet opportunities recur. Recognising the governing story allows individuals to recalibrate, distinguishing between genuine limitation and imagined scarcity, between sustainable capacity and illusory abundance.

The influence of scarcity and abundance narratives is particularly evident in political rhetoric. Leaders frame economic policy to trigger specific mindsets: austerity programmes often rely on metaphors of household scarcity, insisting the nation must "tighten its belt" to weather hard times. Conversely, stimulus spending is justified with abundance language, invoking growth, investment, and limitless potential. Citizens who fail to recognise these narratives risk mistaking metaphor for fact, accepting policies as natural necessities rather than strategic choices. *The real debate is not whether resources exist but how the story of their existence is told and to whom it is directed.*

Cultural context shapes which mindset dominates. In some societies, scarcity is valorised as a moral posture—restraint, frugality, and self-denial are praised, while indulgence is condemned. In others, abundance is seen as virtue—consumption, generosity, and display are celebrated as signs of success. Yet in practice, both stories circulate simultaneously, applied differently depending on class, gender, or ethnicity. For example, working-class families may be admonished for overspending, urged to live within their means, while wealthy elites are praised for risk-taking investments that hinge on abundance narratives. Recognising these patterns highlights how mindsets are not neutral but serve to maintain social hierarchies.

The challenge is not to eliminate these stories but to cultivate awareness of their presence. The narratives we inherit from family, education, and media form the default frameworks through which we interpret financial choices. A child raised in a household where money was always described as scarce may carry those assumptions into adulthood, even when their actual resources are sufficient. Conversely, someone raised in apparent abundance may internalise a belief in perpetual safety, overlooking vulnerabilities until crisis strikes. *To know which narrative governs one's decisions is to see that choices are never purely rational—they are guided by stories lodged deep within memory and culture.*

The capacity to interrogate these narratives offers practical benefits. A professional who recognises that their reluctance to negotiate salary stems from an internalised scarcity mindset may reframe the situation, understanding that resources are not inherently fixed but subject to distribution and bargaining. An entrepreneur buoyed by an abundance story may pause before overextending, realising that not all growth is sustainable. Such awareness does not demand cynicism but clarity—the ability to discern when a story is empowering and when it is misleading.

At the collective level, identifying governing narratives can transform policy debates. When citizens recognise that austerity is not inevitable but a chosen scarcity frame, they are empowered to demand alternative approaches. When they see that promises of abundance are often selective—abundance for investors, scarcity for workers—they can challenge the fairness of distribution.

Democracies function more robustly when citizens are literate not only in economics but in the narratives that cloak economic choices. *To unmask the story is to reclaim agency.*

The task, then, is not to choose once and for all between scarcity and abundance but to understand the conditions under which each narrative proves useful or destructive. Scarcity, properly framed, can foster prudence, conservation, and resilience. Abundance, wisely invoked, can encourage generosity, innovation, and optimism. The danger arises when either narrative is allowed to dominate unchallenged, blinding individuals and societies to complexity. Awareness does not dissolve these stories but equips us to step outside them, to ask: *Whose interests are served by this narrative? What possibilities does it obscure? What choices does it encourage or foreclose?*

In shaping mindsets today, the central question is not whether scarcity or abundance exists, but which story we allow to shape our vision of the world. Every purchase, every investment, every political judgement is coloured by one of these lenses. To recognise the narrative at work is to gain a measure of freedom—the ability to pause, to reflect, and to decide with open eyes. The most valuable form of wealth may not be money itself but the capacity to see through the stories that surround it, and to act not as a passive character in them, but as an author of one's own.

Chapter 8
Fortune and Fate

Few forces exert as enduring a grip on financial imagination as luck. Long before compound interest tables or investment forecasts, people turned to gods, goddesses, and symbols to explain why wealth flowed to some and misery clung to others. Fortuna, perched atop her wheel, spinning lives upward or downward with a flick, embodied the unpredictability of fortune in the Roman world. In South Asia, Lakshmi offered a different vision: wealth as divine blessing, flowing abundantly to the devout. In modern parlance, Lady Luck haunts casinos and trading floors alike, the secular descendant of these ancient archetypes. *The persistence of such figures reveals something crucial: even when economies grow more technical and data-driven, the longing to believe that fate has the final word remains stubbornly intact.*

The tension between planning and chance sits at the heart of financial behaviour. In theory, modern capitalism rewards calculation: budgets, diversification, and long-term strategy are meant to shield against uncertainty. Yet in practice, individuals often behave as though invisible dice are rolling in the background. When a start-up succeeds, when a portfolio outperforms, or when a market collapses, many interpret these outcomes less as the result of skill or preparation than as the favour—or betrayal—of fortune. Economic historians and behavioural psychologists alike have shown how people routinely underestimate the role of structure and overestimate the sway of fate. *Luck becomes the explanation when planning fails, and success is reimagined as destiny rather than design.*

The lottery provides perhaps the clearest case of this dynamic. Despite being statistically one of the poorest financial decisions—odds stacked to near impossibility—lotteries attract disproportionate participation from lower-income households. Economists label this the "lottery paradox": those who can least afford to lose are often the ones who spend the most on games of chance. But seen through the lens of narrative, the paradox dissolves. For many, buying a ticket is not a calculation but a story—a small payment for the hope that fate may yet intervene, rewriting a life trapped in scarcity. The attraction lies less in expected value than in emotional value: the ticket carries with it a dream of abundance unachievable through incremental planning. *Luck promises what discipline cannot: the fantasy of immediate transformation.*

Yet reliance on fortune narratives is not confined to the poor or marginalised. Investors chasing speculative bubbles, corporations gambling on uncertain technologies, and governments banking on unpredictable windfalls all reveal a similar dependence on fate. Venture capital often dresses itself in the language of foresight but frequently operates like institutionalised gambling, hoping that one in ten bets will yield extraordinary returns. Traders toast their "lucky streaks," executives describe successes as "serendipitous," and markets swing wildly on the collective mood. The language of control persists, but the underlying belief in fortune's hand endures. *Planning and luck are less opposites than uneasy partners, entwined in the stories we tell about risk and reward.*

Recognising this entanglement raises deeper questions. Why does the myth of fortune survive in rationalised economies? Part of the answer lies in human psychology: the illusion of control coexists with a need for surrender. To believe that fate governs outcomes alleviates the unbearable weight of responsibility—if ruin comes, it is not entirely one's fault; if wealth arrives, it feels like cosmic validation. Cultures institutionalise this comfort, weaving myths of luck into lotteries, superstitions, and festivals, embedding them within otherwise rational systems. In doing so, they blur the line between planning and faith, between agency and inevitability.

The task is not to eradicate the role of chance—it is undeniable that randomness shapes outcomes—but to shift how stories of fate are integrated into financial decision-making. The modern challenge is to resist narratives that excuse passivity or encourage magical thinking while still acknowledging uncertainty as an irreducible element of life. Rewriting fate means embracing intentional narratives that recognise chance without ceding agency to it. This involves reframing money as neither dictated by capricious deities nor guaranteed by flawless plans but as navigated through an interplay of preparation and unpredictability.

As this chapter unfolds, it will trace how fortune has been personified, how fate continues to colour financial choices, why hope persists in systems like the lottery, and how individuals might reorient their relationship to uncertainty. At stake is more than financial literacy; it is the ability to discern when we are genuinely planning and when we are outsourcing our futures to fortune's wheel. *To understand the myths of fortune and fate is to uncover the hidden drivers behind some of the most consequential choices people make—not just with their money, but with their lives.*

The Goddess of Luck: Traces historical personifications of wealth—Fortuna, Lakshmi, Lady Luck—and their enduring pull

To understand how humans relate to wealth, one must first understand how they have imagined luck. Across cultures and centuries, prosperity has rarely been considered the outcome of effort alone; instead, it has been personified, sacralised, and given a face. *The divine embodiment of fortune reveals how deeply societies seek to negotiate with uncertainty, transforming random chance into a figure that can be supplicated, feared, or celebrated.* By tracing the evolution of these figures—from Fortuna in the Roman world, to Lakshmi in South Asia, to Lady Luck in contemporary culture—we see not just theology or folklore but enduring financial psychology, a set of narratives that shape behaviour in markets as much as in temples or casinos.

In Rome, Fortuna reigned as a powerful and capricious goddess. Unlike gods tied to specific domains such as war or agriculture, Fortuna presided over the unpredictable. Her wheel, endlessly turning, symbolised the oscillation between prosperity and ruin, reminding citizens that stability was illusory. The Roman elite built temples in her honour, generals carried her symbols into battle, and common citizens prayed to her for everything from good harvests to favourable political outcomes. Importantly, Fortuna was not portrayed as consistently benevolent; her favour could shift suddenly, making her both essential and unreliable. *The wheel metaphor, still alive in phrases like "wheel of fortune," captures the uneasy truth that wealth accumulation is never entirely secure, however disciplined one's strategy may appear.* This Roman conception embedded into Western consciousness the idea that financial outcomes remain partly outside human control.

In contrast, Lakshmi, the Hindu goddess of wealth, fortune, and prosperity, reflects a more stable and relational vision of abundance. She is depicted seated on a lotus, pouring out streams of gold coins, her presence signifying not only material wealth but also spiritual prosperity, beauty, and harmony. Unlike Fortuna, Lakshmi's favour is not wholly arbitrary; it is attracted by ritual, devotion, and the cultivation of dharma (righteous conduct). Diwali, the festival of lights, is as much an economic ritual as a religious one: households clean, decorate, and light lamps to invite Lakshmi's blessings for the coming year. Here, wealth is not the spin of a wheel but the product of alignment with cosmic order, suggesting a moral dimension to prosperity. *This model positions wealth as relational: not merely numbers in an account, but signs of right living, mutual obligation, and divine grace.*

The transition from Fortuna to Lady Luck illustrates both continuity and secularisation. Lady Luck emerges in European folklore and later in American idiom, embodying the whims of chance in gambling, lotteries, and speculation. She is less a deity than a figure of speech, yet her influence is no less pervasive. In casinos, the language of players—"luck is with me," "luck has turned"—echoes prayers once directed to gods. Advertisements for lotteries often feature her implicitly: the promise that anyone, regardless of planning or background, can be anointed with sudden abundance. In financial markets, traders toast "lucky breaks," even as they build complex models to predict risk. Lady Luck represents the secular persistence of myth: a cultural shorthand for the same ancient desire to explain and perhaps control uncertainty. *She is the echo of Fortuna, stripped of temples but alive in every roulette spin and lottery draw.*

What unites these figures is their enduring pull across cultures and epochs. Human beings do not simply want to manage money; they want to weave stories around it, to frame prosperity and loss as parts of larger patterns. The goddess of luck, whether divine or secular, provides that pattern, relieving the existential anxiety of randomness. If wealth is the gift of Fortuna or Lakshmi, then loss is not always personal failure; if a gambler loses at cards, it is because Lady Luck has turned her face away, not necessarily because of poor play. *This transference of agency from self to symbol provides both comfort and danger: comfort in externalising misfortune, danger in abdicating responsibility.*

These personifications also shape economic behaviour in measurable ways. Studies in behavioural finance show that investors often speak in terms of luck rather than skill, and superstitious beliefs demonstrably affect decisions. In East Asian markets, traders may avoid certain numbers deemed unlucky, while in Western contexts, individuals may choose lottery numbers based on birthdays or rituals. The invocation of fortune deities or symbols may appear quaint, yet they materially influence billions in financial flows. Anthropologists and economists alike observe that the persistence of these myths is not a sign of irrationality alone but evidence of a universal human need: to map chaos onto meaning.

The persistence of luck figures also highlights cultural divergences in how wealth is moralised. Fortuna, capricious and blind, underscored the precariousness of Roman society, where sudden reversals of power were common. Lakshmi's enduring popularity underscores the Indian view that wealth can coexist with spirituality, provided it is earned and used in line with ethical principles. Lady Luck, meanwhile, reflects a modern world in which chance has been democratised: everyone can buy a lottery ticket, sit at a slot machine, or speculate on risky assets, regardless of social status. *Each figure teaches us that wealth is not merely a ledger entry but a story—a narrative of fairness, fate, and morality projected onto money itself.*

To ignore these narratives is to miss the subterranean forces driving economic behaviour today. When a worker invests a small portion of wages in lottery tickets, when a billionaire attributes success to "luck" rather than solely to strategy, when families prepare ritual offerings at Diwali, they are participating in a continuum of belief that stretches back millennia. These figures of fortune continue to mediate how societies understand wealth, risk, and justice. They reveal that even in highly financialised economies, with algorithms and analytics dominating decisions, the human desire to personify uncertainty cannot be extinguished. *Luck, in her many guises, remains a central player in the theatre of finance.*

The goddess of luck, then, is not an outdated relic but a living symbol. Fortuna's wheel, Lakshmi's coins, and Lady Luck's dice may differ in form, yet they all remind us that wealth is not experienced as mere arithmetic. It is lived as hope, fear, ritual, and story. To trace these figures is not simply to recount mythology but to understand how humans, across cultures and centuries, continue to wrestle with the question of whether money is earned, gifted, or fated. *And until that question loses its power, the goddess of luck will never be dethroned.*

Luck vs. Planning: Explains why people still attribute financial outcomes to fate, even in modern economies

The paradox of modern finance is that while entire industries are built on the promise of prediction—risk models, forecasting tools, and algorithmic trading—people still explain their gains and losses in the language of fate. An investor whose portfolio rises after a volatile week is "lucky," while one who misses a profitable trend blames "bad timing." Even among seasoned professionals, where planning and analysis should dominate, conversations often slip into the realm of fortune, as though numbers alone cannot account for the drama of outcomes. *This persistent attribution to luck is not merely superstition lingering in rational economies; it is a profound reflection of how humans experience uncertainty and responsibility when faced with money.*

Planning is, at its core, a narrative of control. We budget, invest, insure, and diversify because we wish to impose order on the chaos of economic life. Yet every plan sits within an environment riddled with variables beyond our command: political upheaval, natural disasters, technological disruption, or shifts in consumer taste. The 2008 financial crisis remains a striking reminder of this tension. Countless individuals who carefully saved, diversified, and avoided speculation still found themselves caught in the downturn, their pensions halved and their home values collapsing. For many, the sheer scale of the collapse could not be reduced to poor decision-making alone; it was easier, perhaps even more psychologically tolerable, to describe it as being in the wrong place at the wrong time. *Attribution to luck can function as a shield against the unbearable weight of believing one's future is fully self-authored.*

Behavioural finance research has consistently shown that individuals overestimate both their control and their vulnerability. The "illusion of control" leads gamblers to believe their choices influence dice rolls, while the "gambler's fallacy" convinces investors that after a string of losses, a win is "due." Conversely, when faced with outcomes that seem too extreme or too sudden, people retreat into the language of fate. In both directions, luck becomes a convenient explanatory frame, allowing individuals to reconcile the gap between effort and result. *What matters here is not whether luck objectively exists but how belief in luck shapes financial behaviour, encouraging risk-taking in some cases and resignation in others.*

Cultural traditions reinforce this tendency. In East Asia, the Lunar New Year is accompanied by rituals to attract prosperity, from red envelopes of money to the burning of incense for ancestors. In the West, lotteries market themselves as dreams of sudden transformation, explicitly positioning themselves as "games of chance." These practices reveal how societies intertwine planning and fate: one can study hard, work diligently, or save faithfully, but a stroke of fortune is always depicted as decisive. The fact that people from vastly different cultural contexts invoke luck in matters of money suggests a universal psychological need: to interpret randomness not as chaos but as destiny.

Even in environments built to reward analysis, the pull of fate remains strong. In Silicon Valley, successful entrepreneurs often describe their trajectories as a mix of strategy and "being in the right place at the right time." Luck narratives proliferate in venture capital, where countless start-ups fail despite sound business plans, while a few achieve meteoric success. Nobel laureate Daniel Kahneman, who has studied decision-making under uncertainty, emphasised that much of what is attributed to skill in fund management is, on closer inspection, indistinguishable from luck. Yet investors still flock to "star" managers, weaving narratives of genius around what may well be random variance. *The human mind craves stories of causality; luck provides a convenient bridge where causality cannot be proven.*

The persistence of fate language also intersects with moral judgement. In societies shaped by Protestant work ethics, success is often framed as a reward for discipline, while failure signals a lack of virtue. Yet to avoid crushing blame for those who fall despite effort, luck narratives soften the moral calculus. Conversely, those who succeed spectacularly may themselves attribute some portion of their fortune to luck, both to appear humble and to acknowledge forces beyond personal control. This dual function—relieving guilt in failure and tempering pride in success—explains why fate endures as a socially useful category, even when economic systems claim to prize rationality.

There is also a profound emotional dimension. Planning appeals to reason, but living entirely under the banner of rationality is exhausting. Accepting the role of luck offers relief, a way of saying that not every misstep signals incompetence and not every missed opportunity was avoidable. During the COVID-19 pandemic, small businesses that collapsed often did so not from poor planning but from catastrophic external shocks. Survivors sometimes described their endurance as "good luck," even when aided by government support or robust planning. To live without acknowledging luck would be to carry an unbearable burden of total responsibility; to live only by luck would be to abdicate all agency. *The human mind seeks balance by weaving the two together, constructing a financial worldview in which planning and fate coexist.*

Yet there is a danger in leaning too heavily on fate. When individuals attribute success to luck, they may fail to examine replicable strategies; when they attribute failure to fate, they may resign themselves to cycles of poverty rather than seeking systemic reform. This is visible in the lottery paradox: people with limited means invest disproportionately in games of chance, convinced that fortune alone can deliver escape. While this belief in fate sustains hope, it also drains resources that might otherwise be invested in more stable, incremental growth. Similarly, in developing economies, farmers may attribute poor harvests entirely to luck or divine will, overlooking how access to new techniques or insurance schemes could mitigate risk. *The belief in luck provides comfort but can also perpetuate vulnerability.*

The real challenge is not to eliminate talk of luck but to integrate it intelligently into modern financial reasoning. Recognising the role of randomness in markets can lead to more robust planning, emphasising resilience rather than prediction. Portfolio diversification, for example, is an acknowledgement that outcomes are partly governed by chance. Insurance is another: a collective admission that bad luck befalls even the prudent. Rather than setting fate and planning in opposition, a more sophisticated narrative accepts that *planning is the art of preparing for luck—good and bad alike.* This framing allows individuals to honour their agency without denying the role of uncertainty, striking a balance between humility and responsibility.

Ultimately, people continue to attribute financial outcomes to fate because it resonates with how life feels. Even in a world of algorithms and analytics, the lived experience of money—an unexpected inheritance, a sudden redundancy, a market crash—rarely maps neatly onto effort or foresight. Luck gives language to the mismatch between what we plan and what we endure. The task, then, is not to banish fortune from our vocabulary but to use it wisely: to remind us of humility in success, to ease the burden of failure, and to encourage forms of planning that accept the limits of foresight. *In this way, luck remains not the enemy of planning but its silent companion, shaping the financial stories we continue to tell ourselves in modern economies.*

The Lottery Paradox: Examines why the poor spend disproportionately on luck-based games

Few economic behaviours appear more puzzling at first glance than the disproportionate investment of the poor in lotteries and other chance-based games. The people who can least afford to spend on tickets with near-zero odds of return are often those who participate most eagerly. Economists have long called lotteries a "tax on the poor" or, in more caustic terms, a "tax on the innumerate." Yet this explanation, rooted purely in probability and financial logic, misses the deeper psychological, cultural, and social dimensions that make lotteries not merely financial transactions but *stories of possibility.* To dismiss such behaviour as irrational is to underestimate the power of narrative, hope, and identity in shaping economic decisions.

The paradox intensifies when one examines the structure of lottery expenditure. Studies consistently show that lower-income households in both developed and developing countries spend a higher percentage of their disposable income on lottery tickets compared to wealthier households. In the United States, for instance, residents in the lowest income quintile spend several times more on lotteries than those in the highest quintile. In the United Kingdom, National Lottery data reveal similar disproportion. This is not simply a matter of poor financial literacy; it reflects how lotteries serve as vehicles of aspiration in contexts where structural mobility is limited. *For those who feel excluded from traditional pathways to wealth, the lottery represents a democratised chance—one ticket away from escape.*

Historical examples illustrate that this attraction is not confined to modern capitalist societies. The first state lotteries in Renaissance Europe were often explicitly marketed as levellers: anyone, regardless of station, could claim sudden fortune. In colonial America, lotteries financed bridges, schools, and even military campaigns, further legitimising their role as public instruments of progress. Today, governments often defend national lotteries by earmarking revenue for education, healthcare, or cultural projects. For players, this creates a moral paradox: they are simultaneously pursuing individual gain and contributing to collective good. That dual framing softens the stigma and encourages participation, even among those for whom each ticket represents a meaningful sacrifice.

To understand why the poor are particularly drawn to these games, one must move beyond numbers into the terrain of hope and desperation. The poor live in environments where economic gains are marginal and incremental strategies—saving small sums, pursuing modest investments—often feel futile against structural inequalities. The promise of a lottery win, however remote, offers a narrative rupture: instant transformation. Buying a ticket is not simply a calculation of expected value but an act of imagination, a ticket to a parallel life. In this sense, the lottery functions as a modern myth, offering what incremental planning cannot: the possibility of radical escape. *The ticket is not just a piece of paper but a narrative bridge between present deprivation and imagined abundance.*

Psychology adds further depth to this picture. Behavioural economists note the allure of what is called "skewed distribution" games: humans are disproportionately attracted to very small probabilities of very large gains. The prospect of a million-to-one payoff activates a different cognitive and emotional response than a high-probability but modest return. Neuroimaging studies suggest that the anticipation of such jackpots lights up reward pathways in the brain more intensely than smaller, more rational gains. This effect is amplified for the poor, for whom the contrast between current hardship and potential windfall is more dramatic. *The magnitude of change matters as much as the likelihood of change.*

Cultural narratives also play a crucial role. In societies where meritocracy is preached but often not experienced, the lottery stands as a symbolic equaliser. Everyone, from the unemployed to the CEO, has the same chance of drawing the winning numbers. This symbolic fairness is powerful, particularly where structural barriers render real equality elusive. Stories of winners—plastered across news outlets, advertised on billboards, shared in neighbourhood conversations—reinforce the illusion that luck is democratically distributed. Yet these stories are selective: they highlight rare triumphs, not the millions of silent losses. Still, *in environments of systemic exclusion, even selective narratives can create a potent sense of possibility.*

Critics argue that lotteries exploit the poor, effectively siphoning money from those least able to spare it to fund public coffers. There is truth in this, but such criticism often overlooks the agency of participants. To describe the poor as duped or irrational is to strip them of dignity. Many ticket buyers are fully aware of the long odds; they are not under illusions of easy wealth. What they purchase, knowingly, is a dream—the chance to imagine themselves otherwise. The paradox is not that the poor fail to understand probability but that the promise of transformation outweighs mathematical improbability. *The irrationality lies not in misunderstanding but in the weight assigned to hope over arithmetic.*

There are, of course, darker consequences. For some, the lottery becomes less a dream and more a dependency. Research shows that compulsive lottery play correlates with financial stress, depression, and diminished long-term planning. When money spent on tickets displaces essentials—food, bills, education—the cycle of poverty deepens. Governments often position lotteries as "harmless entertainment," but when participation skews so heavily towards the disadvantaged, the entertainment defence rings hollow. Here the paradox turns into a moral quandary: public institutions profit most from those who can least afford it.

Yet not all outcomes are corrosive. There are communities where collective lottery play fosters solidarity. Workplace pools or family syndicates transform individual bets into shared rituals, blurring the line between gambling and communal bonding. Crowdfunding campaigns sometimes adopt lottery-like structures, where participants contribute not for certain outcomes but for the possibility of shared success. In these cases, the symbolic and social functions of lotteries complicate the narrative of exploitation. They reveal that even economically irrational acts can serve psychological and communal needs.

To navigate this paradox, one must distinguish between critique and understanding. Yes, lotteries extract disproportionate revenue from the poor. Yes, they are often marketed in ways that exploit vulnerability. But they also meet real psychological, cultural, and emotional needs. They offer a language of possibility in environments where possibilities are scarce. The task, then, is not merely to condemn but to understand: to ask why structured opportunity feels so unattainable that hope must be outsourced to chance. *The lottery persists not because people are blind to odds but because odds are sometimes kinder than systems.*

In the end, the disproportionate lottery spending of the poor is not a failure of rationality but a reflection of structural and emotional realities. Where economic mobility is blocked, where incremental planning feels impotent, and where cultural narratives glorify sudden fortune, the lottery becomes more than a game. It is a symbolic act of resistance against stagnation, a fragile assertion of possibility in the face of constraint. To dismiss this as folly is to ignore the deeper story: that people invest in luck when they feel denied by design. The paradox, therefore, is not that the poor spend too much on lotteries, but that in societies of inequality, *the lottery may feel like the only fair game left to play.*

Rewriting Fate: Argues for shifting from fate dependence to intentional money narratives

The belief that money is governed more by luck than by effort has proven remarkably persistent across cultures and centuries. Even in modern economies where planning, education, and systems of credit supposedly expand opportunity, a large number of people still attribute financial outcomes to fate, destiny, or divine will. This reliance on external forces reflects a powerful narrative habit: to interpret money not as a field of strategy but as a domain where fortune smiles or frowns arbitrarily. Yet such a stance, however comforting, often leaves individuals passive in the face of financial challenge. To rewrite fate is not to deny uncertainty but to reclaim agency: to shift from dependence on luck to intentional money narratives that foster resilience, clarity, and direction.

One of the striking features of fate-based thinking is how it absolves individuals from responsibility. If wealth is believed to be bestowed by divine grace, astrological alignment, or sheer chance, then planning becomes almost irrelevant. This is visible in the rise of global gambling industries, in which billions are spent annually on lottery tickets, slot machines, and other games of chance that offer astronomical odds against the player. The investment in luck-based strategies often reflects a tacit resignation: a belief that careful budgeting, disciplined saving, or strategic risk-taking cannot yield transformative results. In many low-income households, where structural barriers limit upward mobility, these narratives of fate become especially powerful. *The fatalism does not stem from ignorance but from the deep frustration of living in systems that appear designed to exclude.*

But the problem with fate-dependence is not simply that it promotes unwise choices. It also narrows the imagination. When financial life is understood as dictated by forces beyond one's control, the range of possible futures shrinks. Dreams become binary: either the stroke of luck arrives, or it does not. Planning for gradual growth, for steady improvement, or for collective solutions is abandoned. This fatalistic framework undermines not only individual progress but also broader social change. After all, if poverty is believed to be preordained, then efforts at reform seem futile. Conversely, when individuals embrace intentional money narratives—stories that centre planning, education, collaboration, and effort—they open up a wider horizon of possibilities.

Examples from history demonstrate how shifts in narrative transform financial behaviour. In mediaeval Europe, for instance, wealth was often regarded as the product of divine favour, which made accumulation morally suspicious. The Protestant Reformation altered that story by linking diligence, thrift, and labour with spiritual virtue. Max Weber famously described this shift as the "Protestant ethic," which contributed to the rise of capitalist economies by reframing wealth as evidence of discipline rather than luck. Similarly, in modern Japan, cultural stories emphasising persistence, collective effort, and frugality have shaped distinctive patterns of saving and investment. These cases suggest that when societies alter their financial narratives, they change the very structures of economic behaviour. *Fate, in other words, is never an objective condition; it is a story we tell ourselves, and stories can be rewritten.*

At an individual level, the rewriting of fate often begins with a reframing of setbacks. People who interpret financial hardship as punishment from fortune are less likely to pursue new ventures or rebuild after losses. By contrast, those who view setbacks as temporary challenges are more likely to persist, innovate, and ultimately succeed. This distinction has been observed in entrepreneurial research: successful founders often reinterpret early failures not as evidence of doom but as tuition paid for future success. In this way, intentional money narratives cultivate resilience. They transform uncertainty from a threat into a space for learning. *Fate dependence paralyses, but intentional narratives mobilise.*

Cognitive science offers further insight. Studies in behavioural psychology reveal that humans are prone to what is called "locus of control" bias: the tendency to attribute outcomes either to internal or external factors. Those with an external locus of control believe events are determined by fate, luck, or others' actions, while those with an internal locus of control see outcomes as shaped by their own choices and efforts. Research consistently shows that individuals with a strong internal locus of control achieve higher levels of financial stability, health, and career advancement. This is not because they avoid uncertainty but because they treat uncertainty as a field in which their actions matter. Encouraging intentional money narratives is, in effect, cultivating a more internal locus of control.

There are, of course, dangers in taking intentionality too far. The opposite of fate dependence is not blind self-reliance but balanced agency. Overemphasising personal control risks sliding into unrealistic individualism, where people blame themselves for systemic inequalities beyond their influence. A factory worker cannot erase structural unemployment by budgeting more carefully; a student burdened with unaffordable tuition fees cannot simply "plan better." Intentional narratives must therefore be coupled with honest recognition of systemic constraints. The point is not to deny chance or inequality but to refuse passivity. *To rewrite fate is to hold both truths: that systems matter, but within those systems, stories shape action.*

Modern financial education programmes increasingly attempt to embed this ethos. Rather than teaching compound interest formulas in isolation, they emphasise narratives of empowerment: "Your money choices today shape your options tomorrow." Campaigns encouraging savings among marginalised groups often use storytelling rather than statistics, inviting participants to envision a future self who benefits from consistent action. Microfinance initiatives, particularly in South Asia, have shown how shifting narratives can change behaviour. By reframing loans not as burdens but as tools of empowerment, they encourage repayment, investment, and community solidarity. These interventions succeed not merely because they provide credit but because they cultivate new stories about agency.

The digital age complicates the relationship between fate and intention. On one hand, algorithm-driven trading, viral crowdfunding, and sudden crypto fortunes seem to reintroduce chance into finance at an unprecedented scale. Stories of teenagers becoming millionaires through meme stocks or digital tokens reinforce the appeal of sudden luck. On the other hand, digital tools offer powerful means of intentional planning: budgeting apps, investment platforms, and online education democratise financial strategy. The tension is clear: will technology amplify narratives of luck or narratives of agency? The answer depends on which stories individuals and societies choose to elevate.

Philosophically, the shift from fate to intention reflects a broader human project: the effort to transform contingency into meaning. Life will always contain randomness; fortune and misfortune cannot be eliminated. But how we interpret that randomness determines our orientation to the future. To say "it is fate" is to resign; to say "it is uncertain but open to my influence" is to affirm agency. Money, as both a practical necessity and a cultural symbol, crystallises this choice. Every financial decision—whether to save, to spend, to invest, to take a risk—is an opportunity to rewrite fate by asserting intention.

Ultimately, the movement from fate dependence to intentional money narratives is not a rejection of luck but a rebalancing. Luck exists, but it should not be the primary script by which financial life is read. To live by luck alone is to inhabit a story too fragile to withstand reality. To live by intention is to craft a narrative strong enough to incorporate uncertainty without succumbing to it. The paradox of fortune is that it favours those who prepare: planning does not guarantee success, but it makes one more likely to recognise and seize opportunities when they arise. *Rewriting fate, then, is less about denying fortune than about ensuring that when fortune appears, one is ready to meet it.*

Chapter 9
The Shadow of Inheritance

Inheritance is never just about money. Families pass down stories, silences, expectations, and myths as surely as they pass down property, jewellery, or debt. The accounts we inherit are written not only in ledgers but in whispered comparisons between siblings, in repeated proverbs about thrift or indulgence, in anecdotes about a grandfather's luck or a grandmother's sacrifice. These narratives shape our sense of what money means—whether it is a blessing to be preserved, a curse that corrupts, or a fleeting resource always under threat. In this way, every act of inheritance carries a double weight: the tangible transfer of assets and the intangible transfer of meaning. Understanding this shadow is crucial, for it determines how families remember themselves and how individuals orient their financial lives.

Across cultures, the stories of inheritance oscillate between gift and poison. Biblical literature records quarrels over birthrights and blessings, where the favour of inheritance could fracture families for generations. In Greek myth, the House of Atreus inherited not just lands but curses, the sins of one generation staining the prospects of the next. In more modern contexts, the biographies of wealthy heirs reveal how fortunes intended as safety nets can become snares. Consider the narratives of twentieth-century dynasties, where some descendants turned inherited wealth into flourishing enterprises while others squandered vast sums within a single lifetime. *The paradox is perennial: inheritance is at once stabilising and destabilising, a hand extended and a shadow cast.*

The influence of inheritance stories extends beyond the rich. A family that survived famine may teach its children that security lies only in hoarding, passing on a script of perpetual scarcity. Another family, having known sudden windfalls, may elevate gambling or speculation into a kind of destiny. Migrant households may transmit narratives of sacrifice, where each pound earned is freighted with ancestral struggle. These scripts do not arrive with instruction manuals; they are absorbed at the dinner table, through gestures of pride or shame, through who is spoken about with admiration and who is treated as a cautionary tale. To inherit such scripts is often to mistake them for objective truth, when in fact they are cultural artefacts, reflections of past conditions that may no longer apply.

Psychologists studying financial behaviour increasingly emphasise the role of these unspoken narratives, often referred to as "money scripts." These scripts can persist even when they undermine well-being: a child who grew up hearing that money inevitably corrupts may resist building wealth, sabotaging their own financial stability; another raised to believe that money is the only measure of worth may sacrifice relationships or health in pursuit of accumulation. What is striking is that these patterns often survive long after the material circumstances that generated them have changed. A family that has entered middle-class stability may still operate with the anxiety of poverty, just as a family in decline may still cling to the entitlement of a lost aristocracy. *The shadow of inheritance lingers in habits, anxieties, and blind spots.*

If these inherited scripts shape behaviour unconsciously, they also raise the question of choice. Are we bound to repeat the stories we inherit, or can we rewrite them? History offers examples of individuals and groups who have sought to consciously reshape inherited narratives. Post-war societies, devastated by conflict and deprivation, deliberately cultivated cultural narratives of resilience and rebuilding, framing thrift as patriotic rather than shameful. Social reform movements have often involved the rewriting of money scripts: for instance, the push for universal education reframed the inheritance of opportunity, not just wealth, as a moral obligation. On a personal scale, therapists working in financial psychology report that clients who examine and reframe their family money scripts are more capable of making intentional, values-driven financial decisions.

Yet choosing a different story is not easy. It requires disentangling identity from inheritance, recognising that to honour the past does not mean to be ruled by it. A person raised in a household where generosity was scorned may choose to reclaim giving as an act of liberation rather than betrayal. An heir burdened by wealth may learn to see stewardship as distinct from servitude. Rewriting does not always mean rejecting; it can mean reinterpreting, choosing which elements of the family narrative to carry forward and which to leave behind. In this sense, inheritance is not a fixed legacy but a dialogue across generations, in which each participant decides how to continue the story.

This chapter invites the reader to examine the narratives they have inherited alongside whatever financial assets or liabilities accompany them. The goal is not merely to catalogue family myths but to interrogate their continuing influence. Which stories empower, and which imprison? Which assumptions reflect a bygone world, and which still offer wisdom? By illuminating the shadow of inheritance, we begin to see money not only as a balance sheet but as a biography—one written in advance for us, but never beyond revision. To confront inheritance in this broader sense is to reclaim agency over the most enduring financial legacy of all: the stories we choose to tell, believe, and pass on.

Stories We Inherit, Not Just Money: Explores family myths about wealth, poverty, and legacy

Inheritance is too often imagined as a ledger entry, a simple transfer of money, property, or titles from one generation to the next. Yet the truer inheritance, the one that exerts longer influence, rarely sits in bank accounts or land deeds. What families bequeath most enduringly are stories—narratives about wealth and poverty, sacrifice and entitlement, caution and daring. These stories, carried in proverbs, anecdotes, and silences, do more to shape financial behaviour than the assets themselves. Indeed, it is possible to inherit millions and still live as if money is scarce, just as one can inherit very little and yet carry oneself with the entitlement of great wealth. Family myths, whether whispered or loudly proclaimed, create the frameworks within which individuals perceive financial reality. *To understand what one has inherited, it is not enough to read the will; one must listen for the stories that were never formally written down.*

Consider the role of proverbs. In many cultures, short aphorisms about money act as condensed legacies of past experiences. A Chinese saying such as "wealth never survives three generations" becomes not only a warning but a prophecy, shaping the stewardship practices of heirs who fear squandering their fortunes. In parts of rural Europe, families long repeated maxims that framed poverty as dignified endurance rather than shame, ensuring that future generations approached hardship with stoicism rather than rebellion. These phrases act as scripts, ready-made frameworks for interpreting circumstance. They do not merely reflect conditions; they perpetuate them, as children grow into adults who unconsciously reenact the caution, frugality, or fatalism embedded in their inherited words.

Beyond proverbs lie the personal family stories, which can be even more powerful. A grandparent's tale of starting with nothing and building a modest livelihood through grit may instil deep respect for savings and self-reliance. Conversely, stories of wealth lost through extravagance or betrayal can breed suspicion of luxury, generosity, or risk-taking. Inherited wealth itself often arrives with an accompanying mythology: the founder's entrepreneurial genius becomes a moral exemplar, or their excesses a cautionary tale. These stories shape behaviour precisely because they are personal and emotionally charged. Unlike abstract financial principles, they are tied to identity and lineage, making them harder to challenge. A child who internalises the story that "our family are survivors" may underplay opportunities for growth, choosing endurance over ambition, even when conditions change.

It is not only the content of family stories that matters but their silences. Silence can itself be a legacy. Families that avoid discussing money may transmit shame or secrecy as central features of financial life. For example, heirs who discover only after a death that debts outweigh assets often grapple not just with financial shock but with the betrayal of unspoken truths. Such silence is rarely neutral; it reflects unaddressed fears or unacknowledged conflicts. Sociologists note that these hidden narratives often exert greater power precisely because they remain unarticulated, leaving descendants to interpret through fragments, guesses, and imagination. *An inheritance of silence can be more destabilising than an inheritance of debt.*

Modern psychology has labelled these patterns "money scripts." These scripts, typically formed by age seven, carry unconscious power. A child who hears repeated tales of their family's cleverness with money may develop a script of financial confidence, while one raised on narratives of constant scarcity may operate with a script of perpetual anxiety, regardless of actual circumstances. Research shows that such scripts predict adult financial behaviours, including saving, risk-taking, and even susceptibility to fraud. What is critical here is that scripts are not consciously chosen; they are inherited through exposure, repetition, and the desire to belong to a family identity. They become internalised truths, even when demonstrably false in current contexts.

The cultural dimension of inherited stories is equally significant. In some societies, wealth is framed as divine blessing, with families perpetuating narratives that prosperity reflects moral virtue. In others, wealth is suspected as corruption, and descendants are taught to distrust money's influence. These cultural lenses overlay personal family stories, intensifying or contradicting them. For instance, a family with modest means in a culture that valorises wealth may craft narratives of moral superiority—"we may not be rich, but we are honest"—as a protective identity. Meanwhile, in cultures where wealth confers honour, children may be pressured to preserve or expand fortunes at all costs, internalising obligation rather than choice. These broader cultural stories often amplify the moral weight of inheritance, turning financial outcomes into reflections of virtue or failure.

Inheritance stories also operate through rivalry. Tales of siblings fighting over property, of "black sheep" who squandered their share, or of heirs who upheld or betrayed family honour, become templates for how new generations view fairness and competition. The biblical narrative of Esau and Jacob, or the literary accounts of dynastic feuds, echo in modern inheritance disputes that seem irrationally bitter relative to the sums involved. Here the money is symbolic: what is really contested is legitimacy, identity, and belonging. Psychologists observing inheritance disputes often remark that arguments about money cloak deeper narratives of love, recognition, or resentment. Thus, the story of who received what, or who deserved more, carries forward as a family myth long after the material assets are gone.

At times, inherited stories become curses as much as blessings. The heir to a fortune may feel trapped by narratives of expectation, struggling to forge identity beyond wealth. Conversely, those who inherit stories of deprivation may internalise scripts of unworthiness, carrying poverty's shadow even when materially secure. The challenge lies in recognising that stories are not destiny. While assets and debts are external, stories are interpretive. They can be questioned, reinterpreted, even rewritten. Therapists working with family wealth note that individuals who confront and consciously reframe inherited stories often experience liberation. To acknowledge that "my family taught me money is dangerous, but I can choose to view it as a tool" is to shift from passive inheritance to active authorship.

This reframing is not about rejecting the past but about understanding its influence. Stories of struggle can be honoured without being replicated; stories of fortune can be appreciated without becoming burdens. Indeed, the greatest gift one can give to future generations may not be money itself but the conscious transmission of healthier narratives: stories of resilience without fatalism, of generosity without recklessness, of ambition without greed. Just as financial planners help structure estates, so too can families deliberately shape the narratives they pass down, recognising that words and silences will endure longer than cash accounts.

Ultimately, to explore the stories we inherit is to confront the most enduring form of legacy. Money may be spent, lost, or multiplied, but narratives persist, shaping lives across generations. By recognising that these stories are constructs rather than inevitabilities, individuals gain the power to interrogate them. Which ones are worth preserving, and which are overdue for revision? Inheritance, then, is not only a legal or financial transaction but a cultural and psychological one. *To inherit stories is to inherit a framework for life, but to rewrite them is to claim agency over both past and future.*

The Curse and the Blessing: Analyses inheritance tales—from biblical squabbles to billionaire heirs losing fortunes

Few human experiences carry such contradictory potential as inheritance. It can secure stability, extend privilege, and preserve dynasties; yet it can just as readily ignite conflict, breed resentment, and destroy the very families it was meant to protect. Across centuries, inheritance has been imagined as both gift and test, fortune and burden, blessing and curse. To study its narratives is to glimpse the way societies interpret not only wealth but also justice, destiny, and kinship. *The stories we tell about inheritance reveal less about money itself and more about how communities define belonging, entitlement, and moral worth.*

The biblical record provides some of the most enduring archetypes. The rivalry of Jacob and Esau over Isaac's blessing remains a parable of deception, competition, and the enduring suspicion that inheritance is never fairly allocated. Likewise, the disputes among David's sons over succession established patterns of dynastic intrigue that echo in royal households and corporate boardrooms alike. These stories endure not because they are ancient curiosities, but because they capture a fundamental human anxiety: inheritance rarely divides cleanly. To inherit is not merely to receive assets; it is to take possession of power, identity, and legitimacy. Where those are contested, financial bequests become weapons, proxies for deeper struggles about love, recognition, and survival.

Anthropological accounts reveal how these anxieties were institutionalised. In many societies, strict rules of primogeniture—passing estates to the eldest son—were designed to avoid fragmentation of land and to maintain lineage prestige. Yet these rules created their own tensions, leaving younger siblings dependent, resentful, or forced into alternative paths such as the clergy or military. Inheritance, in such contexts, was less about distributing wealth than about preserving continuity of power. The resentment of disinherited children, however, often persisted, fuelling familial feuds and reinforcing cultural tropes about greedy heirs or wasteful spenders. Literature from Shakespeare to Balzac abounds with plots centred on contested wills, estranged heirs, and squandered fortunes, testifying to the enduring narrative power of inheritance conflict.

The modern era provides equally compelling examples, especially in cases where vast wealth amplified the stakes. The Vanderbilts of America, once the wealthiest family in the world, saw their fortune dissipate within a few generations. Tales of squandered wealth, indulgent heirs, and family estrangement became cultural shorthand for the perils of unearned riches. Similar stories circulate today around heirs to billionaire fortunes who fail to sustain businesses or become tabloid fixtures, embodying the notion that great inheritance is as much a trap as a privilege. These cautionary tales reinforce a cultural suspicion: *what is easily inherited is easily lost.* Inheritance without effort appears to erode discipline, purpose, and resilience.

Yet the opposite stories exist as well—inheritances that secured stability, preserved cultural heritage, or enabled philanthropic legacies. The Rothschilds, for instance, carefully structured family wealth through banking dynasties and intermarriage, ensuring not only financial continuity but also cultural influence across Europe. The Rockefeller Foundation, built on John D. Rockefeller's fortune, transformed an inheritance often criticised as monopolistic into a philanthropic force shaping medicine, education, and global development. These examples demonstrate the blessing side of inheritance: wealth that, when stewarded deliberately, can extend beyond family lines to impact societies for generations. They also highlight the central role of narrative—families who frame inheritance as stewardship rather than entitlement often succeed in sustaining its value.

The duality of inheritance also reflects psychological dynamics. For heirs, sudden wealth can provoke identity crises: Am I valued for myself or only for my fortune? What obligations accompany this wealth? Research into inherited wealth suggests that those who lack a personal narrative of contribution often experience alienation, struggling with meaning and responsibility. On the other hand, those who integrate inheritance into a broader sense of duty—to family, community, or society—report greater fulfilment. Here lies the paradox: the same inheritance that corrupts one life can ennoble another, depending on the story constructed around it.

Cultural variation further complicates the picture. In some East Asian traditions, filial piety frames inheritance not as entitlement but as repayment for loyalty and care, embedding wealth transfer in a moral economy. In contrast, Anglo-American legal frameworks emphasise individual rights, fuelling litigation when heirs perceive unfairness. African communal traditions often treat inheritance as belonging not to individuals but to extended kin, diffusing both benefits and tensions. These differences underscore how inheritance is never simply material; it is always interpreted through cultural lenses of justice, duty, and identity. The same sum of money may feel like a blessing in one context and a curse in another, depending on whether it reinforces harmony or exposes fracture.

Modern legal systems have sought to regulate these tensions, yet even the most precise wills cannot eliminate disputes. Courts around the world are filled with cases of contested estates, reflecting how deeply inheritance taps into emotions of fairness and recognition. Even small inheritances can provoke disproportionate conflict, because the fight is rarely about money alone. To be excluded from a will is to be symbolically excluded from belonging. In this sense, the curse of inheritance lies not only in wealth's corrupting influence but in its capacity to magnify insecurities and resentments that might otherwise remain dormant.

The lesson that emerges from these diverse tales is that inheritance is never neutral. It is always framed as either confirmation of destiny or as a trial to be survived. Biblical squabbles remind us of the timelessness of conflict, while billionaire heirs remind us of the fragility of fortune. Between these poles lie the countless families whose legacies are defined less by the numbers in their accounts than by the stories they tell about what those numbers mean. Whether inheritance becomes blessing or curse depends not only on the assets distributed but on the cultural, familial, and personal narratives that give them significance.

Inheritance is thus best understood not as a mere transfer of wealth but as a transfer of stories. To inherit is to enter into a narrative already in motion, with its promises, warnings, and expectations. The challenge for each generation is to discern whether to repeat, resist, or rewrite that story. When treated as blessing, inheritance becomes a resource for continuity, generosity, and purpose. When allowed to fester as curse, it breeds rivalry, resentment, and ruin. The enduring pull of inheritance tales, from scripture to modern scandals, lies in their reminder that wealth is never simply material—it is a mirror reflecting how we interpret fate, fairness, and family itself.

How Family Narratives Shape Behaviour: Shows how unspoken money scripts determine financial choices

Money is rarely just arithmetic within families; it is storytelling, enacted and reinforced across generations. Beneath explicit conversations about budgets or investments lie the deeper scripts—subtle narratives about security, success, sacrifice, or scarcity—that guide behaviour long before individuals consciously engage with financial systems. These narratives, often transmitted without words, shape attitudes towards saving, spending, risk, and generosity. *The most powerful financial lessons are not those taught deliberately, but those silently absorbed in kitchens, living rooms, and family rituals.*

Consider a child who watches their parents argue every month about bills, punctuated by remarks such as "money doesn't grow on trees." That phrase becomes more than a cliché; it sets a cognitive boundary around possibility, teaching caution and instilling an assumption of scarcity. Conversely, a child raised in a household where investments are discussed openly and losses are treated as learning opportunities may internalise a different script: that money is a tool for growth, risk is manageable, and setbacks are temporary. In both cases, the children inherit not wealth or debt directly, but interpretive frameworks that will influence decisions decades later.

These frameworks can be remarkably durable. Psychologists describe them as "money scripts"—core beliefs, often unconscious, that drive financial choices. Studies have identified recurring patterns: some scripts equate self-worth with net worth, others glorify frugality to the point of self-denial, and others encourage compulsive generosity as a route to validation. Because they operate beneath awareness, money scripts can perpetuate behaviours even when those behaviours contradict conscious intentions. An adult who rationally understands the value of saving may nevertheless sabotage themselves by overspending, compelled by an internalised narrative that equates spending with freedom or affection.

Cultural anthropology shows how such narratives are not merely personal but collective. In some working-class families, money is narrated as survival—something fleeting, never to be relied upon—producing generations who view windfalls as transient and spend quickly before scarcity reasserts itself. By contrast, in families with intergenerational wealth, money is often narrated as stewardship, creating scripts that prioritise preservation, investment, and legacy over immediate consumption. These contrasting narratives can persist even when individuals move across economic classes, suggesting that cultural inheritance of money stories can be stronger than the economic reality they inhabit.

Case studies underscore the potency of these scripts. In research on lottery winners, many individuals from modest backgrounds returned to financial instability within a decade, not because of ignorance alone but because their inherited money narratives treated wealth as temporary, almost illegitimate. The sudden abundance clashed with ingrained scripts of scarcity, leading to self-sabotage through overspending, poor planning, or risky investments. Similarly, studies of entrepreneurs often reveal family narratives that valorise risk-taking, where bankruptcy is reframed as resilience. Such scripts can produce a tolerance for uncertainty that fuels innovation, but they also increase the likelihood of dramatic financial swings.

Family narratives also shape moral attitudes toward money. In some households, debt is described in terms laden with shame, equating borrowing with weakness or irresponsibility. In others, credit is seen as a strategic tool, part of the normal machinery of advancement. These differences explain why two individuals with identical incomes may diverge dramatically in their approach to debt management. One may avoid loans at all costs, even missing opportunities to invest in education or housing, while the other embraces debt as a calculated risk, confident it can be leveraged into greater returns. Both are enacting inherited narratives rather than simply making rational calculations.

What makes these scripts particularly influential is their invisibility. Families rarely articulate them directly; they are woven into everyday life. The silence surrounding money conversations can be as instructive as the words spoken. A household where finances are never discussed openly communicates that money is taboo, private, and potentially shameful. This reticence can stunt financial literacy and leave younger generations vulnerable to exploitation. By contrast, families that normalise discussions of budgets, inheritances, or philanthropy equip children with practical knowledge and emotional readiness for financial responsibility. *The absence of narrative is itself a narrative—one of secrecy, avoidance, and disempowerment.*

Not all inherited scripts are maladaptive. Stories of grandparents who endured poverty yet managed to save modest sums can cultivate resilience and gratitude, shaping a cautious but disciplined approach to money. Narratives of parents who leveraged loans to build small businesses can inspire a respect for risk balanced by persistence. The key distinction lies in whether these stories empower agency or impose limiting beliefs. A script that says, "we come from nothing, so we must always be afraid of losing everything" narrows horizons, whereas one that says, "we have endured hardship before and can build again" expands them. Both originate in scarcity, yet one constricts while the other liberates.

In the corporate and financial sectors, these inherited narratives manifest in professional behaviour. Executives raised with narratives of abundance may be more inclined to pursue bold mergers or high-risk investments, while those shaped by scarcity scripts might emphasise caution and incremental growth. These tendencies are not simply personal quirks; they shape organisational cultures and, by extension, broader economic patterns. Understanding money scripts thus becomes not merely a matter of personal finance but of institutional analysis, revealing how family narratives ripple outward into markets and economies.

Modern psychology and financial therapy suggest that recognising these scripts is the first step toward transformation. By bringing unconscious narratives to awareness, individuals can evaluate whether they serve or hinder present goals. Techniques such as journaling family money stories, reflecting on repeated phrases heard in childhood, or examining emotional responses to financial decisions can illuminate hidden scripts. The aim is not to discard all inherited narratives—many contain wisdom—but to choose consciously which ones to continue, adapt, or abandon.

At the collective level, societies too inherit and propagate money narratives. National myths of thrift, hard work, or entrepreneurial daring influence citizens' behaviour just as family stories do. When these national scripts conflict with individual or familial ones, tensions emerge. For instance, immigrants often navigate between inherited cultural scripts about money and the narratives dominant in their new countries, producing hybrid approaches that blend caution with aspiration. These tensions can be both challenging and productive, generating new strategies for financial adaptation.

Ultimately, *family narratives about money are less about figures than about identity.* They tell us who we are, what we deserve, and what we fear. They explain why some families reproduce patterns of wealth across generations while others remain ensnared in cycles of scarcity despite opportunity. To examine these narratives is to confront the hidden architecture of financial decision-making. The true inheritance passed from parents to children is not just bank accounts or debts but a set of stories—stories that whisper in every financial choice, shaping futures long before those choices are recognised as such.

Choosing a Different Story: Encourages conscious rewriting of inherited narratives

Every family hands down stories about money, yet not every story deserves to be repeated. These narratives, formed through generations of triumphs, failures, sacrifices, and silences, can act as both compass and cage. They explain why one person treats every pound as fragile, saved against disaster, while another spends freely to avoid resembling a parent who hoarded and deprived. What often feels like a rational financial habit is, in truth, the legacy of inherited scripts—scripts that can be rewritten when they no longer serve. *The critical act is recognising that we are not condemned to replay the same financial theatre staged before us.*

The power of rewriting inherited narratives lies in the possibility of choice. Too often, financial behaviours appear deterministic: the child of debt-burdened parents repeats cycles of overborrowing, or the heir of wealth reproduces the same patterns of entitlement or anxiety about losing it. But patterns are not destiny. Research in behavioural finance shows that once people identify the emotional origins of their money habits—fear of poverty, guilt around spending, shame about asking for help—they gain agency to shift them. Recognising that "this is not my story but my family's story" creates space to write a different script, one grounded in current realities rather than inherited fears.

Examples abound of individuals and families who have broken these cycles. Consider the professionals who grow up in households marked by secrecy and conflict over money. Instead of reproducing the silence, they choose radical transparency with their partners and children, teaching not only the mechanics of budgeting but also the values that guide their choices. Others may confront an inherited narrative of scarcity by deliberately cultivating generosity, reframing money not as a fortress against future loss but as a resource for shaping relationships and opportunities. Such deliberate acts do not erase the past, but they reconfigure its meaning, turning restrictive scripts into raw material for new narratives.

Psychologists working in financial therapy often describe this process as narrative reframing. By articulating the family stories one has inherited—"we are always unlucky with money," "women in this family cannot handle finances," "our wealth must be hidden"—individuals expose assumptions that otherwise operate invisibly. The act of naming these scripts diminishes their power. More importantly, it allows new stories to be drafted: "we learn from setbacks," "financial competence is not tied to gender," "our resources can be visible when aligned with purpose." *Reframing does not deny the past but insists on the right to interpret it differently.*

Societal pressures can make this rewriting difficult. In many cultures, filial piety or loyalty discourages questioning family values, especially around money. To adopt a different approach may feel like betrayal. Yet reframing can be understood not as rejection but as evolution—an act of honouring ancestors by refusing to pass forward unexamined burdens. A family that once needed extreme frugality to survive may have instilled habits of fear and withholding. For descendants in more secure contexts, continuing those habits uncritically is not fidelity but stagnation. Choosing a different story can be framed as fulfilling the deeper intent of one's forebears: to ensure resilience, wellbeing, and possibility for future generations.

Modern financial systems provide fertile ground for rewriting narratives. Access to information, diversified investment tools, and platforms for peer support make it easier than ever to step outside inherited paths. Take, for instance, individuals raised in cultures where women were excluded from financial decision-making. Today, online education and communities of practice empower women to challenge and transform those legacies, creating new narratives of agency and competence. Similarly, those raised to distrust banks due to historical experiences of exploitation may now consciously engage with alternative models of finance—credit unions, cooperative savings groups, or ethical investment vehicles—thereby reshaping distrust into cautious, intentional engagement.

Philosophically, the decision to rewrite a narrative reflects a shift from determinism to authorship. Instead of viewing oneself as a passive character in a multi-generational drama, the individual takes up the pen as co-author. This does not erase structural realities—wealth inequality, systemic bias, market volatility—but it does reposition the individual in relation to them. Narratives shape perception, and perception influences behaviour; by choosing a narrative of agency rather than fatalism, people are more likely to act in ways that expand possibility. Behavioural economists note that expectations influence outcomes: those who believe financial success is possible, even incrementally, are more likely to persist through setbacks, while those bound by inherited scripts of futility may give up before beginning.

The challenge lies in discerning which parts of inherited narratives are worth preserving. Not every script is destructive. Stories of resilience, thrift, and sacrifice can serve as ballast in turbulent times. The task is to separate wisdom from fear, discipline from anxiety, prudence from paralysis. For example, a family story about saving every penny may carry the valuable lesson of diligence, but it need not perpetuate an obsession with scarcity that blocks enjoyment or generosity. By consciously selecting which elements to retain, individuals engage in a kind of financial editing—keeping what strengthens identity while discarding what constrains it.

At the level of communities and nations, collective rewriting is equally essential. National myths around money—whether of perpetual scarcity, moralised wealth, or inevitable decline—can paralyse societies just as family scripts can paralyse individuals. Movements that challenge these myths, from financial literacy campaigns to initiatives promoting equitable inheritance laws, represent collective acts of narrative revision. They remind us that money stories are not natural laws but cultural constructions, and as such, they can be reimagined.

Ultimately, *choosing a different story is both a financial and an existential act.* It is about more than altering spreadsheets or rebalancing portfolios; it is about deciding what kind of relationship one wishes to have with wealth, work, and worth. Inherited narratives may whisper that one is destined to fail, to hoard, to squander, or to sacrifice endlessly. But those whispers need not become prophecy. By interrogating them, reframing them, and rewriting them, individuals and communities alike can transform financial inheritance from a shadow into a source of illumination, ensuring that the stories passed forward are ones of agency, resilience, and possibility rather than fear and constraint.

Chapter 10
The Currency of Trust

Money works only because people believe it does. A banknote, stripped of collective agreement, is nothing more than decorated paper; a digital balance in an account is no more tangible than a line of code. Yet societies from ancient marketplaces to globalised economies have thrived on these shared acts of faith. The paradox is striking: the most powerful system shaping human lives relies not on physical substance but on narrative credibility. *To spend, to lend, to invest—all presuppose trust, a fragile and renewable resource that behaves like currency itself.*

The fragility of that trust is evident whenever financial institutions falter. A bank run is not triggered by a vault suddenly emptying; it begins with whispers that ignite suspicion. In 2008, global markets unravelled less because money vanished overnight than because trust did. Complex securities, once vouched for by ratings agencies and respected institutions, were suddenly seen as toxic, and the disbelief spread faster than the contagion of default. More recently, the collapse of high-profile crypto exchanges illustrated the same principle. Digital assets worth billions became worthless when faith in their custodians evaporated. *The core of every financial crisis is not the absence of value but the absence of belief.*

History offers countless reminders that financial trust has always been precarious. The South Sea Bubble of the eighteenth century was propelled by optimism and undone by panic. Ponzi schemes, from Charles Ponzi himself to Bernie Madoff, relied on carefully crafted illusions of reliability, reinforced by social proof and reputation. In each case, fortunes dissolved not because the mathematics changed but because the narrative collapsed. What distinguishes finance from other domains of human activity is precisely this dependence on confidence: bridges may stand or fall regardless of belief, but currencies, credit systems, and speculative markets exist only insofar as people collectively imagine them as stable.

Cultural narratives have long attempted to anchor this unstable edifice of trust in something more enduring. Ancient societies often linked money to divine sanction: coins bore images of rulers whose authority was said to flow from the gods, thus investing the medium with moral and spiritual legitimacy. In Confucian China, trust in financial exchange was tied to the broader virtue of harmony and righteousness, while in mediaeval Europe, usury laws reflected the Church's attempt to align financial conduct with divine will. In each case, money was not merely an economic instrument but a moral test, a measure of one's honour and alignment with cultural ideals. *Trust in finance, then, has always been inseparable from trust in social and moral orders.*

The challenge in modern economies is that the sources of trust have multiplied and fragmented. Where once a monarch's seal or a community's honour guaranteed credibility, today we rely on a lattice of institutions—central banks, regulatory agencies, rating agencies, and auditors. Yet even these guardians are not immune to suspicion. Scandals around manipulated accounts, fraudulent reporting, or political interference erode confidence, creating the sense that oversight itself is compromised. At the same time, decentralised systems like blockchain promise to replace trust in institutions with trust in code, yet the failures of crypto markets reveal that *trust cannot be fully automated; it must still rest on human integrity, governance, and transparency.*

The sociological dimension of financial trust deserves equal attention. Studies show that communities with higher levels of interpersonal trust exhibit greater participation in formal financial systems, while those with histories of corruption or exploitation often rely more heavily on informal networks of exchange. Migrant communities sending remittances home, for instance, often prefer trusted informal couriers over official banks, not because the banks lack resources but because the narrative of reliability is absent. Trust is relational, woven from experience, reputation, and shared values, not merely from technical guarantees.

This brings us to the pressing question: how can trust be restored in an age where scepticism seems the default? Transparency is often cited as the answer, but it is insufficient without narrative coherence.

People do not simply want raw data about a bank's liquidity or a company's balance sheet; they want a story that reassures them the institution is anchored in values beyond short-term gain. Effective rebuilding of trust requires leaders and institutions to articulate narratives of responsibility, accountability, and purpose that resonate with cultural expectations. A regulator who acts swiftly against misconduct tells a story of protection; a company that aligns profit with social impact tells a story of stewardship. *Trust is repaired not by statistics alone but by narratives that people find credible and morally compelling.*

The work of restoring trust also requires acknowledging its fragility. Unlike capital, which can be replenished by investment, or infrastructure, which can be rebuilt by engineering, trust is cumulative and slow to form yet alarmingly quick to shatter. This asymmetry demands humility from institutions and vigilance from individuals. For professionals navigating today's volatile financial environment, the key insight is recognising trust as both asset and liability. It is the invisible balance sheet that underpins every visible one.

To approach money as the currency of trust is to understand finance as an ongoing negotiation of credibility, morality, and shared belief. Readers who engage with this chapter will encounter examples from history and contemporary practice that reveal trust as the unseen foundation of economic life. More importantly, they will be invited to reflect critically on how their own participation in financial systems—whether as investors, borrowers, or everyday spenders—depends on stories they choose to accept or reject. In recognising this, one discovers that to strengthen financial futures is to engage not only in the management of numbers but in the careful stewardship of narratives that sustain belief.

Why Money Needs Belief: Explains how financial systems depend on shared stories of credibility

The most valuable thing about money is not its material form but the belief that it holds value. A gold coin, a paper note, or a digital entry in an online ledger each function as money only because people collectively agree that they do. This is not simply a matter of habit or convenience; it is the foundation upon which every financial system rests. The paradox of money is that it is simultaneously the most practical of human inventions and the most fragile, for its strength is tethered not to physical properties but to stories that people tell each other and choose to trust. *Without belief, money dissolves into meaningless objects or data points. With belief, it mobilises armies, builds cities, and sustains global markets.*

One of the most striking historical examples of money's reliance on belief comes from the island of Yap in Micronesia, where people used massive limestone disks known as Rai stones as currency. Many of these stones were far too heavy to move, sometimes left miles away from the villages that claimed them. Ownership was determined not by physical possession but by collective acknowledgement: if everyone agreed that a particular family "owned" a stone, that was sufficient. If a stone was lost at sea, it could still retain its value if witnesses confirmed that it had once been successfully quarried and transported. The stones had no intrinsic utility, yet their worth endured through shared belief. This illustrates in exaggerated form what modern economies still practice every day: money as a social contract sustained by trust in narrative rather than inherent substance.

Modern fiat currencies operate on precisely the same principle, though on a vastly larger scale. The pound sterling, the dollar, or the yen has no intrinsic worth; their value is rooted in trust that the issuing authority will maintain stability, honour debts, and enforce laws that underpin transactions. Central banks, far from simply minting coins or printing notes, act as guardians of this collective faith. When the credibility of those institutions falters, currencies can unravel with astonishing speed. Hyperinflation in Zimbabwe or Weimar Germany was not merely a function of excessive printing but a collapse in belief that money could hold value tomorrow. Once trust disintegrates, people rush to exchange notes for tangible goods, accelerating the spiral of devaluation. *The health of a currency is measured not only in numbers but in narratives of credibility.*

Financial markets amplify this reliance on belief to extraordinary levels. Stock prices, in theory, reflect the present value of future cash flows. In practice, they are shaped as much by confidence, sentiment, and collective storytelling as by technical fundamentals. A company's valuation can rise or fall billions in a single day based on shifts in narrative—an earnings call that signals confidence, a rumour of fraud, a change in geopolitical climate. The "animal spirits" that John Maynard Keynes identified remain potent drivers of economic behaviour. Investors are not simply calculating machines; they are interpreters of signals, constantly assessing whether others believe the same story they do. The dot-com bubble of the late 1990s exemplifies this dynamic: companies with minimal revenues soared in value because investors collectively believed in a future digital revolution, only to collapse when scepticism replaced faith.

What is often overlooked is how much of ordinary economic life rests on invisible scaffolding of belief. When you deposit money in a bank, you assume it will still be there tomorrow, despite the fact that most of it is immediately lent out or invested elsewhere. This assumption is nothing less than trust in the system's resilience. When you swipe a credit card, you rely on invisible agreements between banks, payment networks, and merchants that settle billions of transactions each day without you ever seeing the exchange. The fact that these processes are so frictionless can obscure the underlying truth: they function only because institutions, technologies, and individuals participate in a web of trust that must be continually reinforced.

It is tempting to imagine that technological innovation can make money less dependent on belief, but evidence suggests otherwise. Cryptocurrencies, for instance, were designed to reduce reliance on centralised institutions by embedding trust in decentralised code. Yet their success has still depended on stories of credibility. The dramatic rises and falls of Bitcoin and similar assets cannot be explained by technological shifts alone; they reflect changing narratives about legitimacy, future adoption, and resistance to established authorities. The collapse of high-profile exchanges such as FTX demonstrated that belief in technology is never enough—people must still believe in the honesty, competence, and stability of human actors running the systems. *No matter how advanced the mechanism, money remains inseparable from collective faith.*

This dependence on belief also raises deeper philosophical questions about the nature of value itself. Economists often draw distinctions between intrinsic value and extrinsic or assigned value, but in practice, even commodities like gold derive much of their worth from cultural narratives. Gold does not corrode, it is relatively scarce, and it can be fashioned into jewellery. Yet its status as a universal store of value stems as much from millennia of human storytelling as from physical properties. Similarly, government bonds are often described as "safe" assets, not because they are immune to default—history shows otherwise—but because societies construct narratives of sovereign reliability. The United States Treasury market is treated as the bedrock of global finance precisely because of the widespread belief that the U.S. government will always honour its debts. *Safety, like value, is a story that enough people find credible at the same time.*

It would be a mistake, however, to interpret the role of belief as a weakness. On the contrary, the flexibility of narrative-based value is what allows financial systems to scale and adapt. Barter economies are constrained by the double coincidence of wants: I must want what you have, and you must want what I have. Money, by contrast, transcends that constraint because it is backed not by immediate utility but by belief that it can be exchanged for something else later. This abstraction is what enables global trade, complex credit systems, and long-term investment. Belief makes it possible to coordinate vast numbers of strangers across space and time, something barter or pure commodity exchange could never achieve. The risk lies not in belief itself but in failing to recognise its fragility and the responsibility required to sustain it.

Recognising money as belief also changes how we think about financial crises. Bank runs, market crashes, and sovereign defaults can be understood less as purely economic phenomena and more as crises of credibility. Once people no longer believe a bank is solvent, their withdrawals will make insolvency inevitable. Once investors doubt a country will repay its bonds, higher interest rates can push that country into genuine distress. In this sense, *financial systems are reflexive: belief shapes reality, and reality reshapes belief.* This dynamic is both empowering and perilous. It means that maintaining credibility can prevent collapse even when fundamentals are shaky, but it also means that panic can destroy value even when fundamentals are sound.

For individuals, the lesson is that participation in financial systems is always an act of trust. We may think we are simply exchanging goods, services, or investments, but underneath lies a reliance on the narratives others accept. Understanding this is not merely academic. It influences how we assess risk, how we evaluate institutions, and how we interpret the promises embedded in financial instruments. When people believe blindly, they become vulnerable to exploitation, as in Ponzi schemes or predatory lending. When they believe reflexively—recognising both the necessity and fragility of trust—they can navigate uncertainty with sharper judgement.

Ultimately, money's dependence on belief underscores the deeply human nature of finance. Behind every transaction lies a story, and behind every story lies a community of believers. Markets may be global and abstract, but their foundations are cultural and psychological. To understand money as belief is to see finance not as a cold machine but as a living organism, responsive to hopes, fears, and collective imagination. The most powerful balance sheets in the world are written not only in numbers but in narratives. And it is within those narratives that economies rise, stumble, or endure.

Trust as Fragile Currency: Uses bank collapses, Ponzi schemes, and crypto scandals to illustrate

The most devastating financial collapses in history have not always been triggered by the lack of money itself but by the erosion of trust. A balance sheet can appear robust, interest rates can look attractive, and innovation can promise dazzling returns, but if people no longer believe in the integrity of the institution, the collapse becomes inevitable. *Trust is the invisible currency that underwrites every transaction, and once that currency loses value, no amount of regulation, collateral, or optimism can restore it overnight.*

Banking has long embodied this delicate balance between confidence and catastrophe. Banks do not hold sufficient cash to cover every depositor's savings at once, nor could they profitably operate if they did. Their model relies on fractional reserves, lending out far more than they keep in immediate liquidity. This system functions smoothly only if depositors collectively believe that their money is secure. The moment doubt spreads, however, rational behaviour flips into destructive panic. A single whisper of insolvency can spiral into a bank run, as history repeatedly demonstrates. The collapse of Northern Rock in the United Kingdom in 2007 was a case study in how fragile that equilibrium can be. The bank's heavy reliance on short-term funding became public knowledge, and despite government assurances, customers queued outside branches to withdraw deposits. In less than a week, what had been an orderly system was thrown into chaos, not by hard evidence of bankruptcy but by the evaporation of trust.

The global financial crisis of 2008 extended this lesson to the systemic level. When Lehman Brothers collapsed, the problem was not only its individual insolvency but the contagion of doubt it spread across counterparties, investors, and governments. Financial markets are intricately interconnected, and once participants began to question the reliability of balance sheets, the entire system seized. Credit froze, not because capital had disappeared, but because belief in its safe circulation had evaporated. *It was not just money that was missing—it was confidence in the stories that money could be trusted tomorrow.* Governments and central banks had to intervene with unprecedented guarantees and liquidity injections, essentially acting as the last guarantors of trust itself.

The same mechanics of faith and betrayal underpin the darker world of financial fraud. Ponzi schemes, despite their predictability, continue to thrive because they exploit the human tendency to trust narratives of success. Charles Ponzi in the 1920s convinced thousands that he could deliver extraordinary returns from arbitraging international postal coupons, when in fact he was simply paying old investors with money from new ones. Decades later, Bernie Madoff ran a far larger scheme, siphoning billions from sophisticated investors, hedge funds, and charities. What made Madoff's fraud especially striking was not the complexity of the mechanism—at its core, it was the same simple ruse—but the power of his credibility. His reputation, bolstered by years of apparent consistency and social proof, lulled individuals and institutions alike into suspending scepticism. Once the illusion shattered, it was not merely money that had been lost but an entire network of trust in professional and personal relationships. *Fraud succeeds when it cloaks itself in trust, and it collapses when trust unravels.*

The twenty-first century has extended these dynamics into digital arenas, with cryptocurrencies offering new frontiers for both belief and betrayal. Bitcoin, at its heart, is an attempt to hard-code trust into mathematics, eliminating reliance on governments and banks. Yet even this "trustless" system remains embedded in human narratives. Its price swings are driven less by computational proof-of-work than by belief in its future legitimacy and adoption. Scandals in the crypto world expose how fragile that belief can be. The collapse of Mt. Gox in 2014, once the largest Bitcoin exchange, saw hundreds of thousands of coins vanish through mismanagement and theft. More recently, the downfall of FTX revealed not a flaw in blockchain technology but in human governance. Sam Bankman-Fried's empire crumbled when revelations of misused customer funds broke trust with investors and users alike. Within days, billions of dollars in value disappeared, not because of technical failures but because confidence collapsed.

What unites banks, Ponzi schemes, and crypto platforms is not their business model but their dependence on collective belief. Each operates as long as participants assume others share their faith in the system's stability. Each collapses once suspicion outweighs confidence. In this sense, *financial institutions are less like fortresses of capital than like delicate ecosystems sustained by fragile social contracts.*

This fragility also reveals a paradox. Trust is both the most resilient and the most vulnerable element of finance. It can withstand years of turbulence, even crises of profitability, as long as credibility is maintained. Yet once broken, it is among the hardest things to rebuild. Northern Rock depositors did not return because of new advertising campaigns. Investors in Madoff's fund could never be repaid fully. Users burnt in FTX's implosion remain wary of the broader crypto market. A scarred community does not easily return to blind faith. Restoring confidence requires time, transparency, and in many cases, intervention by actors powerful enough to substitute their credibility for the system's—be it governments, regulators, or respected institutions.

This dynamic poses an important question for modern finance: how much fragility can societies tolerate? Trust cannot be engineered entirely by regulation, nor can it be left entirely to market forces. It requires constant cultivation, through clear rules, reliable enforcement, and cultural reinforcement of honesty as a value. When societies tie financial trust to morality—as Confucian traditions emphasised—or divine oversight—as in medieval Christian prohibitions on usury—they anchor belief in broader ethical frameworks. When trust is framed purely as a technical or contractual matter, it risks becoming brittle, vulnerable to opportunistic exploitation.

For individuals navigating this landscape, recognising trust as a form of currency is not a call to cynicism but to vigilance. Asking not only "what is the return?" but also "why should I believe this promise?" is a critical discipline. Trust must be extended carefully, sustained consciously, and questioned when signals of fragility emerge. Those who mistake credibility for certainty often find themselves at the mercy of collapse. Those who recognise its fragility are better prepared to distinguish between institutions that deserve belief and those merely borrowing it.

The deeper insight is that money itself, whether managed by banks, conjured in scams, or decentralised through code, cannot escape its dependence on trust. Every deposit slip, every investment certificate, every digital wallet entry is an expression of faith in an institution, a leader, or a community. And faith, while powerful, is never guaranteed. To understand finance as trust is to see clearly both its creative power and its destructive vulnerability. *The invisible currency that underwrites every financial system is not stored in vaults or blockchains—it resides in the shared conviction that the system will hold tomorrow.*

Cultural Narratives of Trust: How societies tie financial trust to morality, honour, or divine will

Money does not float on mathematics alone. It floats on stories—cultural narratives that dictate who is trustworthy, what forms of debt are legitimate, and why promises are believed or doubted. These narratives are rarely neutral. They are tethered to ideas of morality, honour, or divine sanction, embedding financial trust within the deepest frameworks of collective meaning. To study money is therefore also to study the ways societies decide who deserves faith and who does not, who may borrow and who must never default, who can issue credit and under what conditions it can be redeemed. *Trust in finance has always been moralised, ritualised, or sacralised, rather than simply calculated.*

In ancient Mesopotamia, trust was inseparable from divine order. Early clay tablets recording debts were not merely economic instruments; they were bound up with religious rituals that affirmed the gods as guarantors of fairness. Temples themselves functioned as proto-banks, storing grain and precious metals, lending to merchants, and acting as sacred vaults. To default was not only a financial failure but also a transgression against divine authority. This intertwining of economy and theology meant that confidence in currency or credit extended far beyond the ledger—it rested on a cosmological conviction that the gods upheld balance and justice. The same link reappeared in medieval Europe, where the Church's stance on usury cast lending practices as moral or immoral depending on their alignment with divine law. The prohibition against charging interest was justified not as an economic regulation but as a spiritual safeguard, reflecting the belief that exploiting others financially corrupted one's soul.

Other cultures placed honour, rather than divinity, at the centre of financial trust. In Confucian-influenced East Asia, the ideal of *xin*—faithfulness or trustworthiness—was paramount. Commercial exchange thrived in large part because merchants were expected to uphold their word, not simply because courts enforced contracts. The circulation of promissory notes in Ming and Qing China depended less on legal recourse than on reputational capital: a man's creditworthiness was his moral standing, and default could ruin not only his finances but his family's honour for generations. This cultural emphasis endured even into modern corporate Japan, where the concept of *keiretsu*—interlinked networks of firms bound by long-term reciprocal trust—reflects a continuation of honour-based obligations rather than purely transactional logic.

By contrast, Islamic finance offers a distinctive illustration of trust tethered to divine will. Sharia-compliant banking prohibits interest, but far from being a constraint, this prohibition has birthed alternative trust mechanisms rooted in risk-sharing and fairness. Instruments such as *mudarabah* (profit-sharing) or *murabaha* (cost-plus financing) reframe lending not as exploitation but as partnership. Here, trust is not a fragile gamble but a religiously mandated ethic: to invest is to align with divine justice. The growing global market for Islamic finance, now worth trillions, demonstrates how powerful moral narratives can sustain large-scale economic systems even when they diverge from mainstream practices.

Yet trust narratives can also be exclusive, defining insiders and outsiders in ways that shape entire financial landscapes. In early modern Europe, Jews were simultaneously excluded from many professions and compelled into roles as moneylenders, positions that made them both necessary and resented. Their financial trustworthiness was framed not as a matter of honour but as a theological and cultural boundary, with devastating consequences in the form of stereotypes, persecution, and cycles of expulsion and confiscation. Similarly, colonial empires often imposed financial trust systems that privileged European legal and cultural codes over indigenous practices, undermining local credit traditions and declaring them primitive or illegitimate. These hierarchies of trust reveal how financial systems do not merely reflect economics—they inscribe power and prejudice into the very fabric of exchange.

Modern finance might seem to have secularised trust, shifting it from gods or honour codes into institutions and regulations. Central banks, rating agencies, and regulatory frameworks are meant to provide technical assurances, projecting credibility through statistics and oversight. Yet beneath these mechanisms, cultural narratives still shape perceptions. The 2008 financial crisis exposed how misplaced faith in models and ratings substituted for genuine scrutiny. Triple-A ratings became modern-day oracles, their authority rarely questioned until collapse revealed the illusion. Here again, the fragility of trust was not only mathematical but cultural—rooted in an unspoken belief that institutions would act honourably, even when incentives pushed them otherwise.

Crypto communities offer a contemporary example of new trust narratives emerging. Advocates describe blockchain as a "trustless" technology, yet in practice, participants still rely on cultural narratives of decentralisation, fairness, and liberation from corrupt elites. The rituals of transparency—open-source code, public ledgers, algorithmic validation—do not erase the need for belief; they redirect it into the narrative of incorruptible mathematics. Scandals like FTX's collapse remind us that even in supposedly trustless systems, human credibility remains decisive. Investors did not entrust billions to an algorithm alone—they entrusted them to the story of one man's honour, later revealed as hollow.

Philosophically, this intertwining of trust and morality raises critical questions. If financial trust is always embedded in narratives of virtue or divinity, then it is never truly neutral. Markets claim to be rational arenas of exchange, yet the terms of participation depend on deeper cultural scripts. *Every credit system is also a moral system.* Who deserves trust, how much patience is extended to failure, and whether forgiveness is possible—all these judgments draw from traditions of ethics, religion, and honour. To imagine finance stripped of these elements is to misunderstand its human character.

The challenge today is not whether to anchor financial trust in morality, honour, or divine will, but how to reconcile competing narratives in an interconnected world. Islamic finance operates alongside Western capitalist systems; Confucian traditions influence East Asian corporations; secular regulatory states try to enforce neutrality. Global markets, however, demand interoperability between these frameworks. A bond issued in Dubai must attract investors in London; a start-up in Shanghai must secure backing in Silicon Valley. The cultural scripts of trust must therefore coexist, clash, and hybridise.

For the individual navigating this landscape, awareness of these narratives is more than academic. It informs practical decisions about risk, credibility, and alignment. Recognising that one investor may see interest-bearing debt as morally neutral while another sees it as sinful reframes negotiations. Understanding that some communities value honour above legal enforceability explains why handshake deals may be more binding than contracts. Appreciating that for others, divine will underpins financial ethics clarifies why certain instruments thrive despite scepticism elsewhere.

Ultimately, the study of cultural narratives of trust reveals that financial systems are as much about anthropology and theology as about balance sheets. Money circulates not only because we calculate its worth but because we embed it within stories that tell us why it is right, safe, or sacred to believe. And when those stories shift, whether through disillusionment, scandal, or cultural change, the foundations of trust—and therefore the economy itself—shift with them. *To understand finance is to understand the moral and cultural scaffolding that holds belief aloft.*

Restoring Trust in an Age of Skepticism: Provides narrative strategies for rebuilding financial confidence

The collapse of trust in financial institutions is rarely triggered by a single event; it is the result of a slow erosion punctuated by moments of spectacular failure. The bankruptcy of Lehman Brothers, the exposure of Bernie Madoff's decades-long fraud, and the implosions of various cryptocurrency exchanges have all left scars that extend far beyond balance sheets. Each scandal does more than damage portfolios—it deepens the suspicion that money is no longer anchored in reliability, that those tasked with safeguarding it are indifferent to truth, and that systems designed to protect investors are easily manipulated. *In an age where transparency is demanded yet repeatedly betrayed, the challenge is no longer only to rebuild capital but to rebuild belief.*

Trust in finance cannot be restored through technical regulation alone. New oversight bodies, stricter compliance frameworks, and heavier fines might deter future misconduct, but they do not by themselves generate faith. People do not calculate trust by auditing spreadsheets. They infer it from stories: stories about whether institutions act honourably, whether leaders embody integrity, and whether rules are applied fairly. *Restoring trust, therefore, is a narrative task as much as a structural one.* Without compelling narratives of credibility, even the soundest regulations appear hollow.

One of the most powerful narrative strategies lies in radical transparency. Consider the case of the post-crisis reforms in Iceland after the 2008 banking collapse. Instead of shielding the public from the grisly details of mismanagement, Iceland prosecuted bankers, aired the extent of corruption, and let citizens witness accountability in real time. The story that emerged was not merely of technical recovery but of moral reckoning: the public was assured that wrongdoing had consequences. By contrast, in the United States, while financial reforms were passed, very few high-profile executives faced prosecution. The narrative there, for many, became one of impunity—a perception that the system protects insiders while punishing outsiders. The divergence illustrates a critical principle: *without visible accountability, no regulation is sufficient to restore trust.*

Another essential narrative strategy is to emphasise shared vulnerability. When Singapore established its sovereign wealth funds, such as Temasek Holdings, the government consistently framed them not as elite instruments but as custodians of the people's collective future. Annual reports are presented in clear language, and performance is linked to national well-being. The narrative tells citizens: your fate and ours are intertwined. Compare this with the opaque structures of hedge funds or private equity firms, where returns are shrouded in complexity and ownership is concentrated. The latter invites suspicion, the former fosters alignment. Financial trust grows when people sense that those holding power are equally exposed to the risks and outcomes of their decisions.

In an age of digital disruption, narrative restoration also requires embracing openness rather than secrecy. Blockchain enthusiasts argue that distributed ledgers, by making every transaction publicly verifiable, remove the need for trust in institutions. Yet what makes these systems appealing is not just the code—it is the narrative of incorruptibility, the promise that no central authority can manipulate outcomes. Traditional banks, in contrast, have often clung to opacity under the guise of confidentiality, reinforcing the suspicion that secrecy hides misbehaviour. The lesson here is not that blockchain is flawless, but that *transparency itself functions as a narrative asset.* Institutions that tell convincing stories of openness—whether through technology, audits, or public disclosure—gain an advantage in an age of scepticism.

Historical examples reinforce this lesson. After the South Sea Bubble burst in 1720, the British government restored confidence in part by reframing the Bank of England as a bulwark of stability, grounding its image in prudence and continuity. Similarly, after the hyperinflation of the Weimar Republic, West Germany's post-war central bank, the Bundesbank, deliberately cultivated a narrative of discipline and conservatism, binding its credibility to a cultural value of fiscal restraint. These were not merely institutional reforms but deliberate stories that aligned financial practice with public morality. They worked because they resonated with cultural expectations about honour and restraint, demonstrating how narratives of trust must be tailored to their social context.

There is, however, a tension at the heart of rebuilding trust: people demand both certainty and flexibility. Certainty, because they want assurance that rules will not change capriciously; flexibility, because crises inevitably demand adaptation. Narratives that acknowledge this paradox often succeed more than those that deny it. For instance, during the COVID-19 pandemic, governments that openly explained why fiscal and monetary policies were shifting—and admitted the uncertainties involved—retained more credibility than those that insisted on certainty only to reverse course later. *Acknowledged uncertainty builds trust more effectively than false promises of absolute control.*

Trust restoration also requires a new kind of leadership storytelling. Individuals place faith not in faceless institutions but in the people who embody them. Warren Buffett's annual letters to Berkshire Hathaway shareholders are not valued for their financial analysis alone—they serve as rituals of reassurance, projecting humility, clarity, and long-term vision. Christine Lagarde at the European Central Bank has similarly used accessible communication to reframe central banking from technocratic jargon to human-centred stewardship. These examples suggest that *the voice of leadership matters as much as its policies.* Trust is not built in boardrooms; it is narrated to the public through words, tone, and perceived sincerity.

The role of cultural narratives cannot be overlooked. In societies where honour is paramount, such as in parts of Asia, breaches of trust are not just financial infractions but stains on collective reputation. In others, where divine sanction is linked to economic life, such as in Islamic finance, trust restoration requires alignment with religious values. Global financial institutions must therefore adapt their narratives to resonate across cultural contexts. A "one size fits all" story of technical competence will not suffice. Instead, the strategy must be plural: emphasising accountability in one context, shared vulnerability in another, and moral rectitude in a third. *Trust is rebuilt not by imposing a universal narrative but by aligning financial practice with the moral codes of the societies it seeks to serve.*

A final strategy is the conscious crafting of future-oriented stories. People place trust when they believe that systems are not only sound today but sustainable tomorrow. Green bonds, impact investing, and ESG reporting all attempt to position finance within broader narratives of social responsibility. The appeal of these instruments lies less in their mechanics and more in the story they tell: that money can be harnessed for good, that investment aligns with future flourishing. Whether or not every ESG fund delivers on its promise, the cultural hunger for such narratives reflects an urgent need to bind financial trust to purpose. Without this, money risks being seen as mere extraction, deepening cynicism rather than alleviating it.

In the end, restoring trust in an age of scepticism requires more than technical fixes. It demands the deliberate re-weaving of stories that affirm credibility, align interests, and resonate with cultural values. It calls for leaders willing to embrace transparency, institutions prepared to accept accountability, and financial systems ready to acknowledge uncertainty without retreating into denial. *The true currency of finance is not only money but belief—and belief can only be sustained when stories of honour, fairness, and shared destiny are told with conviction and lived with consistency.*

Chapter 11
Time as Wealth

Among the most enduring illusions of modern life is the belief that money, with its tangibility and countability, constitutes the ultimate measure of wealth. Yet when pressed, few would deny that time, slippery and unaccountable though it may seem, is the more precious resource. Unlike money, which can be regained after loss, time once spent is irretrievable, and every choice we make is inescapably a trade between minutes, hours, and years. Cultures across history have attempted to give form to this truth through parables and proverbs, but it is the parable of the wasted hour—the story that reminds us of how easily an hour vanishes without return—that captures the stark symmetry between time and money. The wasted coin can be replaced; the wasted hour cannot. *It is here, in the unrelenting finality of time, that we confront the true boundaries of wealth.*

The ways in which societies have valued time reveal deep cultural assumptions about prosperity and human purpose. In traditional Confucian thought, patience is not a virtue merely for its own sake but a strategy for enduring success. The idea that cultivation, whether of land, scholarship, or virtue, requires decades of persistence sits at the heart of East Asian economic stories of transformation. In contrast, modern Western markets often appear trapped in what one might call quarter-to-quarter myopia, where the rhythm of financial reporting dictates strategy, innovation, and even ethical choices. The divergence is not simply about cultural temperament; it is about the narrative scaffolding through which time is interpreted. *To prize urgency over patience is to live as if compounding did not exist, as if the only value that mattered were immediate return.*

Compounding itself offers perhaps the most powerful metaphor for how time translates into wealth. Mathematically, it is straightforward: small increments multiply over extended horizons. Yet its true power lies not in numbers but in the stories that make those numbers credible to human imagination. When Albert Einstein allegedly called compounding the eighth wonder of the world, he was not celebrating a formula but recognising its narrative seduction. To tell a child that saving £10 today may grow to £100 in adulthood is to seed a story of discipline, foresight, and transformation. Narratives of compounding bridge the gap between abstract patience and tangible outcome, making long-termism a moral and emotional commitment rather than a technical calculation.

The paradox is that many societies appear wealth-rich but time-poor, with individuals tethered to schedules that leave little space for reflection, rest, or meaning. We speak casually of "buying time," as though time could be stored in the same vault as currency, but more often money is exchanged precisely at the expense of time. The professional who works eighty-hour weeks to secure a salary double that of a colleague might appear richer in financial terms but may well be impoverished in lived hours. This trade-off reflects not just individual choices but dominant narratives about success. The danger lies in mistaking money-rich stories for life-rich stories, in failing to ask whether accumulation of capital has silently displaced the accumulation of experience. *Choosing time over money is, at its core, an act of narrative resistance.*

The chapter that follows will show how cultures, corporations, and individuals have wrestled with the tension between time and money, and how these struggles are embedded in the stories we tell ourselves. It will invite readers to reconsider not only their financial strategies but also their life strategies, to question whether urgency has crowded out patience, whether inherited tales of sacrifice and gain still serve them, and whether their own narratives could be rewritten in ways that privilege the wealth of hours over the illusion of unending financial accumulation. If money demands belief to function, then time demands reverence. To treat time as wealth is to reorder priorities, to elevate what is finite above what is fungible, and to measure prosperity not by accounts but by hours consciously lived.

The Parable of the Wasted Hour: Examines stories where time is treated as money's true twin

Few realisations strike with as much force as the awareness that an hour once squandered can never be reclaimed. Money lost may be earned again, assets sold may be repurchased, but time slips irretrievably into the past. This recognition, at once obvious and profound, has echoed across cultures in parables, aphorisms, and cautionary tales. It has fuelled philosophies of labour and leisure, shaped the moral codes of industriousness, and underpinned the modern economic maxim that "time is money." Yet to say that time and money are twins is not merely metaphorical flourish. Both are currencies of exchange, both impose opportunity costs, and both derive value from the stories we attach to them. *The parable of the wasted hour—whether told as a tale of idleness, distraction, or procrastination—captures the central truth that how we value time determines the arc of our prosperity and the limits of our freedom.*

Across history, societies have used narrative devices to impress upon their members the sanctity of time. In Protestant Europe, the work ethic crystallised into moral injunctions: wasted hours were not merely inefficient but sinful, a theft from God's intended purpose. Benjamin Franklin's famous dictum—"Dost thou love life? Then do not squander time, for that is the stuff life is made of"—codified this sensibility into the fabric of early American capitalism. Franklin was not offering a mathematical formula but a moral parable. By framing time as the raw material of existence itself, he elevated punctuality and industriousness from practical virtues into existential imperatives. The wasted hour, in this framework, is not just lost productivity but a forfeited slice of life.

Other traditions have reached the same recognition through different storytelling modes. In Japanese culture, the expression *ichigo ichie*—"one time, one meeting"—captures the uniqueness of a given moment, urging people to treat encounters as unrepeatable opportunities. The wasted hour here is not merely inefficient but disrespectful to the singularity of experience. Meanwhile, in Indian philosophy, time is bound to cycles of karma and rebirth, but each wasted hour still carries weight: it delays the path to liberation. These diverse narratives converge on a single insight: time is not neutral background but the most precious form of wealth humans possess, and every culture has found ways to remind its people that it ought not be squandered.

Modern economics has given this ancient recognition analytical form through the concept of opportunity cost. When an hour is spent on one activity, it cannot be spent on another, and the forgone alternative is the true measure of the cost. Yet opportunity cost is rarely internalised through equations. It becomes vivid through narrative—through the story of the entrepreneur who spent years chasing trivial ventures while ignoring a breakthrough idea, or the employee who stayed at a stagnant job for decades only to look back with regret. These stories function as contemporary parables of the wasted hour, cautioning against the illusion that time can be deferred or recovered. *The arithmetic of economics is only compelling when accompanied by the rhetoric of narrative.*

The urgency of this parable has only intensified in the digital age. While industrial societies once warned against idleness in the form of extended leisure, today's wasted hour often takes the shape of compulsive scrolling, fragmented attention, or endless digital distraction. It is not that these activities provide no pleasure or connection; rather, their cumulative erosion of time undermines intentionality. The wasted hour becomes invisible, scattered across dozens of micro-moments of distraction. In this sense, the modern parable is subtler but more insidious: the danger lies not in dramatic squandering but in incremental erosion, where hours dissolve without recognition. If earlier generations feared idleness, ours must fear the ceaseless consumption of time without memory or meaning.

Still, it would be simplistic to cast every unproductive hour as waste. Philosophical traditions from Aristotle's leisure as the basis of culture to contemporary psychology's recognition of rest as essential for creativity remind us that time's value is not reducible to output. The parable of the wasted hour functions not as a universal indictment but as a lens for discernment. An hour spent in genuine rest, reflection, or unstructured conversation may appear unproductive yet can be profoundly generative. The true waste is not measured by external metrics but by internal misalignment: the hour that contradicts one's values, the hour consumed by inertia rather than chosen for purpose. *What the parable warns against is not leisure but unconsciousness.*

One of the most compelling modern manifestations of this tension lies in the cult of busyness. Many professionals fill their hours with tasks that feel urgent but leave little enduring trace. Meetings without outcomes, emails without substance, reports without influence—all serve as contemporary parables of wasted hours. Sociologists note that busyness itself has become a status symbol, a way to signal importance, even if the hours expended produce negligible value. The parable here flips: waste masquerades as productivity, and the squandered hour is hidden beneath the veneer of diligence. The danger is not merely inefficiency but self-deception, the belief that activity equals achievement.

Counter-narratives exist, and they are gaining cultural traction. Movements advocating "slow living" or "deep work" seek to reclaim the wasted hour by urging conscious investment of attention. The appeal of these frameworks lies in their narrative reframing: they invite people to see each hour not as a unit to be filled but as an opportunity to be aligned with purpose. This shift is crucial, for time is not only scarce but uniquely egalitarian. Wealth can be inherited, talent unevenly distributed, but every individual faces the same twenty-four hours in a day. The parable of the wasted hour, then, is also a democratic reminder: time is the one wealth in which all begin equal, and its use is the ultimate determinant of inequality over the long run.

The practical implications are far-reaching. Economists studying household finance often note that individuals underestimate the long-term value of incremental choices precisely because they discount time. An hour spent learning a new skill, building a relationship, or engaging in healthful practice compounds just as surely as money invested at interest. Conversely, an hour wasted in neglect or avoidance compounds negatively, producing deficits of skill, health, or opportunity. *Time, like capital, grows by the force of compounding, and the wasted hour is the seed of future impoverishment.* Recognising this truth requires narrative, because only stories can bridge the cognitive gap between present sacrifice and future reward.

Perhaps the enduring pull of the parable of the wasted hour lies in its universality. Every person, regardless of culture, wealth, or station, has felt the sting of looking back on time squandered. It is a shared human experience, one that generates both regret and resolve. The wasted hour serves as a mirror in which individuals confront not only their inefficiencies but their mortality, for to waste time is ultimately to squander life itself. Yet it is also a generative parable, for it calls forth the possibility of change. To recognise a wasted hour is to sharpen the urgency of using the next one well.

In the end, the parable of the wasted hour is less a story about loss than a story about awareness. It teaches that the true twin of money is not time in abstraction but time in attention—time consciously directed, intentionally lived. Every culture has tried to preserve this wisdom in tales, sayings, and rituals, because without such reminders human beings are prone to forget it. What emerges is not a formula but a philosophy: that wealth is measured not by the number of coins accumulated but by the scarcity of wasted hours in a life well-lived.

Cultures of Patience vs. Urgency: Contrasts Confucian long-termism with modern quarter-to-quarter thinking

The most consequential difference between civilisations is not always technological prowess or political design but the way they conceive of time. Cultures tell themselves stories about whether patience is a virtue or a weakness, whether waiting is an act of wisdom or of missed opportunity. At one extreme lies the Confucian tradition of long-term orientation, where the moral worth of patience and foresight has been cultivated for centuries. At the other sits the modern obsession with quarterly results, where firms rise or fall on the strength of three months of performance. Both are rational within their own frames, yet their collision defines much of today's global economic landscape. *The tension between patience and urgency is not merely a matter of style but of competing philosophies of value creation and survival.*

Confucianism treats time as cumulative rather than consumable. The Analects teach that virtue is cultivated over decades, that harmony within the family and state arises from rituals repeated across generations. Economic historians often trace the resilience of East Asian development models to this worldview. Japan's Meiji reforms, China's post-1978 opening, and South Korea's industrial ascent were framed not as sudden ruptures but as long arcs, where investment in education, infrastructure, and institutional capacity could be expected to yield returns decades later. Patience in this context was not passivity but disciplined waiting: a willingness to endure present costs for the sake of future stability. It is no coincidence that family-owned conglomerates such as Japan's keiretsu or South Korea's chaebol plan succession across multiple generations, embedding Confucian continuity into corporate DNA.

By contrast, Western capitalism—particularly in its Anglo-American form—has come to valorise speed. The shareholder revolution of the late twentieth century intensified this urgency, tethering executive careers to quarterly earnings reports and investor calls. The discipline of the market is defended on the grounds that it weeds out inefficiency and forces adaptation, but its shadow is evident in underinvestment in long-term assets such as worker training, research, and environmental sustainability. The company that misses expectations for two consecutive quarters may see its leadership replaced, its strategy scrapped, its credibility destroyed. Patience becomes a liability; managers survive not by building enduring value but by producing short-term signals of performance. *The quarterly clock narrows horizons, collapsing the future into the present quarter's ledger.*

The implications of this divergence extend beyond corporations. Families, too, embody cultural orientations toward time. Confucian-influenced households often prioritise education as a multi-generational project, investing heavily in tutoring, savings, and networks that may only bear fruit in the careers of grandchildren. Western families, shaped by credit-driven consumer culture, often emphasise present consumption, with the promise of later adjustment. Neither is wholly virtuous: the long-term orientation risks excessive sacrifice in the present and suffocating pressure on the young, while short-term orientation risks debt traps and generational instability. But each reflects a coherent narrative about how to live in time—whether to see wealth as something to be stewarded for descendants or enjoyed while one can.

Philosophically, patience and urgency rest on different assumptions about control and uncertainty. Confucian long-termism presupposes that stability and order can be cultivated, that the family and state can endure through discipline, and that effort compounds predictably across time. Quarter-to-quarter thinking, by contrast, reflects a worldview of radical uncertainty: the future is unknowable, markets are volatile, and survival requires agility. From this perspective, waiting can be reckless, for tomorrow's rules may be rewritten. Both approaches contain truth. The Asian financial crisis of 1997 demonstrated how decades of patient investment could be undone by sudden capital flight. The 2008 global financial crisis revealed the costs of short-termism in reckless lending and opaque derivatives. The lesson is not that one orientation is superior but that both are vulnerable when carried to extremes.

The contrast is particularly stark in infrastructure. China's Belt and Road Initiative exemplifies patience: projects designed to transform trade routes over half a century, financed through debt instruments premised on generational returns. In the United States, by contrast, infrastructure bills are delayed by political cycles, and projects are scaled to fit electoral timetables. The Chinese narrative is that great undertakings require time; the American narrative is that results must be visible before the next election. Both logics carry risk—the former of overextension and white elephants, the latter of decay through underinvestment—but they illustrate how cultural time horizons shape the material world.

The financial industry provides another lens. Long-term value investing, pioneered by Benjamin Graham and popularised by Warren Buffett, echoes Confucian patience in its insistence on discipline and the compounding of value. Yet such strategies increasingly struggle in a market dominated by high-frequency trading and hedge funds chasing quarterly arbitrage. Even pension funds, once bastions of long-term stewardship, face pressures to deliver immediate returns lest beneficiaries or regulators question their performance. *Urgency has become institutionalised, reshaping not only decisions but the metrics by which success is judged.*

The cultural dimension of patience versus urgency extends into ethics. In Confucian systems, to be patient is to respect the continuity of the family and community, to honour ancestors by ensuring descendants inherit stability. Impatience is seen as disruptive, selfish, and immature. In modern Western capitalism, urgency is valorised as dynamism. To act quickly is to seize opportunity, to show initiative, to demonstrate competitiveness. Patience, by contrast, risks being read as complacency or lack of ambition. Thus, virtues and vices invert across cultures: what one calls prudent, the other calls sluggish; what one calls decisive, the other calls reckless.

Yet these orientations are not fixed. Globalisation is producing hybrids. Chinese tech firms, though rooted in Confucian societies, operate in hyper-competitive markets where quarterly performance matters as much as long-term strategy. Western firms increasingly speak of "sustainable value creation," borrowing language of stewardship from Confucian thought. The cross-pollination reflects recognition that neither patience nor urgency alone suffices. The challenge is to calibrate: to act with urgency when opportunity or threat demands it, but to maintain patience in building foundations that cannot be rushed.

The narratives individuals adopt about time also shape their financial choices. A young professional steeped in quarter-to-quarter thinking may prioritise career moves that yield immediate salary increases, even at the cost of long-term skill development. Someone influenced by Confucian patience may accept lower pay in the short run to gain experience and stability, confident that rewards will come in time. Both strategies can succeed, but both can fail if misapplied. The critical factor is alignment between narrative and context: urgency may be disastrous in a career that requires depth, while patience may be ruinous in an industry disrupted every two years. *The stories we tell about time are strategies, and like all strategies they carry risks as well as rewards.*

At stake in the contrast between patience and urgency is not simply efficiency but meaning. To live within a culture of urgency is to experience life as a series of sprints, each demanding performance, each measured by external validation. To live within a culture of patience is to experience life as a continuum, where progress is slow but steady, and worth is measured by legacy. Both can produce flourishing; both can produce frustration. The art lies in recognising when to lean into one orientation and when to resist it. What Confucianism and quarterly capitalism share, despite their differences, is the belief that time is the ultimate currency of wealth. Their divergence lies in how long they are willing to wait before calling the investment worthwhile.

The enduring question is whether modern societies can recover balance. As crises accelerate—climate change, pandemics, geopolitical shocks—the pressure for urgency will only intensify. Yet without the patience to invest in systemic resilience, the urgent may cannibalise the future. The Confucian story of long-term cultivation and the Western story of urgent adaptation are not irreconcilable. Taken together, they offer a dialectic: patience provides the soil, urgency the harvest. The lesson of contrasting cultures is not to choose one over the other but to recognise when the parable of patience or urgency best fits the moment. Only then can time be harnessed as wealth rather than wasted as noise.

Compounding and Storytelling: Shows how narratives, not just math, make the idea of compounding vivid

The power of compounding is often described as the "eighth wonder of the world," yet for most people it remains an abstraction, reduced to tidy graphs and formulae that fail to capture its real significance. Numbers alone rarely persuade; what persuades are stories. Human beings grasp time, growth, and risk not as mathematical equations but as lived experiences. A chart showing how £10,000 invested at 7 per cent annual growth becomes £76,000 in thirty years is striking, but it seldom changes behaviour. A story about a neighbour who started saving in their twenties and retired decades later with independence, while their equally diligent colleague who began a decade later struggled, has the power to reframe choices. *The lesson is not that the maths is wrong, but that without narrative scaffolding, its impact evaporates.*

Consider the parable of two siblings often used in personal finance education. The first saves a modest amount regularly for the first ten years of her working life and then stops, while the second waits a decade before starting, then contributes twice as much each year. By retirement, the first sibling has more wealth despite investing less overall. This simple fable does what compound-interest tables rarely achieve: it makes time visceral. The audience sees not only the figures but also the injustice of delay, the opportunity cost that feels like a moral warning. It shifts compounding from arithmetic into the domain of human drama. *Stories embed mathematics in emotion, and emotion drives behaviour.*

The ancients grasped this long before financial calculators existed. Agricultural metaphors—seeds planted, harvests reaped, cycles of sowing and waiting—conveyed the essence of compounding in ways that villagers could internalise. Religious texts reinforced the moral of patience: the notion that what is nurtured steadily yields abundance, while what is consumed hastily leads to scarcity. The cultural roots of compounding thus predate its modern financial application; what differs is the unit of growth, whether grain in a field, virtue in a community, or capital in a bank. The continuity of these metaphors underscores how stories, rather than spreadsheets, sustain long-term behaviours across generations.

Yet the modern world complicates compounding with distractions of immediacy. Quarter-to-quarter thinking, day trading, and social media's emphasis on instant returns obscure the patient arc that compounding requires. This is precisely why storytelling remains indispensable. When behavioural economists study why so few people save adequately for retirement, they find that individuals consistently discount the future, treating their sixty-year-old self as a stranger. Narrative is the bridge across this psychological gap. Experiments have shown that when people are asked to visualise and even digitally age their future selves, they are more likely to increase retirement contributions. The math does not change; the story they tell about who they will become does.

Case studies make the same point at a societal scale. Consider Singapore's Central Provident Fund, which mandates savings but frames it as part of a national story of self-reliance and dignity in ageing. The system functions not simply because of compulsion but because the story of independence resonates with citizens. Similarly, Warren Buffett's annual letters to Berkshire Hathaway shareholders work not merely because they explain compounding but because they tell it as a fable of patience triumphing over greed. His folksy retelling of how modest sums in Coca-Cola or American Express grew over decades into fortunes gives flesh to the abstract law of exponential growth. *The genius lies not in discovering compounding but in narrating it so persuasively that millions believe in it enough to act accordingly.*

It is important to recognise that compounding is not only financial. Knowledge compounds when cultivated, skills compound when practised, and reputations compound through consistent action. Narratives play a similar role in these domains. The scientist who dedicates years to research often finds that breakthroughs arrive not as single leaps but as the cumulative result of countless experiments. The athlete who trains daily improves not linearly but exponentially, as skill layers upon skill. Such stories of compounded effort make visible the invisible: the way persistence transforms ordinary beginnings into extraordinary outcomes. Without these stories, the mathematics of exponential growth remains abstract, detached from lived experience.

There is also a darker side to compounding that narratives illuminate more effectively than numbers. Debt accumulates interest as inexorably as savings does. Addiction compounds, small choices snowballing into entrenched patterns. Mistrust in financial systems compounds when scandals are repeated, eroding confidence in ways that no single incident could. Here too, stories capture the phenomenon more forcefully than numbers. A tale of a family overwhelmed by credit card debt resonates far more than statistics on household leverage. The story of Bernie Madoff's victims, some of whom saw lifetimes of savings vanish, illustrates how negative compounding of trust can devastate more swiftly than compound interest can build wealth. *Narratives are not merely illustrative—they shape the moral perception of compounding itself, distinguishing between its promise and its peril.*

Why does narrative work so effectively where raw data falters? Cognitive psychology offers an answer: humans are not natural statisticians, but they are natural storytellers. We remember events as sequences with causes and consequences, not as tables of percentages. When confronted with exponential growth, our intuitions fail. The "exponential growth bias" leads people to underestimate how quickly quantities accumulate. But when this bias is reframed through narrative—such as the classic riddle of the chessboard and the grains of rice, doubling with each square—suddenly the impossibility of keeping up becomes clear. We need the narrative structure to internalise the counterintuitive reality of exponentiality.

In practice, financial educators and policymakers increasingly acknowledge that without compelling stories, compounding fails to penetrate. Governments attempting to encourage pension savings do not only provide calculators but commission campaigns that dramatise the future life of retirees, showing what is lost by waiting. Employers use scenarios of "future you" enjoying stability versus "future you" facing struggle. Charities do something similar: stories of small donations compounding into major impact are far more effective than appeals based on raw figures. The lesson is universal: the arithmetic of compounding may be universal, but *its uptake depends on the stories that give it human weight.*

Contrasting views are worth acknowledging. Critics argue that compounding is often mythologised in ways that obscure structural inequalities. For those without disposable income, stories about starting early are irrelevant or even patronising. Compounding can become a narrative of blame—implying that poverty is the result of poor foresight rather than systemic barriers. This critique reminds us that while stories are essential, they must be honest, accounting for context as well as choice. A story that inspires the privileged but alienates the disadvantaged does not democratise the power of compounding; it entrenches inequity. The responsibility, therefore, lies in crafting narratives that are inclusive, that show not only individual possibility but also the institutional conditions required to make compounding attainable.

The most persuasive stories of compounding, then, balance inspiration with realism. They do not merely showcase the exceptional investor who turned small sums into millions, but also the ordinary saver whose modest, consistent discipline ensured dignity in later life. They reveal the fragility of opportunities to compound, emphasising the importance of protection from predatory debt, market manipulation, and inflationary erosion. They move beyond the sterile exhortation to "start early" by embedding it in human contexts of family, community, and legacy. *Compounding is not only a financial principle; it is a cultural inheritance, sustained or squandered depending on the stories societies tell.*

Ultimately, what endures is not the formula but the fable. The mathematics of compounding is immutable, yet the will to act upon it is cultivated through narratives that resonate with identity and aspiration. The person who saves or invests consistently does so because they believe a story about who they are and who they will become. The nation that embraces long-term planning does so because it believes a story about its collective destiny. In both cases, numbers serve as scaffolding, but story is the architecture. Without it, compounding remains inert; with it, compounding becomes one of the most powerful forces in human affairs.

Choosing Time Over Money: Encourages readers to prioritise time-rich stories over money-rich illusions

A striking paradox of modern life is that those who accumulate the most money often find themselves with the least time. While wealth is pursued as a path to freedom, the pursuit itself can consume decades, leaving little room for the very experiences it was meant to enable. *The true scarcity is not money but hours, days, and years, yet societies have been conditioned to act as though the inverse were true.* To choose time over money requires breaking with dominant narratives that glorify accumulation and redefining wealth as the capacity to live one's life on one's own terms.

The idea that time is wealth is not new, yet it resists cultural adoption. Across history, the affluent classes often defined status not through visible riches but through the leisure to pursue philosophy, politics, or the arts. In ancient Rome, senators prided themselves not only on their estates but on their capacity to devote days to public service and debate. In Confucian thought, wisdom was not measured by material plenty but by the ability to cultivate harmony and learning over generations. Even in medieval Europe, the landed aristocracy guarded time as their true privilege: peasants toiled from dawn to dusk, while nobles claimed the hours necessary for patronage, reflection, and influence. Money provided the conditions, but the real aspiration was liberation from the grind of necessity.

In the twenty-first century, this older understanding of time as wealth has been inverted. The financial elite often live in a state of relentless urgency: executives racing between time zones, entrepreneurs bound by the cycle of start-up valuations, professionals tethered to devices that blur the line between day and night. Meanwhile, those with less financial abundance often find themselves with enforced stretches of time, albeit constrained by precarious resources. The cultural narrative equates value with busyness, such that admitting to having free time is almost stigmatised. Yet research on happiness consistently shows that *time affluence*—the subjective sense of having control over one's hours—is a stronger predictor of well-being than absolute income once basic needs are met.

Why then do so many continue to sacrifice time for money long past the point of diminishing returns? Part of the answer lies in the seduction of money-rich stories. The tale of the tireless entrepreneur who builds an empire is retold endlessly in business media, while the story of the person who deliberately works fewer hours to spend time with family rarely makes the front page. Popular culture frames wealth accumulation as heroic, while time preservation appears ordinary, even indulgent. Narratives drive aspiration, and aspiration drives behaviour. Without alternative stories that dignify choosing time, the cycle perpetuates itself.

Behavioural economics sheds further light on this dilemma. People systematically overvalue immediate monetary rewards and undervalue the long-term benefits of time. Experiments show that when offered the choice between extra cash or additional vacation days, many select the money, even when they later report regretting the decision. The bias is not simply cognitive but cultural: a society that celebrates income as the ultimate metric of success primes individuals to default toward money. Stories that normalise time-rich choices—such as companies publicly adopting four-day workweeks without loss of productivity, or retirees celebrating modest but sufficient lifestyles—can shift these perceptions by providing visible counterexamples. *What people believe to be possible is shaped less by economic theory than by the stories they encounter in their community.*

Real-world examples illustrate this shift vividly. When New Zealand company Perpetual Guardian trialled a four-day workweek, employees reported higher productivity, better health, and greater satisfaction. The financial cost to the company was negligible, yet the time dividend to employees was immense. The story of this experiment spread globally, fuelling debates about the future of work in ways that statistics alone could not. Similarly, movements such as FIRE (Financial Independence, Retire Early) have gained traction not because of the mathematical novelty of saving aggressively but because they present compelling narratives of individuals reclaiming their time decades earlier than expected. Whether one agrees with their austerity or not, the movement demonstrates the hunger for stories that privilege time.

Contrast this with the illusionary power of money-rich stories. Lottery winners, often celebrated as the epitome of financial fortune, provide a cautionary tale. Studies repeatedly show that many winners end up less happy, and in some cases financially ruined, within a few years. The sudden influx of money does not automatically buy meaningful time; instead, it often accelerates consumption and conflict. By contrast, those who consciously design their lives around time—parents who step back from promotions to be present for their children, individuals who relocate to slower-paced communities, artists who accept modest incomes in exchange for creative freedom—may not headline the news, but they embody a more sustainable definition of wealth.

Philosophy reinforces this perspective. The Stoics urged reflection on mortality as a way of valuing time over possessions. Seneca's writings remind us that while life may feel long, much of it is squandered in pursuits that serve neither happiness nor virtue. Modern psychology echoes this insight through studies of *subjective well-being*: experiences, relationships, and autonomy consistently outweigh material goods in predicting life satisfaction. These findings suggest that the richest lives are not those with the most money, but those with the greatest intentional control over time. *Wealth is the ability to spend time as one chooses, not merely the capacity to spend money as one wishes.*

The challenge lies in rewriting the stories we inherit. Families often transmit money scripts that emphasise security, sacrifice, or ambition, but rarely do they pass down narratives that celebrate time. A parent might remind a child to work hard and save, but how often do they tell stories of choosing to leave work early to attend a school play, or of declining overtime to preserve health? When cultural transmission elevates money-rich tales above time-rich ones, individuals struggle to imagine alternatives. It is not enough to lecture on the value of time; one must tell and retell stories where time is the protagonist.

Corporate and political systems also shape this narrative terrain. Policies that guarantee paid parental leave or limit excessive working hours do more than protect workers; they signal what societies value. Countries with generous leave policies, such as the Nordic states, generate cultural stories of normalised balance, where success includes both professional achievement and family presence. By contrast, societies with minimal protections reinforce narratives of endurance and sacrifice, binding identity to labour rather than to the quality of lived time. The divergence shows how collective storytelling interacts with policy: one sustains the illusion that money must always come first, while the other embeds time as a legitimate form of wealth.

Choosing time over money, then, is not only an individual moral act but a cultural reorientation. It requires shifting from seeing time as a cost of earning to recognising it as the dividend that makes earning meaningful. It demands questioning why busyness has become a badge of honour and why rest is treated as weakness. And it invites us to replace the silent narrative of "I'll have time later" with the urgent truth that later rarely comes. The stories we tell about wealth must therefore expand to include hours well spent, not just accounts well stocked.

The task is not to dismiss money but to place it in service of time. Money enables choices, but when it becomes the end rather than the means, it traps rather than liberates. Time, by contrast, once spent, is gone forever. Stories that remind us of this asymmetry—whether the parable of the wasted hour, the lived example of a company embracing shorter workweeks, or the quiet dignity of someone prioritising presence over prestige—are the ones that hold transformative power. To embrace them is to recognise that the true measure of wealth lies not in numbers but in narratives, not in accumulation but in allocation, and above all, not in money hoarded but in time honoured.

Chapter 12
The Price of Security

Security has always carried a paradoxical cost. The more tightly people try to safeguard their assets, their livelihoods, or their very lives, the more they risk being consumed by the effort itself. From ancient walled cities to today's fortress-like financial products, humanity has continually paid a premium—both material and psychological—for the promise of safety. Yet safety is rarely absolute. What appears as protection in one era often reveals itself in hindsight as vulnerability, whether in the form of wealth locked away but rendered idle, or insurance schemes designed more to capitalise on fear than to foster resilience. To understand the price of security is to recognise that security is never free: it is purchased with trust, time, opportunity, and, too often, peace of mind.

The eternal quest for safety is written into the architecture of human civilisation. Archaeologists uncover not only temples and marketplaces but also walls, vaults, and storage chambers—evidence that protection has always been as central to collective identity as worship or trade. The medieval castle, with its concentric fortifications, served not only to deter invaders but also as a symbol of a lord's legitimacy. The same impulse echoes today in the skyscraper bank headquarters, the biometric vault, or the server farm housing the data that underpins global finance. These structures reassure us not only that assets are safe but that the order of society itself is intact. Yet the cost of such fortifications, whether measured in stone, steel, or energy consumption, is immense. In every epoch, the act of securing wealth diverts resources away from creating it. *Security is not neutral; it always requires trade-offs.*

Fear has long been the most effective currency in selling security. Financial products frequently exploit insecurity myths, drawing on narratives that stretch back centuries. Insurance advertising, for instance, often frames protection not in terms of rational risk management but as a bulwark against catastrophe: the fire that destroys the home, the illness that bankrupts the family, the accident that shatters stability. These scenarios resonate because they touch primal anxieties about loss and vulnerability. What is rarely emphasised is that statistical likelihoods often differ dramatically from the scenarios invoked. A homeowner may be more at risk from gradual structural decay than from a catastrophic fire, yet the fire looms larger in the cultural imagination. Financial industries understand this discrepancy and market accordingly. The fear-based narrative, once internalised, reshapes behaviour: people over-insure in some areas, under-invest in others, and maintain products they barely understand out of dread rather than informed choice.

The folklore of protection reveals how deeply embedded these patterns are. Myths across cultures imagine wealth guarded by fearsome obstacles: dragons sleeping atop treasure, sphinxes posing riddles before permitting entry, or jealous gods punishing mortals who dare to hoard. These stories do more than entertain; they encode the recognition that wealth is inherently vulnerable and that protection comes at a price. The dragon may guard the gold, but it also ensures that the gold remains unused, inaccessible to those who might otherwise employ it for growth or generosity. The same can be said of modern safe-deposit boxes filled with heirlooms or bullion: wealth may be secure, but it is also frozen. Such folklore mirrors the paradox of security—it preserves, but it also immobilises.

Today, one sees these narratives playing out not only in tangible vaults but also in digital form. Cryptocurrencies emerged partly as a response to distrust in centralised banking, promising autonomy and incorruptibility. Yet the very attempt to secure value through decentralisation produced new vulnerabilities: lost passwords, hacked exchanges, fraudulent schemes masquerading as safe havens. The irony is that technologies designed to escape traditional fears often generate new ones, shifting rather than resolving the underlying tension. Security remains elusive, because the deeper need is not simply for protection but for confidence that what one has will endure and remain meaningful.

Healthy security stories approach the challenge differently. Instead of portraying wealth as something perpetually under siege, they emphasise resilience, adaptability, and balance. For example, micro-insurance schemes in developing economies provide modest payouts for common risks such as crop failure or localised flooding.

Their power lies not in eliminating vulnerability but in cushioning communities against shocks, enabling recovery without destitution. Similarly, financial planning that frames security as the capacity to absorb disruption—rather than the impossibility of preventing it—creates more sustainable strategies. The emphasis shifts from hoarding to preparing, from wall-building to bridge-building. *True security is less about impenetrable defences than about the confidence to navigate uncertainty without collapse.*

This reframing requires narrative change at both cultural and individual levels. At the cultural level, societies must move away from glorifying impenetrable vaults and secretive wealth preservation towards valuing transparency, mutual support, and collective safety nets. At the individual level, people must be encouraged to ask whether their pursuit of security is driven by informed choice or by inherited fears. Are they buying financial products because they meet real needs, or because the spectre of loss has been magnified through stories designed to provoke anxiety? Such reflection is vital, because the cost of misguided security is not merely financial; it can erode trust, relationships, and quality of life.

The enduring question, then, is not whether security is worth pursuing—clearly it is—but what kind of security we should aspire to. Is it the static protection of walls and hoards, or the dynamic resilience that allows adaptation in the face of change? The former is ancient, compelling, and easy to sell; the latter is less dramatic but far more empowering. By interrogating the stories that shape our perceptions of risk, and by choosing narratives that privilege resilience over fear, individuals and societies alike can begin to pay the price of security more wisely. Security will always demand a cost, but by recognising the nature of that cost, we can ensure it buys not paralysis but the freedom to live with confidence.

The Eternal Quest for Safety: Shows how stories of walls, vaults, and hoards mirror today's insurance and savings

Safety has never been a static condition but a moving target, shaped as much by imagination as by material reality. From the earliest human settlements, people have erected barriers—walls, ditches, watchtowers—not merely to keep danger out but to reassure themselves that life within was predictable, manageable, and less vulnerable to chaos. This desire has persisted in different guises across centuries: medieval keeps with drawbridges, Renaissance vaults lined with iron, Victorian safes with intricate locks, and today's digital firewalls protecting intangible assets. *Security is never only about the object it guards; it is also about the story it tells to those who rely on it.* Every wall or vault functions as much as a narrative device as a technical one, promising continuity in a world where none can be guaranteed.

The symbolism of walls is particularly instructive. The Great Wall of China, stretching across thousands of kilometres, was less effective as a military deterrent than as a cultural statement of unity and permanence. Similarly, medieval city walls in Europe were not simply fortifications; they marked the boundary between civilisation and wilderness, between a safe, governed interior and a threatening, lawless outside. The physical presence of these walls reassured citizens, but their true power lay in the collective belief they fostered. Even when breached, the idea of the wall endured, representing safety and identity. Modern equivalents—border controls, gated communities, or even the encryption protecting online banking—operate in precisely this way. They provide a tangible symbol of security, whether or not their protective capacity matches the narrative attached to them.

Vaults and hoards reveal another dimension of the safety story: the urge not just to protect from outsiders but to immobilise wealth itself. Ancient treasuries often housed offerings to gods, the wealth deliberately locked away to demonstrate reverence as much as power. Later, banks adopted vaults as both practical and theatrical devices. The heavily reinforced doors, polished steel, and weighty locks reassured clients that their deposits were beyond reach, creating confidence in the institution. Yet, paradoxically, the hoarded wealth within such vaults was inert until redeployed into the economy. *The act of securing often involves freezing, preventing assets from being lost but also from being used.* This paradox persists in personal savings behaviour, where individuals over-accumulate in low-yield accounts out of fear, forgoing opportunities for growth in the name of safety.

Insurance, in its modern sense, represents a more sophisticated story of safety—one that extends beyond walls and vaults into promises against uncertainty itself. Medieval merchant guilds first pooled resources to cover shipwrecks or fires, recognising that shared vulnerability could be transformed into collective resilience. That innovation has since expanded into a vast ecosystem of products: life, health, property, and even event insurance. Each policy operates less as a guarantee against misfortune—since many risks remain uncovered—than as a story that converts fear into manageable payments. To pay a premium is to purchase not certainty but *the feeling of certainty*, a psychological comfort that echoes the reassurance once offered by stone walls or sealed chests. The proliferation of these products demonstrates not only the enduring power of insecurity but also the extent to which modern economies rely on packaging and selling peace of mind.

The parallels between past and present forms of protection highlight a profound continuity: people seek structures, both physical and symbolic, that anchor them against the unpredictability of the world. Consider the safe-deposit box, a direct descendant of the medieval coffer, used today more often to protect sentimental artefacts—letters, heirlooms, photographs—than to store negotiable wealth. The contents are less economically valuable than emotionally significant, but the box satisfies the same ancient impulse: to keep what matters away from harm, even if that harm is unlikely. Similarly, the rise of digital password managers and cloud backups reflects a desire to translate the vault into the virtual realm. The story is consistent: whether dragon-guarded treasure or encrypted data, safety is measured not by absolute protection but by the collective belief that the barrier will hold.

At the same time, safety stories often contain a darker side, where overemphasis on protection leads to rigidity, exclusion, or stagnation. Hoarding myths, from King Midas to Smaug the dragon, illustrate the danger of locking wealth away so securely that it becomes destructive, consuming its guardian rather than sustaining a community. In contemporary finance, this dynamic surfaces in households paralysed by fear of risk, who save diligently but never invest, or in nations whose obsession with reserves constrains productive innovation. *The very act of protecting can, if unchecked, become its own form of impoverishment.* This tension underscores the need to question whether the price of security is proportionate to the value it genuinely delivers.

Case studies of financial crises further demonstrate the fragility of security narratives. During the Great Depression, American banks suffered runs not because vaults were empty but because confidence collapsed. The walls and locks remained intact, but the story had broken down. Similarly, in the 2008 financial crisis, institutions once considered "too big to fail" revealed vulnerabilities that no vault could conceal. The guarantees of security—AAA ratings, collateralised assets, insured products—proved illusory when tested. These moments expose the core truth: security is a narrative commodity. Its durability rests less on the thickness of walls than on the persistence of shared belief.

The eternal quest for safety, then, cannot be dismissed as mere superstition or irrationality. It is foundational to the way humans organise both societies and economies. Yet its very persistence demands scrutiny. Are today's financial products truly modern innovations, or are they re-enactments of ancient rituals with updated costumes? A life insurance policy may appear radically different from a medieval city wall, but both function by transforming anxiety into something graspable: a payment, a structure, a promise. Recognising this continuity allows us to see that security has always been as much about psychology as economics.

To move forward, it is essential to cultivate healthier safety stories—ones that balance the human need for protection with the equally human need for growth, generosity, and adaptability. The challenge is not to abandon walls, vaults, or insurance, but to ensure they serve as tools rather than cages. The measure of safety should not be the immobility of wealth but the confidence with which individuals and societies can deploy it without fear of ruin. Only then does the eternal quest for safety shift from a cycle of anxious hoarding to a narrative of resilience, where security provides not just preservation but the freedom to act.

Fear-Based Narratives: Explains how financial products often exploit insecurity myths

Fear is one of the oldest currencies in human exchange, and finance has always been skilled at minting it into value. Where other industries trade in utility, convenience, or aspiration, financial services frequently trade in anxiety—offering products not simply as tools for growth or preservation but as shields against calamity, both real and imagined. The selling of security has long relied on the ability to tap into deep-seated myths of vulnerability, telling stories where the future is dark, uncertain, and perilous unless one purchases the appropriate safeguard. *Fear-based narratives succeed because they do not need to be accurate; they only need to be plausible, and plausibility is enough to ignite the imagination of loss.*

The origins of such narratives stretch back centuries. Medieval moneylenders often cloaked their practices in moral language, warning borrowers of ruin if they failed to secure themselves against uncertain harvests or dangerous voyages. By the eighteenth century, insurers were crafting pamphlets that amplified images of shipwrecks, fires, and widowhood to persuade merchants and households to commit to regular premiums. The message was not subtle: to remain uninsured was to court catastrophe. These stories became more systematised in the twentieth century as financial advertising matured, with campaigns showing destitute widows or ruined families—always with the implicit refrain that foresight (expressed as purchasing insurance, a pension plan, or a savings bond) could have spared the tragedy.

The genius of the fear-based narrative lies in its ability to *personalise risk*. A natural disaster, market crash, or illness is transformed from a statistical abstraction into a vivid possibility that might strike any individual at any time. Consider modern health insurance marketing, which often focuses less on the actuarial realities of illness and more on singular, emotionally charged scenarios: the child diagnosed with a rare condition, the accident that happens "just one street away," the sudden incapacity that turns a provider into a dependent. By dramatising the unpredictability of life, these stories obscure probabilities while amplifying anxieties, steering individuals toward products that may or may not provide meaningful coverage.

Fear narratives also thrive because they resonate with archetypes embedded in cultural memory. The folklore of protection—hoards guarded against thieves, fortresses holding back invaders, villages plagued by famine—provides fertile imagery for financial storytelling. Modern equivalents are advertisements showing burglars prowling darkened homes to sell home insurance, or apocalyptic warnings about stock market crashes to market gold. These tropes endure because they tap into collective memory: *the story of danger is easier to tell, and to believe, than the story of stability.* The consumer who buys the product feels not only insured against loss but aligned with an ancient survival instinct.

Case studies from contemporary finance highlight the potency of these narratives. In the wake of the 2008 financial crisis, sales of gold and other "safe haven" assets surged, fuelled less by rational portfolio balancing than by media narratives of systemic collapse. Investors, unsettled by imagery of bankrupt banks and foreclosed homes, turned to gold bars and coins—objects whose value was bolstered not only by market fundamentals but by centuries of myth depicting gold as imperishable wealth. Similarly, the growth of extended warranty markets for electronics demonstrates how companies harness fear of breakdowns to secure billions in revenue from products that often offer marginal utility. The warranty, like the medieval talisman, operates as much as a psychological amulet as a financial instrument.

Fear-based financial narratives are not confined to traditional products. The explosion of cryptocurrency markets revealed a modern iteration of insecurity myths, often framed around the fear of missing out (FOMO). Here the anxiety is not of loss through calamity but of exclusion from sudden fortune. The story told is stark: either you act now and seize freedom from a decaying system, or you remain enslaved to failing fiat currencies and corrupt institutions. This rhetorical move, though different in form, rests on the same foundation: heightening insecurity to compel behaviour. *Whether through fear of ruin or fear of regret, the emotional logic is the same.*

Yet it would be reductive to suggest that all fear-based narratives are purely exploitative. Fear, after all, has evolutionary value; it is a motivator for prudent preparation. Insurance markets, pensions, and savings products exist in part because genuine risks must be managed. The line between responsible foresight and manipulative scaremongering is blurred, often depending on whether the story illuminates risk or distorts it. For instance, life insurance may be sold through narratives of tragic family breakdown, but it also addresses real vulnerabilities for dependents in households without robust social safety nets. The problem arises when products exaggerate risks, conceal limitations, or inflate prices while cloaking themselves in moral or emotional imperatives.

Critically examining fear narratives requires recognising their structural role in financial capitalism. Economic systems profit not only from managing risks but from sustaining the perception that risks are omnipresent and unmanageable without professional mediation. This perception is cultivated through cycles of media amplification, policy messaging, and industry advertising, ensuring that anxiety itself becomes a resource to be harvested. *The story of insecurity, repeated often enough, becomes inseparable from financial identity; one is responsible not simply for earning and spending but for endlessly insulating oneself from the spectre of ruin.*

To navigate this landscape, individuals must distinguish between *legitimate caution* and *manufactured panic*. The key lies in interrogating the narrative itself: does the product address a real, quantifiable risk, or does it amplify unlikely scenarios to sell a sense of control? For example, travel insurance may reasonably protect against medical emergencies abroad, but the addition of improbable coverages—such as "flight delay due to volcanic eruption"—reflects a layering of exotic fears designed to inflate premiums. Similarly, retirement savings plans promoted through images of impoverished pensioners in bleak nursing homes may oversimplify the diverse realities of ageing, reinforcing a singular myth of decline to compel participation.

What makes fear-based financial narratives especially powerful is their resistance to disproof. A fire that never occurs, a market crash that does not happen, or an illness that does not arise cannot negate the story—rather, it is taken as evidence that the protective product worked. The absence of calamity is reinterpreted as validation of foresight, closing the loop and entrenching the product's legitimacy.

This is the paradox of financial fear: *security becomes unfalsifiable because the very stability it ensures erases the evidence of its necessity.*

The challenge, then, is not to eliminate fear from financial storytelling but to place it in proportion. Fear must be acknowledged as an enduring feature of human decision-making, but it should not be allowed to dominate it. A healthier financial culture would foreground narratives of resilience, adaptability, and empowerment, where protection is framed not as submission to fear but as a rational extension of prudence. To move in that direction requires both industry accountability and individual literacy—an ability to recognise when a story serves the customer's interests and when it serves only the product's.

Fear-based narratives will not disappear; they are too deeply entwined with human psychology and too lucrative for financial industries to abandon. But awareness of their mechanics allows for resistance. The myths of insecurity may be perennial, but they need not dictate behaviour uncritically. The task is not to deny fear but to interrogate it—asking whether it reflects reality, whether it has been amplified for profit, and whether the story being sold offers genuine protection or merely the illusion of it. Only by doing so can individuals and societies reclaim financial storytelling from the grip of anxiety and reframe it around strategies that empower rather than exploit.

The Folklore of Protection: From dragon-guarded gold to safe-deposit boxes, how cultures narrate security

Across cultures and centuries, wealth has rarely been imagined as sitting unguarded. It is not enough to possess treasure; the deeper psychological need is to believe that treasure is defended against intrusion. This impulse is not merely practical—it is profoundly narrative. From ancient myths of serpentine guardians to modern institutions encased in marble and steel, societies construct elaborate stories of protection. These narratives serve two purposes at once: they deter imagined threats and reassure the possessor that what is valued will remain intact. *The desire for security is as much about the story we tell ourselves of invulnerability as it is about actual defence mechanisms.*

The dragon is perhaps the most enduring folkloric figure of financial security. In European and Asian traditions alike, dragons coil themselves around mountains of gold, embodying the paradox of protection: the wealth is safe precisely because it is inaccessible. To reach the hoard requires heroism of the highest order, which means that for ordinary mortals, the treasure remains untouchable. The dragon, in this sense, is less a literal adversary than a narrative device that conveys the weight of guarding wealth. The hoard is safe, but its safety comes at the price of perpetual inaccessibility. Here lies a striking resonance with modern finance: savings locked in vaults or inaccessible investment vehicles promise preservation, but often at the cost of liquidity. The dragon has simply changed form, from mythical beast to contractual clause.

Cultural variations on this theme reveal how different societies have imagined protection in line with their own anxieties. In Norse sagas, cursed rings and guarded gold are defended not only by monsters but by the very weight of fate—wealth becomes entangled with doom, suggesting that protection is less about keeping outsiders away than about protecting the owner from their own greed. In Chinese folklore, wealth is often safeguarded by celestial beings or ancestral spirits, linking protection to moral order and filial piety. In both cases, the message is clear: wealth cannot stand naked in the world; it must be embedded within a protective narrative that elevates it beyond mere possession.

Modern financial institutions replicate these myths with remarkable fidelity. The grand facades of nineteenth- and early twentieth-century banks—columns modelled on temples, vaults advertised as impenetrable—were not just architectural choices but narrative statements. They told depositors a story: your money is not simply held, it is *guarded.* The heavy doors, reinforced steel, and even the intimidating silence of marble halls functioned as the modern equivalent of dragons and curses. The ritual of walking into a bank and placing one's savings in a vault was not merely transactional but performative; it enacted a cultural myth of invulnerability.

Safe-deposit boxes exemplify this modern folklore of protection. To the rational mind, a small locked box within a larger vault provides little more than storage. Yet the allure is disproportionate. People place in them not only deeds, jewellery, and bonds but also keepsakes with no financial value—letters, photographs, heirlooms. The box becomes sacred because of its layered protection: locked within a vault, housed in a bank, guarded by both physical security and the cultural aura of financial institutions. What is being purchased is not safety alone but *the story of safety*—a tale that reassures the owner that their valuables have been entrusted to forces larger, stronger, and more permanent than themselves.

Contemporary parallels extend beyond banks. Insurance policies, cybersecurity packages, and investment guarantees are all narrated through metaphors of protection. The firewall is a digital moat, anti-virus software a shield, pension funds a fortress against the uncertainties of age. Each draws on deep cultural memory that equates protection with fortification. *The financial product succeeds not only because it functions but because it activates an archetypal narrative already waiting in the mind of the consumer.* This is why advertisements so often reach for metaphors of walls, locks, and guardians: they are updating myths that have been culturally tested for centuries.

Yet embedded in these stories is a paradox. The stronger the guard, the less accessible the wealth. A treasure behind dragon fire, a deposit locked behind multiple layers of steel, or a pension fund inaccessible until late life all share the same ambivalence: what is protected is not immediately usable. Narratives of security therefore often involve a trade-off between protection and freedom. The owner is reassured by the guard but simultaneously constrained by them. This tension is rarely acknowledged explicitly in financial storytelling, but it underlies many modern frustrations with financial products—insurance claims denied, funds locked by penalties, savings inaccessible at moments of urgent need. The folklore promises invulnerability, but the lived experience reveals entanglement.

Critically, these protective myths do not only serve individuals; they function socially. In societies with weak institutions, folklore often compensates by embedding protection in spiritual or familial frameworks: ancestral curses on stolen land, divine oversight of sacred wealth. In societies with strong institutions, the state itself narrates protection through deposit guarantees, central bank authority, and visible regulation. What differs is the source of trust, but the underlying narrative logic remains the same: wealth requires guardianship, and guardianship must be made visible and believable.

The modern fascination with cryptocurrencies provides a new lens on this folklore. At first glance, crypto assets appear to abandon traditional protections—no vaults, no bank clerks, no marble facades. Yet the community has created its own protective myths: impenetrable blockchains, incorruptible algorithms, decentralised guardianship by a global network. The same human need persists: to believe that wealth is safe not only through mathematics but through stories that make mathematics emotionally intelligible. When enthusiasts describe blockchains as "unhackable" or wallets as "unbreakable," they are invoking the same cultural archetypes as dragons and fortresses, updating them for the digital age.

There is also a moral dimension to protection folklore. Stories of guarded wealth often carry implicit judgements about worthiness. In myths, only the noble hero or rightful heir can access the guarded treasure. In finance, similar moral undertones persist: creditworthiness, respectability, or social status often determine access to the safest institutions and products. The folklore thus reinforces not only security but hierarchy. To be deemed trustworthy enough to place wealth in the vault is to be marked as belonging to the circle of the protected. Those excluded from such circles face not only economic insecurity but the narrative stigma of being unworthy of guardianship.

Understanding this cultural and historical continuity sheds light on the enduring grip of protective narratives in financial life. They remind us that security is not merely technical but symbolic, sustained by shared myths that reassure us against the fragility of fortune. *What is being protected is not only wealth but the psychological need to believe that wealth can be made invulnerable.* From dragons to digital ledgers, the human imagination insists that treasure must have a guardian, and it is this story—more than the locks, the vaults, or the code—that sustains our confidence in the systems we build.

Healthy Security Stories: Encourages reframing security as resilience rather than fear

Security is one of the oldest human aspirations, yet it is also one of the most misinterpreted. Too often, it has been equated with the elimination of threat or the possession of unbreachable defences. But history shows that walls crumble, vaults are broken, and insurance schemes collapse under pressure. What endures is not absolute safety—which is an illusion—but the capacity to absorb shocks and continue. *True security lies less in the eradication of risk than in resilience, the ability to adapt and recover.* To reframe our financial narratives around resilience rather than fear is not simply a semantic shift; it is a profound reorientation of how we understand wealth, risk, and wellbeing.

The stories we tell ourselves about security matter because they shape the choices we make. A fear-driven narrative frames the world as hostile, teeming with dangers from which we must withdraw. It is the voice that urges us to hoard, to over-insure, to build fortresses around our assets. A resilience-oriented narrative, by contrast, accepts that uncertainty is inevitable but insists that we can endure it. It asks not "How can I make myself invulnerable?" but "How can I prepare to withstand the blows I cannot predict?" This distinction is critical: one leads to paralysis, the other to strength.

Consider the difference between a family that believes their security lies in locking every penny into fixed assets versus one that invests in education, networks, and flexible opportunities. The first strategy, rooted in fear, may provide a sense of control but leaves the family exposed to unforeseen disruptions—currency crises, health emergencies, shifts in technology. The second, rooted in resilience, recognises that wealth can vanish but skills and adaptability cannot be confiscated. *Security becomes the cultivation of capacities rather than the accumulation of locks.*

Fear-based financial products thrive on magnifying vulnerability. The marketing of many insurance policies is instructive: advertisements highlight calamities—house fires, theft, sudden illness—not to encourage prudent planning but to invoke anxiety so acute that buying protection feels compulsory. Similarly, savings products often lean on images of frail retirees and warnings of destitution. These strategies succeed precisely because fear narrows attention and compels immediate action. Yet they also impoverish our imagination, conditioning us to define security only as protection against loss, never as preparation for growth.

A resilience framework, by contrast, directs attention to flexibility and continuity. Take the example of microfinance in developing economies. Its impact is not primarily that it eliminates poverty overnight, but that it provides households with modest buffers to weather fluctuations—be it a poor harvest, a medical emergency, or school fees. These small cushions enable participants to continue working, educating children, and planning for the future. Security here is not the absence of risk, but the assurance that risk does not force total collapse.

The COVID-19 pandemic underscored this lesson on a global scale. Nations, firms, and households that relied solely on rigid protections—stockpiles, cash reserves, or temporary fixes—soon discovered their limits. Those that fared better were often those with diversified resources, strong social networks, and institutional trust that allowed for rapid adaptation. The pandemic revealed that resilience is not built by avoiding shocks but by having systems—financial and social—that can bend without breaking. *Security as resilience is not about building walls but weaving nets.*

Cultural traditions also highlight this distinction. In many Indigenous communities, wealth has historically been measured less by accumulation than by circulation—the ability to share, redistribute, and sustain the group. In these frameworks, security is guaranteed by relationships, reciprocity, and shared responsibility rather than by fortresses of personal wealth. Contrast this with the Western fixation on inheritance as protection, where fear of future vulnerability drives the obsessive guarding of assets. Both models aim at security, but only one prioritises resilience through community interdependence.

Resilience-oriented security stories can be integrated into modern financial life. For individuals, this might mean focusing less on maximising savings locked away and more on maintaining employable skills, health, and strong networks—resources that endure even when money evaporates. For organisations, it may mean prioritising adaptability over efficiency: keeping redundancies in supply chains, investing in staff training, and holding reputations built on trust rather than short-term profit. For states, it suggests that social safety nets, while costly, function as resilience infrastructure, enabling populations to absorb shocks without spiralling into crisis.

Critically, reframing security requires narrative change. Fear-based messages will always have a primal grip on the human psyche because they tap into survival instincts. Shifting towards resilience means cultivating a collective imagination that finds reassurance not in promises of absolute safety but in stories of endurance, renewal, and recovery. Literature and myth already provide ample material: from phoenixes rising from ashes to societies rebuilt after disaster, the human tradition is rich with tales that valorise resilience. These stories, if applied to finance, can shift expectations from invulnerability to adaptability.

One striking modern example comes from the growing popularity of financial independence movements. While some strands descend into extreme austerity rooted in fear of insecurity, the more constructive narratives focus on resilience—achieving flexibility, having the freedom to choose work, and the confidence to navigate economic turbulence. Here, financial security is not hoarded wealth but *the optionality that allows one to respond to life's unpredictability without panic.* Such a mindset is fundamentally different from the fear-based marketing of traditional financial products.

Ultimately, a society's dominant security stories reveal its relationship with uncertainty. A fear-based society equates uncertainty with disaster, constructing ever larger walls that paradoxically amplify vulnerability when the unexpected occurs. A resilience-based society accepts uncertainty as the natural state of affairs and invests in systems that make uncertainty survivable. The stories we choose to tell about protection, therefore, do not merely reflect our financial strategies; they shape our cultural identity. To choose resilience is to accept the fragility of human life without succumbing to paralysis, to build institutions and habits that honour adaptability as the true form of strength.

Healthy security stories, then, are not about denying fear but about refusing to let fear dictate the frame. They invite us to see insurance as continuity rather than calamity, savings as preparation rather than panic, and wealth as capacity rather than a fortress. By reframing security as resilience, individuals, families, and societies can liberate themselves from the exhausting and impossible task of seeking invulnerability. *The measure of true security is not how rarely one falls, but how surely one rises when one does.*

Chapter 13
Money as Identity

Few aspects of human life are as revealing as the way people use money to define themselves. A bank account is not merely a ledger of transactions; it is a script of choices, a catalogue of values, and a stage on which identity is performed. The clothes worn, the homes purchased, the experiences chosen or declined—each decision tells a story not only about means but about meaning. *Money does not simply buy things; it buys symbols, affiliations, and self-narratives.* What makes financial identity so powerful is not its abstraction but its daily visibility, expressed in decisions as small as a coffee order and as monumental as a mortgage.

Across cultures and centuries, money has been inseparable from the construction of identity. Consider the dowry systems that made wealth a prerequisite for honourable marriage, transforming gold and livestock into markers of family dignity. Or look to the ancient Roman elite, whose patronage of games and monuments broadcasted status far more loudly than private savings ever could. These practices were not incidental; they wove financial acts directly into the social fabric, embedding wealth within the definition of who one was and how one belonged. Today, luxury handbags, exclusive clubs, and curated Instagram feeds serve the same function. The names and symbols change, but the mechanism—using money to anchor identity—remains remarkably consistent.

Thorstein Veblen's concept of conspicuous consumption still resonates because it captures a truth too often ignored: spending is seldom neutral. When someone buys an expensive watch, the act communicates something beyond timekeeping. It signals belonging to a group, aspiration toward a lifestyle, or the cultivation of an image. In this sense, every purchase is an act of storytelling. Some stories strive for subtlety—craft beer signalling artisanal taste, eco-friendly cars conveying moral commitment—while others lean into spectacle. What unites them is their reliance on money as a vehicle for identity performance. *Consumption is less about the object itself than about the narrative it sustains.*

Yet these narratives are not always authentic. A financial identity built on external validation can be both fragile and exhausting. The pressure to maintain appearances often drives individuals into debt, working long hours not to secure essentials but to uphold an image crafted for others' consumption. Credit markets have learned to monetise this vulnerability: easy loans and instalment plans allow people to purchase identities they cannot afford. The result is not only economic strain but an identity crisis, where self-worth is tethered to possessions rather than personal conviction. In such cases, money ceases to be a tool and becomes a master, dictating identity rather than reflecting it.

Cultural comparisons illustrate how malleable financial identities can be. In Japan, the ethic of *mottainai*—a disdain for wastefulness—has historically shaped consumer behaviour, with thrift and durability seen as moral virtues. In contrast, American consumer culture has often valorised abundance, equating identity with acquisition and variety. Meanwhile, Scandinavian societies, influenced by the egalitarian spirit of the Law of Jante, often regard overt displays of wealth as socially suspect, tying identity to moderation rather than extravagance. These contrasts reveal that *financial identity is not merely personal; it is culturally coded, a dialogue between individual choice and collective norms.*

The digital age has intensified these dynamics. Social media platforms collapse traditional distinctions between public and private consumption, making every meal, outfit, or holiday a potential broadcast of identity. The performative aspect of money is amplified by algorithms that reward spectacle and aspiration. This environment accelerates the creation of identities tied not to lived reality but to curated presentation, encouraging financial decisions driven less by need or value than by the hunger for visibility. The marketplace and the stage have fused; the act of spending is simultaneously economic and theatrical.

Amid this complexity, the challenge is to cultivate financial identities that are both authentic and sustainable. Doing so requires a confrontation with the stories we inherit and the pressures we internalise. If one spends to signal belonging, what group is truly being joined? If purchases communicate values, are those values genuinely held or merely borrowed from cultural scripts? Reframing money as a means to express rather than to distort identity opens the possibility of alignment—where spending reinforces rather than undermines one's convictions.

Such alignment is not only a matter of personal satisfaction but of resilience. A financial identity grounded in authenticity provides a buffer against economic turbulence. When spending is tethered to core values—education, community, creativity, wellbeing—financial setbacks are less likely to dissolve self-worth. Conversely, when identity is staked on luxury or status, even minor losses can feel existential. *The healthier the narrative we attach to money, the more durable both our finances and our sense of self become.*

The task, then, is not to deny that money and identity are intertwined but to make that intertwining conscious and deliberate. Recognising that every transaction tells a story, individuals can begin to edit those stories with intention: choosing experiences over appearances, value over vanity, resilience over display. In doing so, they participate in a broader cultural shift, away from fear-driven and status-obsessed narratives and toward identities that reflect authentic values.

Money as identity is unavoidable, but it need not be corrosive. It can be a mirror of aspiration, a declaration of belonging, or a tool of self-expression. The question is whether the story it tells is one authored by us or imposed upon us. To understand money as identity is to grasp that our financial lives are inseparable from our personal lives, and that both can be rewritten with greater honesty, dignity, and coherence.

Who We Are, What We Spend

Every purchase carries a trace of autobiography. When someone chooses a local café over a global chain, buys a well-worn book from an independent shop rather than a glossy new copy online, or selects a practical family car instead of a sleek sports model, these choices narrate aspects of who they are—or who they aspire to be. *Spending is never just economic; it is expressive.* Money may appear to flow outward, but it leaves behind a pattern of signals that reveal identity, status, and belonging. Understanding this dynamic is not merely about consumer psychology; it is about recognising how financial behaviour weaves into the larger story of selfhood.

The idea that consumption expresses identity is not new. Anthropologists have long studied how objects serve as markers of culture, class, and aspiration. Pierre Bourdieu's concept of *distinction* captures how taste and spending habits reflect and reinforce social hierarchies. For Bourdieu, even seemingly trivial preferences—whether for opera or popular music, for fine dining or fast food—were loaded with symbolic meaning, demarcating boundaries of belonging and exclusion. This theoretical lens remains strikingly relevant today. A branded sneaker, a designer handbag, or an organic vegetable box may look like mundane transactions, but they operate as emblems within social systems, revealing how individuals align with—or resist—the expectations of their milieu.

What complicates matters is the tension between authenticity and performance. Few people consciously declare, "I buy this to signal who I am," yet purchases inevitably function as forms of self-presentation. The individual who invests heavily in home fitness equipment may well care about health, but the act also communicates discipline and modernity. The minimalist who prides themselves on owning little might insist on rejecting consumerism, but the choice itself is often a performance of purity and detachment that communicates just as loudly as the luxury brand they renounce. *Even renunciation becomes a kind of consumption, albeit one coded as virtue rather than extravagance.*

Modern advertising has institutionalised this process, blurring the line between what we buy and who we are. No longer do campaigns simply describe the utility of products; instead, they promise transformations of identity. A car is not marketed as a vehicle but as freedom, masculinity, or environmental conscience. A handbag is not presented as a container but as confidence, status, or taste. The product becomes secondary to the narrative it enables. In this sense, we are not merely consumers of goods but consumers of identities. The result is a market where selfhood is continuously constructed and reconstructed through transactions.

Globalisation has widened the stage for these performances. In many emerging economies, rapid access to global brands creates opportunities to adopt identities previously unavailable. A young professional in Lagos might wear European luxury labels as a declaration of cosmopolitan belonging, while a teenager in Jakarta might signal subcultural identity through Korean fashion imports. At the same time, localisation and counter-currents thrive: Nordic consumers emphasising sustainability, or indigenous communities reclaiming traditional crafts as symbols of identity against homogenised global markets. These contrasts remind us that *financial self-expression is both universal and deeply contextual, shaped by cultural scripts and economic structures alike.*

The digital revolution has intensified the visibility of financial choices. In a pre-digital world, consumption often remained semi-private, observed mainly by neighbours, colleagues, and family. Now, social media platforms turn spending into spectacle. Holidays, meals, fashion, and hobbies are shared instantly, making financial decisions part of a curated personal brand. The act of consumption becomes intertwined with the act of broadcasting. It is no longer enough to buy; one must be seen buying, or seen having bought. This accelerates the conversion of financial behaviour into identity performance, creating pressure not just to live but to live narratively.

Yet the relationship between spending and identity is not merely performative; it is also aspirational. Purchases often anticipate the person one hopes to become. A stack of unread books on a nightstand signals not current knowledge but desired erudition. Gym memberships unused past January reveal not present discipline but the aspiration toward fitness. This phenomenon illustrates how money functions as a bridge between present and imagined selves. *The story money tells is not only descriptive of who we are but projective of who we hope to be.* The gap between these two narratives—real and imagined identity—often fuels cycles of both motivation and disappointment.

The darker side of this dynamic lies in how financial systems exploit the fragility of identity. Easy credit allows individuals to perform identities beyond their means. Buy-now-pay-later schemes, targeted online advertising, and peer comparison culture encourage spending that exceeds capacity, all in pursuit of a self-image maintained through consumption. The pursuit of narrative coherence—wanting to appear successful, stylish, or generous—can lead to financial incoherence, where debt undermines the very security that identity construction depends upon. This reveals a paradox: the more one relies on purchases to express selfhood, the more vulnerable one becomes to economic manipulation.

Still, it would be reductive to see all spending as shallow performance. Financial choices can also be profound declarations of values. A family deciding to allocate resources to education rather than luxury goods signals a prioritisation of knowledge over display. An individual supporting local artisans rather than global chains communicates commitment to community resilience. A consumer who chooses ethically sourced products over cheaper alternatives affirms moral responsibility. These decisions show that money, far from corrupting identity, can serve as a powerful medium for aligning actions with convictions. *The key distinction is whether spending reinforces values or replaces them.*

The challenge for contemporary individuals is navigating a landscape where every financial decision is both private necessity and public statement. Housing choices reflect not only affordability but taste, status, and lifestyle. Food purchases carry implications about health, ethics, and social class. Even digital subscriptions—from streaming platforms to productivity apps—signal affiliations and self-image. In such a context, reflection becomes essential: are these expenditures deliberate expressions of self, or are they scripts written by marketers, peers, and cultural pressures?

Ultimately, to examine who we are by what we spend is to confront the interplay between autonomy and influence. Money offers agency, but it also invites manipulation. Financial decisions express identity, but they also expose it to external judgment. To spend consciously, therefore, is to take responsibility for one's narrative, choosing not only goods but the stories they sustain. It requires the courage to step outside of scripts—whether of status, rebellion, or conformity—and to craft a financial life that resonates with authentic values rather than borrowed ones.

Purchases may seem trivial, but they are chapters in a larger story of identity. The choice between fast fashion and enduring quality, between indulgence and restraint, between performance and authenticity—all shape the tale that money tells about us. The question is not whether money reflects identity but whether the reflection is one we recognise and embrace. By acknowledging this, we reclaim the possibility of making our spending not a hollow performance but a meaningful narrative of selfhood.

Cultural Status Tales: From dowries to luxury brands, money's role in identity

Money has never been only a medium of exchange; it has always been a language of status. Across cultures and centuries, wealth has operated as both an intimate and public performance of hierarchy, belonging, and aspiration. From the carefully negotiated dowries of ancient societies to the glossy storefronts of luxury fashion capitals today, financial resources are marshalled not simply to meet needs but to communicate worth. *Status is money's second skin*, and the stories societies tell about wealth often reveal more about identity than about economics.

The practice of dowry provides one of the clearest examples of this intertwining of wealth and identity. In South Asia, Europe, and parts of Africa, dowries functioned not merely as material transfers but as symbols of familial honour and social positioning. A lavish dowry could elevate a family's reputation, signalling generosity, stability, and prestige. A modest one might imply fragility, even if the bride's family was otherwise respectable. The dowry thus encoded the identity of not only the bride but her entire lineage. It was not simply wealth moving across households; it was a performance of continuity, legitimacy, and standing. The persistence of disputes over dowry, sometimes escalating into violence or litigation, underscores how profoundly these transactions shape social identity.

In pre-modern Europe, the dowry was equally central, not only as a form of inheritance but as a statement of dynastic ambition. Aristocratic families measured their influence in the size and splendour of dowries, using them to forge alliances and cement power. The Medici family, for instance, deployed dowries strategically to integrate their banking wealth into noble bloodlines, translating financial capital into cultural legitimacy. Here, money was not simply a resource to be spent but a tool for embedding identity within a broader network of recognition. The echoes of such practices linger in modern societies, where weddings—though rarely framed in the language of dowry—still function as grand displays of family status.

Fast forward to the twenty-first century, and the logic of status through wealth persists, albeit in new forms. The global luxury industry thrives on its ability to convert material goods into markers of prestige. A Hermès handbag, a Patek Philippe watch, or a Ferrari is rarely purchased for functionality alone. These items serve as potent signals of identity, affirming not only financial capacity but discernment, taste, and belonging to a particular cultural stratum. Thorstein Veblen's notion of *conspicuous consumption* remains strikingly apt: luxury goods are valuable not for what they are but for what they say about their owner. In this sense, the modern luxury brand operates as a globalised dowry, translating wealth into narratives of identity that others recognise and decode.

The comparison between dowries and luxury brands reveals a consistent truth: wealth expressions are never neutral. They are interpreted within cultural frameworks that imbue them with meaning. In India, for example, gold remains a central status marker, both as a financial asset and as a cultural symbol of purity and permanence. In China, conspicuous consumption often centres on gifting, where expensive alcohol, watches, or jade serve as tools of social reciprocity and prestige. In the United States, homeownership has long been mythologised as a marker of respectability and identity, symbolising both independence and civic belonging. Across contexts, *the form changes, but the function persists: wealth is translated into status through shared cultural codes.*

What complicates matters is the tension between authenticity and performance. A dowry may express devotion and honour, but it may also conceal coercion or social pressure. A luxury purchase may reflect genuine aesthetic appreciation, or it may mask insecurity and the desire for recognition. The ambiguity of these gestures is what makes them culturally powerful: they are never purely personal, nor purely performative, but an unstable mixture of both. This duality explains why debates around conspicuous consumption often carry moral undertones. The critique of lavish spending is rarely about the waste of money alone; it is about anxieties over identity, fairness, and social hierarchy.

Modern consumer culture has amplified the stakes. Social media ensures that displays of wealth circulate more widely than ever, turning personal choices into public performances. A luxury holiday or designer outfit posted online becomes a status tale consumed by thousands. The audience is no longer a wedding hall or a small community but a global stage. This visibility intensifies both aspiration and critique. On one hand, it democratises access to status narratives, enabling individuals without inherited privilege to craft identities through curated spending. On the other, it heightens the risks of exposure, fuelling resentment, comparison, and sometimes outright backlash against perceived excess.

The cultural narratives of status are not uniform. In Japan, subtlety and understatement often define elite consumption, with a preference for craftsmanship and discretion over loud branding. In contrast, in parts of Africa and Latin America, visible displays of wealth are integral to affirming success and redistributing prestige within communities. These differences remind us that *money's role in identity is not inherent but contextual, shaped by historical experience, cultural values, and social expectations.* To understand status spending is to understand the cultural scripts that give it meaning.

The moral dimension of status tales also demands attention. Historically, religious traditions have both condemned and sanctified wealth displays. In medieval Europe, the Catholic Church often criticised ostentatious spending while simultaneously benefiting from grand donations that signalled piety and ensured social prestige for patrons. In Islamic traditions, wealth is often balanced with the expectation of *zakat* (charitable giving), tying financial identity to moral obligation. These tensions remain visible today. Philanthropy by billionaires is framed not only as redistribution but as reputation management, a way of reframing personal wealth as collective benefit. Here, the act of giving becomes another status tale, one where generosity, not luxury, secures social legitimacy.

The persistence of these narratives raises a deeper question: do humans need wealth as a mirror of identity, or have we been conditioned to believe so? Psychological studies suggest that material symbols can provide a sense of belonging and recognition, but they also show diminishing returns. The satisfaction derived from status goods often fades quickly, replaced by new desires as social benchmarks shift. This endless pursuit risks trapping individuals in cycles of consumption that sustain identity externally rather than internally. *If who we are is always tethered to what we can display, we are perpetually vulnerable to the shifting tides of social recognition.*

And yet, there is an opportunity to rewrite these tales. Just as dowries evolved into different forms of familial and social expression, and luxury brands adapted to globalised markets, contemporary societies can reshape the narratives of status. Sustainable consumption, for instance, increasingly functions as a status signal, where restraint and responsibility carry prestige equal to, if not greater than, extravagance. Investing in education, health, or community initiatives may become new status tales, signalling depth of character rather than depth of pockets. The challenge is to recognise that money will always play a role in identity, but the story it tells need not be limited to hierarchy and display. It can also tell stories of responsibility, resilience, and authenticity.

Ultimately, cultural status tales—from dowries to luxury brands—remind us that money is never just financial. It is woven into the very fabric of identity, shaping how individuals are seen and how they see themselves. These tales endure because they offer a script for belonging, even as the props change. The question for modern readers is not whether to participate in such narratives but how to do so consciously, deciding whether their financial choices reinforce borrowed scripts of prestige or craft more meaningful stories of identity.

The Performance of Wealth: Explains Veblen's 'conspicuous consumption' as storytelling

Few ideas in economic thought have proved as enduring and provocative as Thorstein Veblen's notion of *conspicuous consumption.* First articulated in his 1899 book *The Theory of the Leisure Class*, it described the tendency of elites to spend not for necessity or utility, but to signal status, power, and cultural superiority. To wear an impractically fine suit, to throw an extravagant banquet, or to acquire an ornate but functionless trinket was, in Veblen's account, to make a performance out of wealth. What often goes unnoticed, however, is that this performance is not just an idle flourish—it is a form of storytelling. Each act of ostentatious consumption is a narrative, crafted for an audience, about who the spender is, who they aspire to be, and how they wish to be seen. *Wealth, when performed, becomes biography made visible.*

Consider the modern luxury car. From a purely functional perspective, most vehicles in advanced economies can provide safety, speed, and reliability. Yet to buy a Lamborghini or a Rolls-Royce is to participate in an elaborate form of self-expression. These cars are rarely about transport; they are about story. They narrate their owner as exceptional, victorious, or possessing refined taste. The car becomes a character in a tale the driver wishes others to read in passing. It is not the leather interior or horsepower alone that matters—it is the inscription of status into a shared cultural script. Without an audience capable of recognising the signal, the purchase loses much of its meaning. A Lamborghini in a desert with no onlookers is not a Lamborghini in the Veblenian sense; it is simply a fast, expensive machine.

This dependence on an audience highlights a key feature of conspicuous consumption: it is inherently theatrical. The wealthy are not only buying objects; they are staging identities. An expensive watch gleaming on a wrist at a business meeting says something more than "I can tell the time." It proclaims membership in a class of discernment, seriousness, or affluence. Similarly, a designer handbag carried into a restaurant operates as a silent script, narrating access, taste, and even moral qualities like discipline or sophistication. The story told may vary across cultures—what impresses in Paris may puzzle in Jakarta—but the logic is the same. Conspicuous consumption is a drama in which wealth is both the costume and the script.

What makes this performance compelling is that it is not always consciously manipulative. Many people who buy luxury goods or stage lavish weddings do not perceive themselves as actors; they are participating in cultural rituals whose scripts have been written long before them. Veblen argued that such consumption reflects "pecuniary emulation"—the tendency of individuals to imitate the spending patterns of those above them. Yet this is not a matter of raw envy so much as a desire to inhabit an existing narrative of respectability and success. The performance of wealth, in this sense, is as much about continuity as invention. Families may purchase large homes not simply for space, but because the house narrates a story of stability and permanence. Parents may fund costly private schooling not only for educational outcomes, but because such schools script their children into a tale of distinction.

Modern consumer capitalism has only amplified these dynamics. Social media platforms function as vast theatres of conspicuous consumption, turning private gestures into public broadcasts. A holiday in the Maldives, once shared with a handful of acquaintances, now becomes part of a curated digital story consumed by hundreds or thousands of followers. Each post is a chapter in a narrative of lifestyle, success, and identity. The performative aspect is heightened: consumption no longer merely whispers status across a dining table, it shouts it across a network. At the same time, the proliferation of digital influencers shows how consumption can itself become a livelihood, where narrating a life of apparent luxury translates into financial gain. Here, conspicuous consumption is not merely a story—it is a business model.

Yet not all performances of wealth are received as authentic. Audiences are critical. Excessive display can be read as vulgar, desperate, or fraudulent. A banker flaunting bonuses in the wake of a financial crisis may find his performance derided rather than admired. Similarly, counterfeit goods complicate the script: if a luxury bag can be faked, its storytelling power diminishes. The performance requires credibility, and when the audience no longer believes, the story collapses. This fragility underscores that conspicuous consumption is always negotiated. It depends on shared cultural codes, on trust in symbols, and on the tacit agreement of spectators to play along.

The historical dimension is equally revealing. In the early modern period, sumptuary laws in Europe attempted to regulate clothing and luxury, explicitly recognising that consumption was a visible marker of identity and hierarchy. Peasants were prohibited from dressing above their station, not for economic reasons but because their doing so disrupted the narrative order of society. Today, no such laws exist, but the underlying concern persists: who gets to tell certain stories with money, and who is excluded from them? When a middle-class family stretches to buy designer goods, they are attempting to access a narrative once reserved for elites. Their participation destabilises hierarchies but also perpetuates the cycle of status storytelling.

There is, however, another layer worth recognising. Conspicuous consumption not only tells others who we are; it tells ourselves. The act of buying an expensive dinner or attending an exclusive event often operates as self-narration, reinforcing one's identity internally. The spender does not simply perform wealth outwardly; they consume a story inwardly, convincing themselves of their place in a desired social script. This is why conspicuous consumption can be so psychologically potent—and why it can also be precarious. The self built on such performances requires constant reinforcement, vulnerable to comparison, critique, or financial disruption.

The philosophical question emerges: is conspicuous consumption inevitable in human societies, or is it a particular pathology of capitalism? Anthropological evidence suggests that the performance of wealth is far older than industrial capitalism. Ancient potlatch ceremonies among indigenous peoples of the Pacific Northwest involved chiefs giving away or destroying large quantities of goods to demonstrate power and prestige. The ritual made visible that true status lay not in hoarding but in the ability to give lavishly. In this sense, conspicuous consumption can take many forms, from accumulation to distribution, from ostentation to sacrifice. What unites them is not the object but the story. Wealth, when performed, narrates hierarchy, belonging, and identity, whether through gold-plated watches or ritual bonfires of blankets.

The contemporary challenge lies in the kinds of stories conspicuous consumption sustains. When a society valorises extravagance, it risks reinforcing narratives of inequality, fuelling envy, and corroding solidarity. Yet conspicuous consumption can also be harnessed for constructive ends. The rise of eco-luxury goods, where wealth is performed through sustainability—electric cars, ethical fashion, carbon-neutral estates—demonstrates how the logic of performance can be redirected. Here, the story told is not only "I am wealthy" but "I am responsible." The storytelling power of consumption, in other words, can evolve, offering scripts that align with broader social values rather than undermine them.

Veblen's insight remains indispensable because it reframes consumption as narrative rather than transaction. The wealthy are not simply buyers; they are authors of stories written in currency and objects, stories that audiences read, critique, and replicate. To understand conspicuous consumption is to see economic life not as a ledger of numbers but as a theatre of meaning. *When money performs, it speaks in stories, and those stories shape the identities of both individuals and societies.*

Writing a Truer Financial Identity: Suggests ways to align spending with authentic values

Every act of spending, whether deliberate or casual, tells a story about who we are. A cup of takeaway coffee purchased daily might narrate convenience and routine, while a carefully chosen book or a charitable donation speaks of priorities more deeply tied to identity. The paradox is that much of this storytelling occurs unconsciously, shaped by advertising, cultural scripts, and inherited assumptions about what is valuable. To write a truer financial identity requires more than budgeting techniques or abstract theories of personal finance. It demands a conscious interrogation of what our money is already saying on our behalf, and a willingness to edit that script until it reflects our own values rather than someone else's.

The first step in understanding the relationship between money and identity is to acknowledge that spending is rarely neutral. Economists often describe consumption as the fulfilment of needs, but anthropologists see it as the performance of meaning. A wedding ring is not simply metal and stone—it is a public declaration of commitment. A child's education is not merely a transaction in services but a statement about future horizons. Even the choice of supermarket brands reflects affiliations, signalling thrift, discernment, or solidarity with local producers. *What we buy and how we save are not just economic acts; they are narrative acts.* Recognising this narrative dimension gives us the tools to question whether the stories our finances tell are ones we truly want authored in our name.

In practice, many of these stories are inherited rather than chosen. A family may have grown up believing that debt is shameful, while another considers it a natural stepping stone to opportunity. Some cultures invest heavily in communal celebrations, seeing them as duties of honour, while others prioritise individual accumulation. Marketing exploits these embedded narratives, amplifying insecurity and aspiration. Luxury advertisements rarely dwell on the material properties of a handbag or watch; they craft narratives of elegance, belonging, and superiority. The consumer buys not the leather or the mechanism, but the script in which they play the leading role. To resist manipulation, one must first uncover the extent to which one's financial identity is borrowed rather than authored.

This raises the critical question of authenticity. Authenticity in financial life is not about asceticism or self-denial; it is about coherence between one's values and one's economic choices. If someone believes strongly in environmental stewardship, yet regularly invests in industries that accelerate climate change, there is a rupture between belief and financial behaviour. If another values generosity yet structures their life around fear of scarcity, the contradiction undermines both peace of mind and integrity. *Authenticity emerges not when one spends less or more, but when one spends in alignment with what one claims to stand for.* The task is not to erase consumption, but to ensure it supports rather than erodes the identity one seeks to inhabit.

Examples of this principle are increasingly visible in modern financial trends. The growth of ethical investment funds reflects a desire to reconcile financial returns with broader social commitments. The rise of minimalism, with its emphasis on quality over quantity, is partly a pushback against identities diluted by clutter and overstimulation. Even the increasing popularity of experiences over possessions can be seen as a recalibration of narrative: to travel, learn, and create memories is to foreground stories of growth and connection rather than accumulation. Each of these trends, though sometimes co-opted by commercial forces, reveals a widespread yearning to write financial stories that resonate more closely with genuine values.

Yet aligning money with identity is not without tension. Sometimes values themselves conflict. A parent may value frugality but also wish to provide their child with costly educational opportunities. A professional may desire financial independence while also valuing generosity to family members. These tensions are not evidence of hypocrisy; they are evidence of complexity. The task is to navigate them consciously, to prioritise without losing sight of the plural nature of values. In this sense, writing a truer financial identity is not a one-off declaration but an ongoing editorial process. Like any serious manuscript, it requires revisions, redrafting, and the occasional deletion of chapters that no longer serve the larger narrative.

One useful lens is to treat money not as an end but as a medium of expression. If money is a language, then each expenditure is a sentence, each investment a paragraph, and the whole of one's financial life a story. To ask "What does my spending say about me?" is akin to reading one's own diary aloud. Does it reflect care for others? Does it narrate curiosity, security, or creativity? Or does it tell a story dominated by anxiety, imitation, or contradiction? This self-examination, though often uncomfortable, can be transformative. *When we read our financial story with fresh eyes, we can choose to rewrite it.*

The rewriting process requires both imagination and discipline. Imagination allows individuals to conceive of financial identities beyond the ones marketed to them. Discipline ensures that intentions become practices. For instance, someone who wishes to narrate themselves as a patron of local culture might commit to spending part of their disposable income on independent businesses or community projects. Another who seeks to tell a story of resilience might prioritise building an emergency fund, not out of fear but out of a desire to embody steadiness in turbulent times.

These are not abstract strategies; they are practical edits to the financial manuscript of life.

At the societal level, the collective stories we tell about money also shape individual possibilities. In cultures where financial worth is equated with moral worth, it is difficult to write an authentic financial identity that privileges community or simplicity without social resistance. By contrast, in societies that celebrate moderation, thrift, or shared prosperity, individuals find greater freedom to align money with their chosen values. This interplay underscores that authenticity is not only a personal project but also a cultural negotiation. To write a truer financial identity is to resist or adapt cultural scripts as much as to craft personal ones.

Ultimately, the goal is not to achieve a perfect alignment—such a state is illusory—but to cultivate integrity in the face of complexity. Money will always carry the weight of competing demands, shifting contexts, and cultural pressures. But when individuals consistently return to the question, "Does this financial decision reflect who I truly am and wish to be?" they ensure that their economic life is not dictated by inherited myths or manipulative marketing. *They become the authors of their own financial story, rather than characters written by others.*

The pursuit of a truer financial identity is not a luxury reserved for the wealthy. It matters as much for the student choosing between fast fashion and sustainable clothing as it does for the executive balancing investments and philanthropy. It matters in everyday groceries, in the shaping of debt, in the structuring of work-life balance. Wherever money circulates, identity is at stake. To treat money merely as a tool of exchange is to overlook its deeper role as a mirror of the self. To treat it as a narrative device is to reclaim the power to tell stories that ring true.

Authenticity in finance, then, is less about numbers than about narratives. It is about ensuring that the material record of one's life aligns with the moral and personal convictions that give it meaning. Each purchase, each saving habit, each gift becomes a line in a story worth owning. The reward of this alignment is not only financial clarity but existential coherence: the knowledge that the story our money tells about us is, finally, one we recognise as our own.

Chapter 14
The Marketplace of Morals

Few aspects of human life are judged with as much suspicion, admiration, and contradiction as the making of money. Trade, the oldest and most enduring of human exchanges, has always been accompanied by moral commentary. Merchants have been hailed as innovators, builders of prosperity, and bridges between cultures. Yet the same figures have also been derided as cheats, profiteers, or symbols of greed. This oscillation reflects an ancient truth: commerce has never been a purely economic act. It is also a moral drama, in which every price, every profit, every bargain is weighed against questions of fairness, exploitation, and virtue. To pretend otherwise—to treat markets as neutral arenas of supply and demand divorced from values—is not only naïve but historically inaccurate.

Consider the seemingly simple question: is profit ever pure? For centuries, societies have drawn lines between fair and unfair gain, often with passionate disagreement. In the medieval bazaars of Europe, local guilds regulated not just the quality of goods but also the margin of profit deemed acceptable. Islamic jurisprudence established detailed rules against unjust enrichment, embedding trade within a larger moral framework. Even in modern capitalist economies, where deregulation is celebrated, debates over "windfall profits," executive compensation, and tax avoidance reveal how instinctively people attach ethical weight to economic outcomes. *To earn is not merely to receive; it is to be judged.*

Religious traditions have been particularly influential in shaping the moral imagination of finance. The Hebrew Bible warned against charging interest to the poor, framing debt as a tool of oppression. Christianity, through centuries of canon law, denounced usury as a sin, seeing it as profit extracted without labour or risk. Islam continues to prohibit riba, a prohibition that has spurred the creation of vast alternative financial systems. Across these traditions, money was never morally inert: its use could elevate or corrupt, redeem or condemn. To lend, to invest, to speculate—all were seen not just as technical activities but as spiritual ones, carrying consequences for the soul as much as the ledger.

These moral concerns are not relics of the past. They re-emerge every time financial innovation disrupts existing norms. When payday lenders charge triple-digit interest rates to desperate workers, critics reach for the language of exploitation, echoing medieval anxieties about usury. When multinational corporations shift profits to tax havens, citizens instinctively frame the act not merely as legal manoeuvring but as a violation of social trust. When luxury brands charge extraordinary sums for items manufactured cheaply, questions of value and deception cut through the glamour. Each controversy reminds us that commerce cannot be disentangled from the moral frameworks societies use to interpret it.

Cultural narratives of wealth, too, reveal the ambivalence at the heart of economic life. In ancient Rome, merchants were often treated with disdain, viewed as socially inferior to landowners. Yet the fortunes they accumulated fuelled the empire's expansion. In Confucian China, scholars were placed above traders in the social hierarchy, but the prosperity of markets proved indispensable for dynastic stability. Even today, entrepreneurs are celebrated as visionaries in one breath and condemned as monopolists in the next. *We oscillate between venerating wealth as evidence of genius and condemning it as proof of exploitation.* This ambivalence underscores the reality that money is never interpreted in a vacuum; it is always judged through cultural lenses of honour, morality, and fairness.

What makes these moral narratives especially potent is their persistence. A medieval sermon denouncing avarice and a twenty-first-century debate on corporate social responsibility may seem far apart, yet both spring from the same concern: the fear that financial systems left unchecked erode the bonds of trust that hold societies together. The language may shift from "sin" to "regulation," but the underlying anxiety remains. People want assurance that their economic lives do not corrode their moral ones.

This chapter invites readers to confront these questions directly. Instead of treating financial systems as separate from ethics, it positions them as deeply entangled. We will examine stories of fair and unfair trade, from biblical injunctions to modern controversies, and consider how religious traditions have shaped enduring narratives about money, sin, and exploitation. We will explore the cultural judgments societies have placed upon merchants and entrepreneurs, showing how ambivalence continues to shape our collective understanding of wealth. And finally, we will consider how to reclaim moral narratives of finance, asking whether it is possible to align the pursuit of profit with the pursuit of integrity.

The argument is not that finance must be sanitised of ambition or risk—such a demand would be both impossible and undesirable. Rather, it is that financial practices must be re-situated within the wider moral stories that give them legitimacy. *To act in the marketplace is to act in the moral sphere, whether or not one acknowledges it.* The true challenge, then, is not to escape morality but to choose which moral frameworks will guide our economic lives.

What the reader will gain from this exploration is not a simple formula for ethical finance—no such formula exists—but a set of sharper questions, historical insights, and conceptual tools for navigating the marketplace with integrity. By the end, the ambition is that each reader can recognise the moral narratives already shaping their economic world and consciously participate in rewriting them. For whether one is a consumer, investor, policymaker, or entrepreneur, one is also a storyteller, and the stories we tell about money carry consequences far beyond the balance sheet.

Is Profit Ever Pure?

Profit, at its simplest, is the surplus left when revenues exceed costs. Yet this definition, precise in an accountant's ledger, dissolves under moral scrutiny. For centuries, societies have asked whether profit is ever entirely legitimate, free from exploitation, or whether it always carries some trace of asymmetry—of someone winning more than another loses. What looks like efficient exchange in one narrative can appear as unjust gain in another. The question, then, is not only economic but ethical: can profit be pure?

Ancient societies grappled with this tension long before modern capitalism sharpened its edges. Aristotle distinguished between *oikonomia*, the management of household resources for sustenance, and *chrematistics*, the pursuit of wealth for its own sake. The latter he regarded with suspicion, seeing in it a departure from natural needs towards artificial accumulation. This philosophical unease foreshadowed debates that persist today: when does profit signal ingenuity and service, and when does it drift into exploitation? The very distinction between fair and unfair gain is as old as markets themselves.

Religious traditions encoded these anxieties in rules and prohibitions. Medieval Christian canon law restricted usury, not simply out of dogma but from the belief that money should not breed money without labour. Islamic finance, in its enduring rejection of riba, continues to structure systems that frame profit as just only when it is tied to risk-sharing and tangible assets. Jewish teachings, too, tempered commercial exchange with ethical constraints, particularly when dealing with the vulnerable. In each case, *profit was not denied, but it was bounded.* The moral community sought to draw a line between fair recompense for effort and exploitation cloaked as enterprise.

Such boundaries were never fixed, however, and they shifted with context. In medieval marketplaces, guilds regulated not only the quality of goods but also the permissible margins traders could charge. A cobbler could profit from his craft, but exorbitant prices risked social censure. This was not simply about protecting buyers; it was about preserving the moral fabric of a community. Profit, in this worldview, was not a solitary achievement but a social relationship, and its legitimacy depended on collective judgement.

Modern capitalism reframed profit as a mark of efficiency and innovation, often detaching it from the ethical conversations that once constrained it. Yet even in the contemporary world, claims of "pure" profit rarely stand unchallenged. The debate over pharmaceutical pricing illustrates this vividly. When a life-saving drug is priced beyond the reach of the majority, defenders argue that high prices fund research and reward innovation, while critics see it as profiteering at the expense of human dignity. The same balance sheet, depending on the story told, can symbolise progress or moral failure. *Profit is never only numbers; it is narrative.*

Case studies from financial crises reinforce the fragility of claims to purity. During the 2008 collapse, banks defended complex mortgage-backed securities as efficient instruments of risk distribution. Yet when those instruments unravelled, the profits extracted in prior years came to be seen as gains built on systemic deception. What had once been heralded as innovation was reframed as exploitation. The reinterpretation of those profits—first as legitimate, later as illegitimate—demonstrates how the moral status of gain is always provisional, subject to re-evaluation in the court of public opinion.

Contrast this with businesses that deliberately anchor their profits within narratives of fairness. The rise of fair-trade certification in commodities such as coffee and chocolate reflects a consumer desire for profits to be shared equitably across supply chains. While sceptics argue about its efficacy, the movement itself reveals something profound: that profit is legitimised not only by its size but by the story of its distribution. Consumers increasingly demand not just cheaper goods but cleaner consciences, seeking assurance that their purchases do not enrich one party at the unjust expense of another.

The cultural ambivalence about merchants, present since antiquity, continues to colour debates today. In some societies, entrepreneurial wealth is lionised as evidence of vision and courage. In others, it is treated with suspicion, the sign of cunning rather than virtue. The same billionaire can be framed as a philanthropist reshaping the world or a monopolist hoarding resources. *Profit is a mirror in which societies project their anxieties, aspirations, and moral codes.* Its purity or impurity often lies less in the numbers themselves than in the interpretations layered upon them.

One of the most striking examples of this interpretive flexibility lies in the digital economy. Companies like Facebook or Google generate extraordinary profits by monetising user data. Defenders hail these profits as the fruits of innovation, providing services for free while creating new industries. Critics contend that the profits are "impure," extracted from surveillance, behavioural manipulation, and the erosion of privacy. The debate illustrates a deeper truth: the pureness of profit cannot be separated from the question of what, precisely, is being commodified and whether society consents to that commodification.

Philosophically, one might argue that pure profit is an illusion. Every exchange involves unequal information, shifting power, or contextual constraints that shape the terms of trade. Yet to embrace such cynicism entirely would be to erase the possibility of legitimate gain. A more balanced view sees profit as morally contingent. It can be closer to purity when it arises from genuine value creation—solving problems, meeting needs, innovating responsibly—and further from purity when it depends on deception, coercion, or the exploitation of asymmetry.

The challenge, then, is not to search for an unattainable ideal of "pure" profit but to refine the frameworks by which societies distinguish fair from unfair gain. This requires continual negotiation between markets, laws, and moral imagination. Regulations can set boundaries, but they cannot by themselves confer legitimacy. Cultural narratives, religious traditions, and civic debates all play a role in shaping how profits are judged. What is deemed fair in one generation may be condemned in the next, and vice versa. Profit, in this sense, is always provisional: its moral standing depends on the stories we agree to tell about it.

Seen in this light, the question "is profit ever pure?" is less about a definitive answer and more about a diagnostic tool. It compels us to examine the moral scaffolding of economic life, to ask not only *how much* is earned but *how* it is earned and at whose expense. It reminds us that profit cannot escape judgement because it exists within a web of relationships—between buyer and seller, investor and worker, present and future. And it challenges us to accept that the purity of profit is not a fixed state but an ongoing negotiation between ethics, culture, and commerce.

For the intelligent reader navigating today's global economy, this recognition matters. It reframes profit not as a neutral surplus but as a contested space where values, narratives, and interests converge. Whether one is an entrepreneur, policymaker, or consumer, the implication is the same: profit cannot be passively received. It must be continually interrogated, its sources scrutinised, its uses evaluated.

Only then can societies hope to distinguish between gains that sustain the common good and those that corrode it. And perhaps, in that distinction, lies the closest we may come to answering the question of whether profit can ever truly be pure.

Money and Sin

Few subjects reveal the moral unease of human societies more sharply than the act of charging interest. To many modern observers, lending at interest seems natural, even indispensable to functioning economies. Yet across history and civilisations, the practice has been repeatedly cast as sinful, predatory, and corrosive to the moral fabric of community life. The condemnation of usury is not simply a matter of finance; it reflects deep anxieties about power, justice, and the proper ordering of human relations. By scrutinising how religions have framed interest and exploitation, we uncover not only historical prohibitions but also enduring questions about whether money can ever truly be neutral.

The Hebrew Bible provides some of the earliest and most influential prohibitions. In Deuteronomy and Exodus, lending to fellow Israelites at interest is explicitly forbidden, though lending to outsiders is treated differently. This asymmetry reveals how the prohibition was embedded in notions of kinship and covenant: to exploit a brother in need was a betrayal of divine trust, while extracting profit from foreigners was framed as less morally fraught. Debt forgiveness, enshrined in the Jubilee year, underscored the principle that wealth should never become an instrument of permanent domination. The biblical condemnation of usury thus reflects not only economic restraint but a vision of community in which money was subordinated to divine justice.

Early Christianity absorbed and radicalised this suspicion. The Church Fathers warned that usury corrupted both lender and borrower, reducing human relationships to mere transactions. By the Middle Ages, canon law enshrined prohibitions on interest as a form of theft—profit without labour. Thomas Aquinas, drawing on Aristotelian thought, argued that money is sterile, a medium of exchange rather than a source of intrinsic growth. To demand interest on money was, in his eyes, to demand payment for something that did not exist. The force of this moral argument was so strong that even when economic realities made lending indispensable, financial actors had to devise elaborate workarounds—contracts disguised as partnerships, fees framed as penalties, or clever distinctions between "interest" and "compensation for risk." The ingenuity of medieval finance illustrates how moral prohibitions did not eradicate profit-seeking but redirected it into more complex, sometimes opaque, forms.

Islamic finance developed its own robust critique of usury, encapsulated in the prohibition of *riba.* The Qur'an condemns doubling and redoubling of debts, presenting it as a manifestation of greed and injustice. In Islamic jurisprudence, the problem is not simply the level of interest but the very idea of guaranteed, risk-free profit. Legitimate trade requires risk-sharing: profit and loss must be borne jointly, reflecting a principle of fairness rooted in divine will. This framework continues to shape contemporary Islamic banking, which emphasises instruments such as *mudarabah* (profit-sharing partnerships) and *murabaha* (cost-plus financing) as alternatives to conventional interest-bearing loans. What might appear to outsiders as mere legal formalism is, within the tradition, a deeply moral stance: that finance must be tethered to real economic activity and reciprocal responsibility.

While Jewish, Christian, and Islamic traditions share a scepticism of usury, their treatments of exploitation extend beyond interest alone. The Hebrew prophets denounced unjust weights and measures, reminding merchants that cheating buyers was no less sinful than charging exploitative loans. The Christian Gospels, too, portray Christ driving money changers from the temple, signalling that finance could desecrate sacred space when it crossed into exploitation. Islamic teachings warn against *gharar*—excessive uncertainty or deception in contracts—further reinforcing the moral imperative of transparency and fairness in financial dealings. Across these traditions, *money becomes sinful when it is detached from reciprocity, honesty, and the dignity of human need.*

The persistence of these prohibitions across centuries raises a pressing question: why have human societies so often equated financial exploitation with sin? Part of the answer lies in the asymmetry of power inherent in lending. When one party is desperate and another controls surplus, the risk of coercion is high. Religious authorities, seeking to protect the vulnerable, drew hard lines around lending, transforming what might appear as neutral contracts into moral battlegrounds. Usury became symbolic of avarice unchecked by compassion, a sin not against efficiency but against fraternity.

Yet the march of capitalism altered these boundaries. By the Renaissance, growing trade and the emergence of banking challenged rigid prohibitions. The Medicis in Florence, for instance, operated in tension with Church doctrine, legitimising their wealth by patronage of the arts and service to civic life. In Protestant regions, attitudes began to shift more explicitly. Max Weber famously argued that the Protestant ethic, with its valorisation of disciplined work and reinvestment, laid the cultural foundations for capitalism's embrace of profit. Interest, once condemned, was gradually reframed as a legitimate return for time preference, risk, and opportunity cost. The theological framing of money as sin gave way to a secularised narrative of money as neutral capital.

Still, the older moral frameworks never fully disappeared. Modern debates about payday lending, credit card debt, and predatory mortgages echo the biblical and Qur'anic anxieties about exploitation. Critics denounce triple-digit annual percentage rates as usury by another name, exploiting the desperation of those with few alternatives. Advocates defend them as providing access to credit for underserved communities. The arguments mirror ancient tensions: is interest a fair price for risk, or does it become sinful when it takes advantage of vulnerability? These debates remind us that the language of sin, though less visible in secular economies, continues to shape our intuitions about fairness.

Consider also the controversy surrounding student loans in the United States. With outstanding balances exceeding a trillion dollars, many borrowers feel trapped in obligations that limit life choices—marriage, home ownership, family formation. Religious traditions would not struggle to categorise this: to burden the young with unpayable debts in exchange for access to education would be viewed as a structural form of exploitation. The fact that such lending is legal does not dissolve its moral ambiguity. Once again, the ancient suspicion of debt as bondage reverberates in contemporary settings.

At the same time, the modern financial system has sought ways to frame lending as socially constructive. Microfinance institutions, for example, position themselves as vehicles of empowerment, offering small loans to the poor in developing countries. Yet even here, questions of morality surface. While many borrowers have benefited, cases of over-indebtedness and coercive collection practices have sparked criticism. What began as a celebrated innovation for development has in some contexts replicated the very dynamics of exploitation it aimed to remedy. The fact that such institutions often invoke the language of empowerment and dignity highlights how, even now, finance must borrow from moral vocabularies to defend itself.

The interplay of religion, finance, and morality extends beyond interest into broader narratives of sin and virtue. Prosperity theology within certain Christian movements, for instance, recasts wealth itself as a sign of divine favour, softening earlier suspicions of profit. Conversely, strands of liberation theology in Latin America treat structural poverty and exploitation as sins perpetuated by unjust financial systems. Islam, too, wrestles with modern financial engineering, seeking to balance compliance with *sharia* against participation in global capital markets. These debates reveal a common thread: money cannot escape moral interrogation. Whether condemned as sinful or sanctified as virtuous, it is always judged in relation to human well-being and divine order.

The enduring lesson across traditions is that interest, usury, and exploitation are not merely technical matters but reflections of deeper questions: What does it mean to treat others justly in conditions of economic inequality? When does the pursuit of gain undermine solidarity? Can financial contracts ever be morally neutral, or are they inevitably moral acts dressed in economic language? By framing these questions in terms of sin, religions remind us that finance is not just about efficiency but about justice, not just about growth but about dignity.

For the contemporary reader, living in societies where credit pervades daily life, these lessons are not antiquarian curiosities but urgent reminders. The fact that charging interest is legal does not absolve us from asking whether it is fair. The fact that exploitation can be profitable does not make it defensible. To read money through the lens of sin is to recover a moral vocabulary that refuses to treat finance as a world apart from human responsibility. It suggests that the purity of profit, the legitimacy of debt, and the morality of markets are not questions settled by law or economics alone but by the ethical commitments that communities choose to uphold.

Money and sin, then, are not opposites but entangled realities. Finance carries the potential to enable flourishing or to deepen bondage, and societies have long known that the difference between the two is measured not only in numbers but in justice. The prohibitions of the past, whether biblical, Qur'anic, or ecclesiastical, may no longer bind in the same form, but their essence endures: *that wealth gained through exploitation is never merely gain but a distortion of what it means to live rightly with others.* This recognition—ancient and yet startlingly relevant—demands that we continue to interrogate money not only as capital but as a moral force shaping the very soul of society.

Cultural Judgments of Wealth

Few figures in human history embody ambivalence as sharply as the merchant. Across cultures, merchants have been both lauded as the lifeblood of prosperity and denounced as parasites who profit without producing. They have been celebrated as pioneers who connect societies through trade routes and condemned as corrupters who thrive on greed. This oscillation is not incidental but reveals something fundamental: wealth accumulation and exchange touch the deepest cultural nerves about fairness, virtue, and the meaning of human labour. Examining how societies have judged wealth and its agents shows us how moral, political, and economic narratives are inseparably bound.

The Greeks of antiquity already wrestled with the duality of trade. Aristotle drew sharp distinctions between *oikonomia*—the natural management of household resources—and *chrematistics*, the pursuit of wealth for its own sake. While the farmer and craftsman were seen as honourable for producing tangible goods, the merchant's profit was suspect, arising from the manipulation of exchange rather than the creation of value. Commerce was tolerated as necessary but rarely revered as noble. Yet paradoxically, it was the merchant fleets of city-states like Athens that fuelled their military and cultural ascendancy. Even in societies that disparaged the merchant class, their success underpinned collective flourishing. The contradiction was never fully resolved.

Roman society shared this ambivalence. The patrician elite idealised land ownership as the highest form of wealth, considering commerce beneath the dignity of a gentleman. Senators were forbidden from direct involvement in trade, even as vast fortunes were quietly amassed through intermediaries. The disdain for merchants contrasted sharply with Rome's dependence on their networks for supplying armies, cities, and colonies. The cultural judgment of wealth was thus double-edged: merchants might be essential, but their pursuit of profit was imagined as morally tainted compared to the rootedness and stability of agricultural wealth.

Religious traditions reinforced this tension. In medieval Europe, shaped by Christian doctrine, merchants occupied a precarious moral space. On the one hand, itinerant traders were often depicted as dishonest, associated with trickery, price manipulation, and exploitation. On the other hand, the great merchant families—such as the Medici in Florence or the Fugger in Augsburg—became patrons of art, education, and political stability, embedding themselves into the very identity of their societies. Their wealth bought suspicion but also legitimacy, as they recast their commercial gains into civic and cultural capital. *The merchant was redeemed not by trade itself but by what he did with the fruits of trade.*

Islamic societies of the medieval period offer a contrasting perspective. The Prophet Muhammad himself was a merchant, and commerce enjoyed a degree of honour absent in contemporary European contexts. Markets were celebrated as spaces of exchange blessed by divine sanction, provided they operated under principles of fairness and transparency. Yet even within this framework, suspicion of excess remained. Hoarding and profiteering during times of scarcity were condemned as violations of communal trust. Thus, while Islamic culture afforded merchants a more dignified role, wealth remained under constant moral scrutiny. The merchant was honoured when embodying trust and fairness but rebuked when veering towards exploitation.

The rise of mercantilism in early modern Europe marked another shift. States began to view merchants less as social outcasts and more as strategic assets, capable of expanding national wealth and influence. Maritime traders, chartered companies, and financiers were instrumental in building empires. Yet admiration for their audacity coexisted with criticism of their methods: the East India Company symbolised both the grandeur of global commerce and the violence, monopoly, and exploitation that underpinned it. The merchant became a symbol of national pride and imperial overreach simultaneously, reinforcing the sense that wealth was never judged in purely economic terms but always through a moral and political lens.

In the modern era, the oscillation persists. Capitalist societies often celebrate entrepreneurs as embodiments of innovation, risk-taking, and meritocratic achievement. Silicon Valley founders, Wall Street financiers, and global tycoons are heralded in some narratives as visionaries shaping the future. Yet in moments of crisis—financial crashes, corporate scandals, or glaring inequality—the same figures are vilified as symbols of corruption and moral decay. The 2008 financial crisis exemplified this swing: bankers who had been lionised as architects of prosperity were suddenly branded as reckless exploiters whose greed plunged millions into hardship. Societal judgment shifted almost overnight, illustrating how fragile the legitimacy of wealth remains.

What makes merchants uniquely vulnerable to these oscillations is that they deal in intangibles: risk, trust, information, and opportunity. Unlike artisans or farmers, their contribution is less visible, and their profit appears detached from labour. This opacity fuels suspicion. Yet precisely because their work relies on bridging gaps and creating connections, they are also indispensable. Merchants embody the paradox of wealth itself: necessary, powerful, transformative, yet always morally contested.

The cultural judgments of wealth also extend beyond merchants to wider debates about inequality and legitimacy. In East Asian societies influenced by Confucian ideals, merchants historically ranked lower than scholars, farmers, and artisans in the moral hierarchy. Yet in practice, wealthy merchant families often wielded substantial influence, sometimes even purchasing official titles. The dissonance between ideological disdain and practical dependence reflects a universal theme: societies may condemn the pursuit of wealth rhetorically while relying on it structurally.

Contemporary consumer culture provides a modern analogue. Luxury brands, advertising, and celebrity endorsements transform merchants into curators of aspiration. Far from being disparaged, many merchants are celebrated as tastemakers and cultural leaders. Yet beneath the glossy surface, critics question the morality of such wealth: are these not modern forms of conspicuous consumption, reinforcing inequality and shallow status competition? The judgment swings once again, with wealth treated as both cultural capital and social liability.

The oscillation between celebration and condemnation reveals an enduring truth: *wealth is never judged in isolation but always in relation to the values of the society that beholds it.* When merchants are seen as serving the community, expanding opportunity, or embodying fairness, they are elevated to symbols of progress. When they are perceived as hoarders, exploiters, or manipulators, they are condemned as corruptors of virtue. The pendulum swings not simply because of the actions of merchants themselves but because wealth touches on anxieties about justice, power, and the moral limits of gain.

This insight matters profoundly today. As global inequality widens, debates about billionaires, corporate responsibility, and the ethics of profit intensify. Are the tech titans of Silicon Valley modern visionaries lifting humanity or monopolists distorting democracy? Are financial innovators democratizing access to credit or exploiting the vulnerable through opaque systems? These questions echo the same judgments that societies have cast upon merchants for millennia. To examine cultural judgments of wealth is to recognise that the marketplace has always been a moral stage, where applause and condemnation intertwine.

What we learn from this long history is not that societies should decide once and for all whether merchants are heroes or villains but that *wealth itself is a narrative battleground.* Merchants do not simply trade goods; they trade in meanings, embodying competing visions of virtue and vice. Their fortunes rise and fall not only with markets but with the shifting tides of cultural judgment. To understand this oscillation is to see clearly that the moral story of wealth is inseparable from the human story of what we choose to honour, what we choose to condemn, and what we expect from those who carry the burdens and privileges of prosperity.

Reclaiming Moral Narratives of Finance

Finance has always been more than numbers. It has carried moral weight, even when institutions and individuals have tried to disguise it behind technical jargon or mathematical inevitability. The way money is earned, distributed, and invested has historically been a matter of profound ethical scrutiny. Societies have praised fair exchange and condemned exploitation; religions have imposed rules on lending and warned against greed; communities have celebrated generosity and frowned upon avarice. Yet in the contemporary world, finance often appears detached from this moral heritage. Technical language, algorithmic trading, and a relentless emphasis on quarterly returns make it easy to forget that financial practices are embedded in stories about what is right, just, and worthy. To reclaim moral narratives of finance is not to turn back the clock nostalgically but to insist that finance cannot be separated from ethics without losing its legitimacy.

What makes this task urgent is that financial systems are now more powerful than ever, shaping the lives of billions. From the mortgages that determine where families live, to the pensions that secure retirements, to the credit that underpins entrepreneurship, finance is woven into the fabric of everyday existence. Yet when asked who benefits, who bears the risks, and whose voices set the rules, the answers often reveal asymmetries of power and justice. *The narratives we tell about finance matter, because they either legitimise these structures or challenge them.* When the story emphasises efficiency, self-interest, and technical neutrality, it leaves little space for moral reflection. But when the story foregrounds fairness, resilience, and community, finance can be reimagined as a force for shared well-being rather than private extraction.

The roots of moral narratives in finance can be traced back to ancient traditions. Aristotle's suspicion of usury was not a rejection of commerce altogether but a critique of practices that generated profit without productive contribution. In the Christian tradition, medieval prohibitions on charging interest were grounded in the idea that money, as a sterile medium, should not breed money without labour. Islamic finance today embodies a similar concern, structuring contracts to avoid exploitative asymmetry between lender and borrower. These examples demonstrate that financial practices have always been subject to moral boundaries, shaped by cultural convictions about justice. Modern finance often frames itself as amoral, but this too is a narrative choice: it replaces old ethical concerns with a new story that markets are neutral arbiters of value. The effect is not to eliminate morality but to displace it.

Contemporary society shows the limits of this displacement. The global financial crisis of 2008 was not only an economic event but also a moral reckoning. The anger directed at banks, regulators, and political leaders revealed widespread perception that finance had strayed too far from its social obligations. The crisis exposed the dangers of financial products sold with little concern for the borrowers' ability to repay, and of institutions that privatised profits while socialising losses. The narrative that emerged was one of betrayal: financial elites had failed in their moral duty to society. This disillusionment created space for calls to re-anchor finance in principles of fairness, transparency, and responsibility.

One way to reclaim moral narratives is to examine how investment is framed. Traditional measures of success often emphasise returns on capital, treating financial gain as the ultimate metric. Yet the rise of socially responsible investing, environmental, social, and governance (ESG) criteria, and impact investing represents a deliberate attempt to tell a different story. These approaches signal that investors are not only seeking profit but also outcomes aligned with ethical commitments, whether reducing carbon emissions, promoting gender equity, or strengthening communities. Critics rightly point out that these frameworks can devolve into box-ticking exercises or marketing ploys, but their very existence underscores a cultural hunger for moral accountability in finance. They reveal that many participants in financial markets wish to see themselves not just as profit maximisers but as custodians of broader values.

Philosophically, reclaiming moral narratives requires us to reconsider the ends of finance. Is money merely a means for individual accumulation, or should it serve as a tool for collective flourishing? The answer is not merely academic. If finance is understood as a neutral system of exchange, then ethical concerns are always external, tacked on after the fact. But if finance is seen as a practice inherently tied to moral purpose, then questions of justice, responsibility, and fairness are integral. The stories societies tell about finance shape whether we see speculative bubbles as clever innovation or reckless endangerment, whether we view philanthropy as noble redistribution or as a patch for structural inequality, and whether we imagine debt as empowerment or as exploitation.

Real-world examples illuminate these competing narratives. Microfinance was once heralded as a moral innovation, providing small loans to empower the world's poor. For a time, it seemed to embody the story of finance aligned with human dignity. Yet in some cases, aggressive lending practices led to cycles of indebtedness, revealing how easily noble intentions can be subverted by profit motives. Similarly, the emergence of decentralised finance (DeFi) has been framed by its advocates as a liberation from centralised control and exploitation. But it too faces scrutiny for creating new risks, concentrating wealth among insiders, and enabling speculative bubbles. These tensions underscore that *finance cannot escape moral judgment; it only shifts the terrain of debate.*

Reframing finance around resilience rather than fear is another step towards reclaiming moral narratives. Traditional financial products often sell security by preying on anxiety—insurance framed around catastrophe, savings accounts marketed as shields against uncertainty. But resilience as a story emphasises strength, adaptability, and shared support rather than fragile protection. For instance, community-based credit unions not only provide financial services but also embody narratives of mutual aid and solidarity. They remind participants that financial security does not need to be rooted in fear of collapse but in trust that communities can support each other.

This is not to suggest that reclaiming moral narratives is easy. Global finance is complex, transnational, and driven by powerful interests. Yet even within this system, individuals and institutions can make choices that signal different stories. Pension funds that divest from fossil fuels, governments that regulate predatory lending, firms that prioritise long-term stability over short-term gain—all are acts of narrative revision. They challenge the idea that finance must be amoral, asserting instead that finance is always a moral practice, whether acknowledged or not.

The role of storytelling here is not ornamental but foundational. Humans interpret finance through narrative lenses, whether those are tales of risk and reward, myths of security and fear, or parables of fairness and exploitation. To reclaim moral narratives of finance is to consciously choose stories that align with ethical commitments. It is to reject the myth that money is value-neutral and to insist that financial practices should reflect the kinds of societies we aspire to build. *The question is never whether finance has a moral narrative, but which narrative we will allow to dominate.*

Ultimately, reclaiming these narratives requires imagination. It means envisioning financial practices that do not merely minimise harm but actively contribute to human flourishing. It means asking whether the tools of finance can support ecological sustainability, reduce inequality, and expand dignity. Such questions challenge the fatalism that markets are beyond moral reach, reminding us that finance has always been shaped by human choices, cultural norms, and collective stories. To reclaim moral narratives of finance is to accept responsibility for shaping them deliberately, rather than leaving them to be dictated by the narrow logic of profit.

The path forward is not about moral perfection or utopian ideals but about moral clarity. It is about recognising that every financial practice—from the terms of a loan to the priorities of an investment fund—embodies values. Some of those values may entrench fear, exploitation, and inequality. Others may cultivate trust, resilience, and shared prosperity. By reclaiming moral narratives, individuals, institutions, and societies can realign finance with ethics, ensuring that money serves as a means of collective flourishing rather than an end in itself. The challenge is not whether this alignment is possible, but whether we will have the courage to tell—and to live—the stories that make it real.

Chapter 15
Choosing the Story You Live By

Every person carries with them a set of financial fables, often unspoken yet quietly determinative, shaping choices about saving, spending, investing, and even self-worth. These stories are rarely chosen deliberately; they are inherited from families, absorbed from cultures, whispered through advertising, reinforced by institutions. A child growing up in a household where scarcity was a constant refrain may internalise a story that money is always fleeting, no matter how much they earn later in life. Another, raised in an environment where consumption was the currency of affection, may unconsciously equate spending with love. Such narratives are powerful not because they are true in any universal sense, but because they feel inevitable. They become part of one's identity, guiding decisions long after their origins have been forgotten. To recognise these money myths is the first step towards agency. One cannot reframe a story one does not first acknowledge, and financial self-determination begins not with a new spreadsheet or investment plan, but with an act of narrative awareness.

The human mind is not well-equipped to process money purely as numbers. We gravitate toward meaning, context, and metaphor, and money becomes a canvas for these deeper psychological needs. The myth of the "self-made" millionaire, for instance, is not simply a statistic about entrepreneurial success; it is a cultural narrative that valorises independence, discipline, and exceptionalism, while often erasing the roles of inherited privilege, structural advantage, or collective effort. Likewise, the tale of "money as freedom" serves as a powerful motivator for countless individuals, shaping decisions about career, savings, and retirement. Yet beneath this story lies another: that freedom is conditional, that autonomy can only be bought, that one is not free until one has accumulated enough. By examining the stories behind financial behaviours, individuals begin to see not immutable truths but scripts that can be edited, challenged, or discarded.

Ignoring these narratives is not a solution. Repression is rarely effective, because repressed stories do not disappear; they resurface in disguised forms. A person who tries to suppress anxiety about scarcity may still hoard wealth, but frame it as prudence. Another who rejects the family narrative of frugality may rebel with excessive consumption, only to find themselves trapped by debt. The problem is not the existence of financial stories but the lack of conscious authorship over them. *Retelling is more powerful than repressing, because it allows one to integrate the truth of past experiences while reshaping their meaning.* A childhood marked by instability may leave scars, but it can also inspire a narrative of resilience, adaptability, and resourcefulness. A history of overindulgence may teach the value of discernment rather than lead to endless shame. Retelling does not erase; it reorients, allowing individuals to live with coherence rather than contradiction.

The art of financial storycraft is not mystical; it can be approached with the same rigour as any meaningful practice of reflection and design. Reflection prompts serve as tools for surfacing the implicit. What phrases about money echo from childhood? Which purchases produce pride, and which produce regret? What feelings accompany payday, or a large expense, or the sight of a bank statement? By tracing these emotional contours, one uncovers the stories beneath the numbers. Journaling, dialogue with trusted peers, or even structured financial therapy can provide the scaffolding for this process. The goal is not merely to catalogue the old stories but to ask whether they serve or constrain. *A useful financial narrative is one that enlarges agency rather than diminishes it, one that aligns with values rather than undermines them.*

Consider the practical implications. Someone living by the myth that "money equals security" may prioritise hoarding assets far beyond what is needed, sacrificing joy and opportunity in the process. By reframing this into a narrative of "security as resilience," they might choose to invest not only in savings accounts but also in relationships, skills, and health—forms of wealth that money alone cannot guarantee. Another, shaped by the tale that "spending proves success," may constantly chase status markers, only to feel hollow. Retelling this as "spending reflects values" shifts consumption from signalling to others toward affirming the self, turning financial choices into authentic expressions of identity. These are not minor semantic changes; they are tectonic shifts in the landscape of decision-making.

Living a different financial fable is less about rejecting old myths outright and more about choosing consciously among them. All societies are saturated with narratives about money: cautionary tales about greed, heroic tales of risk, parables about thrift, hymns to generosity. The question is not whether one will live by a story, but which story one will embrace. This is where financial literacy, too often reduced to numbers and formulas, must expand into narrative literacy. *To live wisely with money is to understand that it is not just an equation to be solved but a plotline to be authored.* The accounts we keep are not only in ledgers but also in the stories we tell ourselves and others.

What makes this perspective transformative is that it reframes money from master to medium. If one believes that money is merely math, then the challenge is always accumulation and optimisation. If one accepts that money is narrative, then the challenge becomes authorship. Do you wish your story to be one of anxiety or of sufficiency? Of envy or of integrity? Of imitation or of originality? The recognition that choice exists is liberating, for it positions the individual not as a passive character trapped in inherited myths but as an active narrator capable of redirection. This does not deny the structural realities of inequality, privilege, or access—these are real constraints—but even within them, narrative reframing provides psychological clarity and practical empowerment.

As this chapter unfolds, it invites the reader to recognise the myths that have silently governed their financial behaviours, to resist the temptation of repression, to embrace the practice of retelling with intention, and to begin crafting stories that better align with who they wish to be. It does not promise perfection or guarantee prosperity. What it offers instead is a more profound form of freedom: the freedom to live not by default narratives but by chosen ones. Money, in this view, is less a verdict and more a vocabulary, a language through which each person composes the story of their life. The task is to choose that story with the same deliberation and care that one might devote to any other work of enduring authorship.

Recognizing Your Money Myths: Guides readers in identifying the fables silently shaping their financial decisions

Few forces influence human behaviour as quietly and as powerfully as the stories we tell ourselves about money. These are not simply opinions or strategies; they are myths—deeply ingrained narratives that operate below the level of conscious choice. A myth can be as blunt as "money is the root of all evil" or as seductive as "money buys freedom." It may come in the form of a family mantra—"we can't afford that"—or an unspoken cultural script—"success means owning property." What unites these myths is their invisibility: they shape perceptions, decisions, and priorities while masquerading as common sense. To recognise them is to take the first step toward autonomy, because myths cannot be dismantled or rewritten if they are not first brought into the light.

Money myths are rarely the product of deliberate reasoning. They emerge from experience, tradition, and cultural conditioning, often reinforced before an individual has the capacity to challenge them. A child raised in a household scarred by unemployment may internalise the myth that financial stability is fragile, regardless of their later income. A teenager surrounded by advertising that equates consumption with popularity may absorb the idea that self-worth is measured in brands. Even the supposedly rational world of financial planning is steeped in myth: the unquestioned faith that home ownership is always the best investment, or that career advancement invariably leads to greater happiness. These narratives are sticky not because they are true in every case, but because they provide coherence in a complex world. *Myths supply meaning where numbers alone cannot, turning financial life into a story with heroes, villains, and outcomes.*

Consider how myths manifest in adult decision-making. The professional who continues to chase promotions long after financial needs are met may be living under the myth that status equals security. The couple delaying experiences and pleasures until retirement may be entrapped by the myth of deferred life—that sacrifice today guarantees fulfilment tomorrow. At the other end of the spectrum, the individual who spends compulsively at the first sign of distress may be operating under the myth that money alleviates emotional pain. These are not minor quirks; they shape entire lifecourses, influencing where people live, what careers they pursue, and how they judge themselves and others.

What makes these myths so compelling is that they are often reinforced collectively. Religions, governments, and markets alike have long recognised the power of financial storytelling. The Protestant ethic elevated thrift into a moral virtue, shaping generations of Western attitudes toward work and saving. Consumer capitalism, by contrast, thrives on myths of self-expression through purchase, persuading individuals that identity can be bought. Even modern technology companies craft myths around financial behaviour: that frictionless spending is progress, that "buy now, pay later" is empowerment. These cultural stories are persuasive not because they are logically airtight but because they resonate emotionally, embedding themselves in daily routines until they feel like truth.

Recognising money myths requires a form of intellectual archaeology. It is the work of digging beneath surface-level behaviours to uncover the assumptions that fuel them. One practical method is to examine repeated patterns of financial behaviour and ask what belief sustains them. Why does a person feel guilt when spending on themselves but not when buying for others? Why does another avoid looking at their bank statements altogether? These behaviours reveal the stories beneath: perhaps that self-indulgence is shameful, or that confronting reality is too painful. Another strategy is to pay attention to language. Phrases like "throwing money away on rent" or "splurging" are not neutral; they carry embedded judgments about what is responsible, respectable, or reckless. By interrogating these judgments, one begins to see the narrative scaffolding propping up financial choices.

Yet recognition alone is not easy, because myths often defend themselves. They cloak themselves in logic or morality, making resistance feel like irresponsibility or even sin. The myth of endless growth, for example, insists that questioning the pursuit of more is naïve or defeatist. The myth of scarcity frames cautiousness as virtue, discouraging any suggestion that abundance might exist. These self-reinforcing loops are why money myths endure across centuries, persisting even in the face of evidence that contradicts them. To recognise them, one must develop both intellectual scepticism and emotional courage: scepticism to question inherited wisdom, and courage to confront the discomfort of challenging what feels familiar.

There are also dangers in misrecognition. Not every financial habit is myth-driven; some behaviours are pragmatic responses to circumstance. To dismiss frugality as a mere story of scarcity, for example, would ignore the lived reality of those who truly lack resources. Likewise, not all cultural myths are harmful. The narrative of communal responsibility, which underpins practices such as mutual aid or cooperative saving groups, can be a powerful counterweight to the myth of rugged individualism. The task, therefore, is not to reject all financial stories but to discern which serve flourishing and which constrain it. *A myth becomes dangerous when it limits possibilities, obscures truth, or drives behaviour at odds with authentic values.*

Practical recognition can be aided by reflective exercises. One might map the earliest memories of money and note the emotions attached: Was money a source of conflict, pride, secrecy, or generosity? Another approach is to track recurring financial decisions and identify whether they align with stated values. A person who claims to value freedom yet repeatedly takes on unnecessary debt may be living by a myth of instant gratification rather than their conscious ideal. These exercises are not meant to produce immediate answers but to make visible the hidden scripts. Visibility is power: once a myth is named, it loses some of its hold.

The broader implication is that recognising money myths is not just an individual task but a cultural one. Societies, like individuals, live by fables that shape institutions and policies. The myth of trickle-down prosperity, for instance, has justified tax regimes that disproportionately favour the wealthy. The myth that poverty reflects moral failure has influenced welfare systems worldwide. By identifying these collective myths, citizens can question whether the stories guiding public life are equitable, sustainable, or even accurate. Just as personal recognition leads to greater autonomy, cultural recognition opens the possibility of reform.

Ultimately, the recognition of money myths is not about cynicism but about choice. To see the myth is to reclaim the ability to decide whether to continue living by it. The individual who discovers they have been driven by the myth of endless accumulation can choose to stop chasing status and pursue sufficiency instead. The person raised on the myth of scarcity can choose to reinterpret it as a call to resilience rather than fear. Recognition is the hinge upon which transformation turns. Without it, people remain characters in stories they did not choose; with it, they can begin to act as authors.

Every financial life is lived within stories, some empowering, others constraining. The myths that once offered comfort can become cages, while those that once limited can, when reinterpreted, become sources of wisdom. The act of recognition is not a one-time event but a lifelong practice, for myths evolve as circumstances change. The critical task is to remain attentive: to notice which stories are speaking through one's decisions, to discern whether they are allies or adversaries, and to choose deliberately which deserve to endure. Only then can money serve not as an unconscious myth-maker but as a conscious medium for living with integrity and purpose.

Retelling, Not Repressing: Shows why rewriting narratives is more powerful than ignoring them

Silence does not erase a story; it buries it alive. The fables we inherit about money—whether of scarcity, abundance, sacrifice, or indulgence—do not simply dissolve when we refuse to acknowledge them. They linger beneath the surface, shaping choices with a quiet insistence, sometimes more potently than if we had confronted them head-on. Repression is not liberation but displacement, and repressed money myths often return in disguised forms: anxiety about spending, guilt over success, compulsive saving, or reckless indulgence. The more one insists on ignoring the story, the more insistently it writes itself into behaviour. *Transformation comes not from silencing these myths but from retelling them, giving them new endings, fresh protagonists, and alternative lessons.*

This distinction matters because financial stories are rarely neutral. They are carried in the language of morality—what is "responsible," "greedy," "secure," or "wasteful." To repress such stories is to pretend they have no claim on us, when in fact they quietly adjudicate every decision. A person raised on the myth that debt is a moral failure may repress this belief in adulthood, dismissing it as old-fashioned, yet still feel disproportionate shame at the sight of a credit card bill. Another who absorbed the myth that wealth signals virtue may reject materialism in theory but still crave the validation that comes with outward displays of success. In both cases, the story is not gone; it is merely unacknowledged. By retelling, however, one can reposition debt as a tool rather than a sin, or wealth as a responsibility rather than a badge of honour.

History offers ample evidence of the dangers of repression. Consider the long-standing stigma surrounding discussions of money in polite society. For generations, people were encouraged to avoid financial conversations, to repress curiosity about wages, inheritances, or debts. Yet this silence allowed myths of inequality to fester. Employers justified wage gaps with moral narratives of merit, while families passed on advantages cloaked as "hard work" rather than inheritance. Repression created opacity, and opacity allowed exploitation. By contrast, moments of cultural retelling—such as the labour movements that reframed wages as justice, not charity—shifted public understanding and policy. Retelling made visible what repression sought to conceal.

Psychology underscores the same lesson. Cognitive behavioural therapy, for instance, recognises that unwanted thoughts cannot simply be repressed; they must be reframed. The patient who attempts to ignore intrusive worries only strengthens them, while the one who learns to reinterpret those worries gains agency. Similarly, financial myths lose their grip when reinterpreted rather than denied. A narrative of "never enough" can be retold as a call to gratitude and sufficiency. A myth of "money corrupts" can be rewritten as "money reveals character and can amplify generosity." The difference lies in agency: repression concedes power to the myth, while retelling asserts authorship.

Contemporary finance illustrates how pervasive repression remains. Take retirement planning. Many individuals, uncomfortable with the story that old age brings vulnerability, repress financial preparation altogether. They avoid looking at pensions, dismiss the thought of frailty, and tell themselves they will "figure it out later." Yet repression does not shield them from reality; it simply magnifies the eventual shock. Contrast this with those who retell the story of ageing not as decline but as a stage of freedom, purpose, and reallocation of resources. Their financial decisions reflect empowerment rather than avoidance, precisely because they have rewritten the myth in which retirement is not a tragedy but a chapter to be crafted deliberately.

Repression also thrives in families. Parents may repress their own anxieties about money to shield children, only for those anxieties to seep through in unspoken tensions. A family that refuses to talk about a history of bankruptcy may still pass on a legacy of fear around spending. In contrast, families that retell such experiences as learning opportunities transmit resilience rather than silence. A narrative of "we lost everything" can be retold as "we learned how to rebuild." The facts remain the same, but the meaning shifts radically, opening space for healthier attitudes in the next generation.

Crucially, retelling does not mean fabricating. It means choosing interpretation. Myths are not eliminated; they are recontextualised. Consider the ancient fables of hoarded treasure guarded by dragons. Taken literally, they reinforce the myth of money as something to protect obsessively. Retold through a modern lens, they highlight the futility of hoarding and the risks of letting fear define wealth. In this retelling, the dragon is not a guardian but a prison-keeper, and the lesson becomes one of circulation rather than stagnation. By shifting the emphasis, a myth that once justified greed now warns against it.

There is also a collective dimension. Nations and economies live by financial myths that cannot be repressed without consequence. The myth of endless growth, for example, has dominated much of modern economics. Attempts to repress environmental critiques of this myth did not extinguish them but forced them underground, where they resurfaced as crises—ecological collapse, financial instability, social unrest. Only when societies begin to retell the story—by framing prosperity as sustainability rather than sheer expansion—does the narrative open paths to resilience. Retelling at scale requires courage, but it is the only way to prevent old myths from reasserting themselves destructively.

The act of retelling demands imagination. It requires asking: What is the story beneath my financial choices? Who wrote it? What if I changed the plot? For instance, the entrepreneur haunted by the myth that failure is shameful might retell failure as apprenticeship, transforming losses into investments in learning. The saver paralysed by the myth that risk is ruin might retell risk as necessary for growth, recasting investment not as gambling but as participation in shared futures. These retellings are not naive optimism; they are deliberate reconfigurations of meaning. *The facts of financial life cannot always be changed, but the story told about them always can.*

Retelling is also more sustainable than repression because it honours memory rather than denying it. People cannot simply excise childhood lessons or cultural imprints. A community that experienced famine, for example, may never abandon the story of scarcity, nor should it. But it can retell that story as one of resilience and solidarity rather than perpetual fear. In doing so, the past is acknowledged without being allowed to dictate the future. This is the difference between living as a prisoner of history and living as its curator.

At its heart, the choice between repression and retelling is the choice between passivity and authorship. Repression pretends the story does not exist, ceding control to its unconscious influence. Retelling accepts the story's presence but insists on reshaping its meaning. The former breeds anxiety, rigidity, and recurrence; the latter fosters resilience, creativity, and freedom. To retell is to take the pen back from inherited myths and write lines of one's own. It is the quiet yet radical act of recognising that while we do not choose the stories handed to us, we can always choose how they end.

Practical Storycraft Tools: Provides reflection prompts for reshaping financial stories

Every financial decision carries a narrative, whether we recognise it or not. Buying a house may tell a story of belonging, ambition, or stability. Investing in education may symbolise hope, self-belief, or duty to family. Even mundane acts—choosing a brand at the supermarket, delaying a purchase, tipping generously—are embedded in scripts shaped by upbringing, culture, and imagination.

The challenge is not that these stories exist, but that many of them were written without our conscious input. They are inherited, absorbed, or imposed. If they remain unexamined, they can quietly dictate the plot of our financial lives. *The craft of retelling begins with the discipline of reflection: pausing to name the stories, testing their truth, and rewriting their direction.*

The first tool is simple yet profound: questioning the origin of a financial belief. Many people live by unspoken axioms such as "money must always be saved for a rainy day" or "spending on yourself is indulgent." Such phrases, often uttered in childhood homes, carry moral weight long after their context has changed. To interrogate them is not to dishonour those who passed them down but to ask whether they still serve the life one wishes to live. A person who grew up in scarcity may have internalised a myth of perpetual threat, hoarding even when stability has been achieved. By asking, *Whose voice is this? Where did I first hear it?* one begins to separate inherited story from current reality.

Another powerful tool is re-authoring through counter-narrative. This involves taking a well-worn story and deliberately seeking evidence for its opposite. For example, someone convinced that risk always leads to ruin might recall moments when risk-taking produced growth, community, or opportunity. By balancing the ledger of memory, the narrative gains nuance. It is not about erasing the original lesson—perhaps risk did indeed once cause loss—but about refusing to let a single episode monopolise the narrative. This method mirrors practices in psychology, where trauma is not denied but placed within a broader, more textured account of experience. The same principle applies to money myths: broaden the storyline, and the myth loses its absolutism.

Journaling provides another practical mechanism. Rather than recording numbers alone, individuals can write financial diaries as story records: *What story did today's spending tell? What story did today's saving reinforce?* Such questions shift focus from mere transactions to meaning. Over time, patterns emerge—perhaps of self-denial masked as prudence, or generosity used as a way to secure belonging. The act of naming these patterns transforms them from unconscious scripts into deliberate choices. A small prompt like "If this purchase were a sentence in my life story, what would it say?" can radically change awareness.

Dialogue is equally crucial. Stories thrive in conversation, and many distortions arise because financial myths are rarely spoken aloud. Discussing money narratives with trusted peers, partners, or mentors can reveal both commonalities and blind spots. A spouse may notice that generosity always accompanies guilt, or a colleague may observe that professional identity seems tied too tightly to income. Externalising the story allows it to be examined rather than simply enacted. This is why support groups or financial coaching sessions often prove transformative: they provide arenas where unexamined stories can be retold in community.

Visualisation can also serve as a reframing tool. Instead of abstracting money into numbers on a screen, one can imagine financial decisions as scenes. A person might picture themselves as the protagonist of a fable: guarding treasure, sharing harvest, planting seeds. These images make visible the underlying narratives that might otherwise remain implicit. If the recurring visualisation is one of guarding, perhaps the dominant myth is scarcity. If it is one of sowing, perhaps abundance and trust are the guiding principles. Once surfaced, these metaphors can be reshaped deliberately: the guard can be recast as a steward, the sower as a collaborator.

Equally important is practising narrative substitution: consciously replacing a destructive story with a healthier one. For instance, the myth "I am bad with money" is not merely inaccurate; it is paralysing. Substituting it with "I am learning to steward money wisely" reframes the identity from failure to progress. Similarly, the refrain "money is the root of all evil" can be substituted with "money magnifies values." This does not trivialise the moral risks of wealth but repositions money as a mirror of choices rather than an inherent corruption. Each substitution is a subtle but powerful act of authorship.

The stories we live by often have archetypal roots—heroes, victims, villains. A useful tool is to ask: *What role am I cast in by my financial narrative?* Someone might discover they habitually position themselves as the martyr, sacrificing for others at all costs. Another might find they default to the victim, always acted upon by forces beyond their control. Recognising these roles allows one to consider alternatives: hero as collaborator rather than solitary saviour, victim as survivor with agency. By shifting roles, the same financial events can carry entirely different meanings.

Reflection is not solely introspective. It must engage with the cultural myths that surround us. Advertising, for example, constantly crafts stories: the car as freedom, the handbag as confidence, the holiday as self-discovery. To treat these not as products but as narratives is to reclaim interpretive power. A practical tool here is narrative decoding: asking, *What story is this company trying to sell me? Do I accept that story, or do I prefer to write my own?* By practising this consistently, one cultivates resilience against external myths and strengthens internal authorship.

At a societal level, storycraft becomes a form of resistance. Communities can collectively retell economic myths. Consider how microfinance initiatives reframed the story of the poor: not as helpless recipients of aid but as entrepreneurs with dignity. Or how ethical investment reframes profit: not as exploitation but as alignment with shared values. These examples illustrate how deliberate storycraft can reshape collective behaviour and institutions, not just individual decisions. Thus, practising reflection at a personal level also contributes to broader cultural change.

Importantly, storycraft is not a one-time exercise but an ongoing practice. Just as financial circumstances evolve, so too must financial narratives. What served in youth—a story of striving, risk-taking, or frugality—may become constraining in middle age or irrelevant in retirement. Regularly revisiting one's narratives ensures that they remain aligned with present values rather than fossilised in past anxieties. A simple yearly ritual of asking, *What financial story served me this year? Which one do I need to retell for the next?* can prevent myths from hardening into dogma.

Underlying all these tools is a philosophical insight: money is not merely a medium of exchange but a medium of meaning. Numbers on a balance sheet do not tell us why we work, save, spend, or give. Stories do. And stories can be crafted, like any art, with care, creativity, and discipline. By treating money as narrative material rather than brute fact, individuals reclaim authorship of lives that might otherwise be scripted by forces beyond their control. *Reflection is not indulgence; it is governance of the self at the most practical level.*

To practise storycraft is therefore to exercise freedom. It is to refuse the tyranny of silence, the inertia of inheritance, and the seduction of external myths. The tools—questioning origins, re-authoring through counter-narratives, journaling, dialogue, visualisation, substitution, archetypal role analysis, decoding cultural stories, and periodic renewal—are not abstract techniques but disciplines of autonomy. Each one chisels away at the unconscious myths that shape behaviour and replaces them with stories chosen deliberately. In doing so, financial life becomes not a script imposed from without but a narrative authored from within—lived with clarity, coherence, and integrity.

Living a Different Fable: Ends with the invitation to treat money not as math to be solved, but as a story to be authored

The dominant cultural view of money casts it as a problem to be solved—an equation of income and expenditure, growth and risk, assets and liabilities. This arithmetic framing has its uses, but it is ultimately impoverished. To live only by the ledger is to imagine life as an endless balancing act, where the goal is the elimination of error rather than the pursuit of meaning. *What if, instead, money were treated not as a puzzle of mathematics but as a narrative material, capable of shaping the stories we live by?* To adopt this stance is to move from the role of accountant to that of author, from reactive problem-solver to deliberate storyteller.

The idea that financial life is a story rather than a sum is not mere rhetoric. Our economic choices already carry narrative weight. A person who pays off a mortgage is not only reducing debt; they are completing a chapter of striving and arrival. The graduate with a student loan is not simply managing interest rates but inhabiting a story of investment in potential. Even indulgent purchases are rarely about numbers alone; they are about identity, belonging, or rebellion.

Numbers measure, but stories explain. To recognise this is to see that the task is not to reject mathematics but to put it in its place—as the supporting grammar, not the plot itself.

Living a different fable begins with choosing which stories to reject. Many people unconsciously live out financial myths that do not belong to them: the myth that wealth is the only measure of success, that debt is always shameful, or that generosity must wait until abundance. These narratives often persist because they are socially reinforced. Cultures reward certain stories—heroic entrepreneurs, frugal savers, charitable donors—while stigmatising others. To live a different fable is to examine these scripts and decide which to keep, which to rewrite, and which to abandon altogether. This process is neither abstract nor indulgent; it directly shapes practical behaviours. A person who reframes debt not as moral failure but as a tool may approach borrowing with discernment rather than paralysis. Someone who rewrites the story of generosity may give consistently rather than sporadically, aligning financial practice with deeply held values.

The act of authorship demands imagination. If money is only a technical problem, then creativity is irrelevant. But if money is narrative, then imagination becomes central. Consider the rise of the FIRE (Financial Independence, Retire Early) movement. At its core, it is not just about numbers; it is about the story of freedom—the plot twist that one can exit the conventional script of lifelong labour. Similarly, the increasing popularity of social impact investing rests on a narrative shift: profit no longer has to conflict with ethics, but can instead advance it. These examples demonstrate how entire communities have re-authored their financial lives by imagining new stories, then building systems to sustain them.

There is also courage involved in storycraft. Narratives carry emotional risk because they expose values. To say, "I spend on travel because I value experience over possessions" is not just a financial decision; it is a declaration of identity. To say, "I give away a portion of my income because I see wealth as stewardship rather than ownership" risks critique in a society that idolises accumulation. Numbers can be defended with spreadsheets, but stories demand justification at the level of meaning. Yet this vulnerability is precisely what makes narrative life richer than purely mathematical life. It invites alignment between inner conviction and outer action, producing coherence that arithmetic alone cannot offer.

One might object that stories are subjective, whereas numbers are objective. But even the most technical financial systems are built on narratives. Insurance, at heart, is a story about fear and resilience. Pensions are a story about continuity and trust. Stock markets function not merely on numbers but on collective narratives of confidence and panic. To imagine that financial life can ever be free of story is an illusion. The choice is not whether to live by narrative but whether to live by narratives authored by others or crafted deliberately for oneself. *The invitation, therefore, is not to abandon calculation but to place calculation within the service of story.*

A different fable also means recognising money as relational rather than solitary. Mathematics often isolates: your income, your savings, your debt. Narrative reminds us that financial life is entwined with others. Dowries, inheritances, shared mortgages, collective investments—all remind us that money flows through webs of relationship, binding one life to another. To treat money as story is to acknowledge this social dimension openly, rather than concealing it behind impersonal figures. By reframing financial decisions as acts within relationships—acts of care, reciprocity, or justice—we move towards stories that honour interdependence rather than deny it.

Practical implications of this narrative view are profound. Retirement planning shifts from an obsession with "the number" to a reflection on what kind of elderhood one wishes to inhabit. Budgeting ceases to be about cutting costs mechanically and becomes a method of ensuring one's values are visible in daily life. Career choices become less about maximising salary and more about weaving together income, meaning, and contribution. Even the act of teaching children about money becomes less about arithmetic drills and more about embedding values through shared narratives of work, saving, and generosity.

The richest aspect of living a different fable is its open-endedness. Mathematical models promise certainty—if one saves a set percentage, invests in particular vehicles, and avoids specified risks, the outcome is projected with precision. Stories, by contrast, embrace contingency. A story can twist, surprise, and evolve. This unpredictability is not a flaw but a feature. It allows adaptation when life deviates from forecast, whether through illness, opportunity, or discovery. A narrative life accepts that the future cannot be solved like an equation, but it can be authored with intention. *The point is not to eliminate uncertainty but to script meaning within it.*

By living a different fable, individuals reclaim agency from systems that often treat them as data points. They refuse the reduction of life to spreadsheets and instead embrace the role of storyteller. They accept the tools of mathematics but subordinate them to the higher task of authorship. They discover that money, when approached as narrative material, becomes not a source of anxiety but of coherence—a medium through which values are enacted, identities expressed, and communities shaped.

The invitation, then, is clear: step into authorship. Do not merely solve for "enough" or "more." Write, instead, the fable you wish to live by. Ask not only, *What do the numbers say?* but also, *What story do they tell?* In that question lies the power to transform financial life from an exercise in arithmetic to an art of meaning. And unlike numbers, which eventually exhaust themselves in sums, stories carry forward, weaving lives into legacies that outlast calculation.

About the Author

Adrian Vale writes about money the way people actually experience it—through stories, instincts, and the quiet rules we inherit without noticing. His work blends behavioral insight, economic history, and cultural anthropology to reveal why rational plans often collide with the narratives we live by. With a calm, plain-spoken style and a bias toward practical clarity, Adrian explores how myths about wealth, risk, debt, and luck shape everyday choices—and how readers can rewrite those scripts for steadier, saner financial lives. His earlier work on resilience and preparedness informed a clear worldview: build systems that hold under stress, question seductive narratives, and choose habits that outlast hype. Adrian lives simply, reads widely, and believes the most useful money lessons are old, portable, and human.

www.ingramcontent.com/pod-product-compliance
Lightning Source LLC
Chambersburg PA
CBHW031340230926
51848CB00002B/313
* 9 7 8 9 3 7 1 7 7 6 3 6 3 *